David —

to wish you a very

happy birthday!

lotsa love

from

Big Sis!.

HIGH
WIDE
A · N · D
Handsome

IAN
BOTHAM

The story of a very special year
— BY —
FRANK KEATING

Willow Books
Collins
8 Grafton Street, London W1
1986

TO JANE AND KATHY WITH LOVE

Willow Books
William Collins Sons & Co. Ltd
London · Glasgow · Sydney · Auckland
Toronto · Johannesburg

First published 1986

© Newschoice Ltd/Frank Keating 1986

BRITISH LIBRARY CATALOGUING IN PUBLICATION DATA

Botham, Ian
   High, wide and handsome.
   1. Botham, Ian   2. Cricket —— History —— 20th
   century
   I. Title   II. Keating, Frank
796.35'8'0924   GV915.B5/

ISBN   0 00 218226 2

Set in Melior
by Thomas/Weintroub Associates, Wembley
Printed and bound in Great Britain by
Billing and Sons, Worcester

Contents

Author's Preface

IT seemed about time for someone to have a crack at doing justice to Ian Botham from a purely cricketing point of view. In more than a decade, he has been increasingly garlanded in such adjectival sermonizing, puff, huff and hyperbole that it has become ridiculously easy to forget that it has been his continued exploits at the national game that have made him one of the pre-eminent figures in Britain's folklore of the last quarter of the century. 'A working-class hero is something to be', sang John Lennon, and in the summer of 1985 Ian Botham trenchantly celebrated the fact with a sustained string of accomplishments that invigorated the cricket crowds of England. It included a series of valiant and chivalrous jousts against the ancient enemy from Australia, as well as a voluptuous obliteration of the game's 50-year-old six-hitting record. More often than not, Botham manhandled sport from the newspaper back-pages to the front (sometimes, it must be said, through his own careless zest for living dangerously), and it struck me to attempt a redress of that trend and inquire about the regard, or otherwise, in which he is held by his sporting rivals and colleagues.

Thus, many of them – from some of the game's legendary Test players to the bread-and-butter apprentices in the endearing freemasonry of the county grind – have contributed to cobbling together this little memoir of one special man's special year. I did not know what the response would be. In the event I found their commentaries as surprising as they were illuminating. To all of them, my thanks for their time and generosity. Gratitude, too, to the man himself, not only for occasionally slowing down to reminisce during his epic tramp from John o'Groats, but just for the utter *hooraymanship* of his cricket since I first saw him bat as a gawky teenager at Taunton one lovely golden, shadowed summer's evening in 1974. (He made a boisterous and precociously breezy 45 against Bedi and Willey, of Northamptonshire, and I mentioned it with a warm glow in the last paragraph of my report for *The Guardian*. It was cut out. Not many mentions of Botham have gone the same way since).

The book would scarcely have been possible without crucial help from my two friends, Patrick Murphy and Trevor Grant. Particular thanks as well to those moles in the England and Somerset dressing-rooms, especially Nigel Popplewell, who will be much missed in county cricket in 1986 as he swots to follow his distinguished and judicial father round a different type of circuit. In this dottily glorious pastime of cricket, statistics provide some folk with an almost orgasmic joy; in my view Derek Lodge's lists of figures are contrived to tell the most intriguing tales. My father burrowed deep in West Country libraries to unearth some fascinating snippets, and my editor, Michael, of the cricketing family Doggart, was, as Mike Brearley once said in another context, 'particularly helpful and helpfully particular'. As Ian Botham begins his tenth consuming year as a Test match cricketer, we know, alas, that England's star cannot continue to flame so bright for long. If the summer of 1985 was to be one of his last at centre-stage, it is gratifying at least that it is here on record, however skimpily, for any great-grandchild to digest. Certainly it was rewarding to keep the log.

Frank Keating
January 1986

1 Is Botham In?

BOTHAM'S In! The dumpy, middle-aged Wessex farmer's wife emerged from her cottage doorway to shout, with a burring, butter-fly-startling urgency, across the sleepy Wiltshire hamlet on one of the few blue-bright, bee-buzzing midsummer Saturdays of 1985. Across a field yonder, her gnarled, nutbrown, countryman husband was at work, knee-deep in nettles. On hearing his woman's shout, he threw down his billhook and, cap in hand now, he loped hurriedly back to the house. To watch the Test match cricket on television. When he had left for work he had switched on the set. His kitchen-wife had kept an ear cocked as she pottered and panned – and, when the time came, she had obeyed instructions. '*Botham's In!*'

On another afternoon that same summer, a driver crossing the Severn Bridge from Wales to England was listening to the same Test match commentators on his car radio. He slowed as he approached the sombre line of pay-booths that serve as barrier at this barren border, this tar-macked, exhaust-fumed no-man's-land between two countries. Inside these upright coffins sit anonymous guards in perpetual silence and navy-blue Millett's overcoats: you never see their faces, just a blue-clad metronomic arm (stiff and regular as a royal wave) that extends one human hand to accept your money and dispense your change. Certainly, precious few travellers could vouch on oath that these men had learned to speak: if, indeed, it was men they were. This time, the car edged, window down, towards the toll when – all of a sudden and most surprisingly – from the dark sentry-box emerged a tall man with a pallid complexion and a desperate cast to his eye, half pleading, half expectant. In the local dialect of those parts, he demanded of the driver the answer to two urgent questions. '*Is Botham In? How many's he got then?*'

Not, you notice, 'Are *England* In? How many have *they* got?' Mean-while, around the narrow High Streets and cluttered, over-peopled 'pedestrian precincts' of the land, the similar, *singular* query was being muttered as groups of the citizenry scurried to join hunched huddles that

The final cheque. On the balcony, at the Houses of Parliament MP Harry Greenway and two of the children who walked

had gathered before the flickering plate-glass shopfronts of Messrs Multibroadcast. Out of the side of the mouth it came, furtively yet fraternally: '*Is Botham In?*' For as long as he was in, as the writer Miles Kington pointed out, it showed that Britain itself could not be counted out – 'even though, of course, there's still a great deal to do and it's up to Ian now to consolidate Britain's position, safeguard our herring stocks in the North Sea, turn back the flood of Golden Delicious apples from France and get the economy on a sound footing. But given what he has done already, there's no reason why he should not do this as well.'

One hundred years ago they used to have a stock of posters ready to pin to the turnstiles at the Bristol cricket ground – '*Entry 6d. If W.G.'s Batting, 1s 6d.*' A modern entrepreneur could do the same only for Ian Botham. To be sure, since the days of that bluff and bearded Dr Grace, what British sportsman has heard his name mentioned more times – pro and anti, ayes and noes, it must be admitted – in the Houses of Parliament itself. Indeed, the year under review ended with the Prime Minister herself hosting a reception devoted totally to honouring Ian Botham and, you might say, all his works and pomps.

In the event, the day turned out to be just about the most convulsive of the Government's year: it was Prime Minister's Question Time over what was known as the 'Westland crisis'. Ian and his family of friends had already assembled in the Lady's chamber and were tinkling the teacups with assorted courtiers of MPs and Peers when Mrs Thatcher sent word apologising for having to miss her own tea party – but had she turned up, I imagined her entering the room, looking round and turning to tug the sleeve of an aide to enquire: '*Is Botham In?*'

In autumn 1985, the man they call 'Both' (as in 'broth') – or 'Beefy' – had turned 30, having just played his 79th Test match at the end of his ninth season for England, and his eleventh for Somerset. Exactly half a century earlier, in 1935, another Somerset all-rounder, Arthur Wellard, had set one of cricket's most spectacular records. He scored 66 sixes in the season – that is, 66 times in a first-class match he hit a cricket ball which cleared the perimeter of the field without bouncing. Americans call them 'home runs'. It seemed an inviolate record and Wellard's place was surely secure in the game's logbook of legend for, with the preponderance of limited-overs professional cricket in the second half of the century ('one-day' competition was not deemed first-class though, oftentimes, it was more fiercely and skilfully fought), a modern batsman had many fewer opportunities in which to attempt to beat a record of 66 'first-class' sixes.

In his *annus mirabilis*, the tall, jet-haired, brilliantined Arthur needed 46 innings for his rollicking 66 sun-scorchers. He averaged 1.43 sixes each time he went to the wicket. Fifty years later, Botham's astonishing 80 sixes came in only 27 innings, fully 19 less than Wellard. Botham averaged 2.96 each innings, and just one more six and Ian's average would have been 3 per knock. Most times too, as we shall see, he arrived at the wicket with his injury-wracked Somerset side bogged down in troubled waters – almost literally sometimes, for 1985 was one of the most notoriously wet summers of memory. The pitches, when playable, were like puddings, the ball 'heavy', and it did not, as they say, 'come onto the bat': a batsman had to go out and 'fetch it'. Yet in all, from April to September, Botham averaged 124 runs from every 100 balls he received. Through the summer he scored at the phenomenal rate of over 60 runs per hour – and 74 of each 100 runs came in boundaries. There can have been no more vigorous or sustained assault by bat on ball in all first-class cricket's history.

In the first two Test matches of the series of six against the traditional enemy, Australia, Botham played two glistening innings of 60 and 85 at Headingley and Lord's respectively. The rubber then seemed wide open: thereafter England's suddenly prolific top order made such a mountain of hay in the next four Tests that Botham was not called on to bat again till England were, successively, 365, 304, 572 and 405. He had never been one to take candy from kids. Those totals, however, gave him something

Opposite: 'If Botham's in, Britain itself could not be counted out'

Left: In off that bullish, economical run – swerving, seaming, sometimes seething with vim and verve and menace

Below: Athleticism and daring bravado at slip

to bowl at and, with his impulsively magnificent obsession with getting 'into' any game he played, he bowled his boots off, bounding in with that bullish, economical run – swerving, seaming (and sometimes seething) with vim and verve and menace. He was the fastest bowler in the series, indeed his tally of 31 wickets was fully a dozen more than the next English bowler, Emburey. It almost went without saying that, although he spent half the series bowling - 251 overs, more than anyone on either side – no fieldsman, either English or Australian, caught more catches than Botham with his athleticism and daring bravado at slip.

It went without saying, too, that the Common Man perceived these heroics (either in the flesh or at the window of Messrs Multibroadcast) and was enthralled. Indeed, as the season ended the solemn, tractful, magazine *New Socialist* ran a fulsome cover treatise: *Botham – the Last Working Class Hero*. No question mark, even. The People's Choice – himself a very Independent Tory it must be said – did not even read it, preferring to pepper a few final far pavilions.

And yet, while the people purred content, a large section of the sporting Press of Britain – and a couple of Fleet Street tabloids in particular – continued to treat Botham with a wariness, even suspicion that bordered, it must be said, sometimes on the malevolent. Such regular and snide iconoclasm astonished the rival Australian team – no strangers at home to the virulent excesses of downmarket journalism – to such extent even that midway through the summer, the visiting captain, Allan Border, publicly chided his hosts that if England's establishment, as it seemed to him, wanted to deport Botham, then the Autralian cricket board would

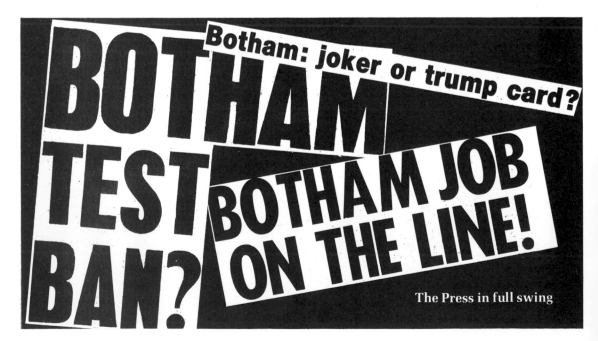

The Press in full swing

push through his naturalization papers in time for the next Test and with a speed unmatched even by Ms Zola Budd's Fleet Street string-pullers.

Botham remained uncomplicatedly English, becoming aggrieved and sullen only once or twice a week when he carried on his spats with the Press by sniping back with scarcely-veiled scorn by way of his own, ghosted, column in the bingoist pop of populars, the mass circulation *Sun* (whose new quiz game of skill in the not-too-distant future must surely be Spot the Journalist). Typically, Ian saw nothing illogical in accepting over £20,000 a year to be able to retaliate with his enemies' very own weapons of short, sharp sentences, scurrulous innuendo, and headline overkill. Meanwhile, back in *real* life – smiling wolfishly out in the middle with a bat in his hand, he would sometimes curl his lip in the direction of the reporters in their glasshouse press-box eyries, prior to launching a mighty dangerous whizzer in their general direction. He enjoyed seeing the gentlemen of Fleet Street spilling sweat, ink-wells, and half-empty bottles of the best of vintages as they cowered for cover in clusters.

Some of Fleet Street's attitudes, admittedly, could reek of jealousy – only occasional and possibly unconscious, but envy nevertheless. Down below them on the field was a young man achieving things with a carefree swagger and an insubordinate grin – achieving things that other great, good, upright men could never manage for all their practice and application. Men whose names are held revered in the whole canon, the whole litany of our saints. Yet this insolent young pup does not even practice. A 'net', the sacred homework, is a bore to Botham. He plays a 'net' as if he is on the beach at Weston-super-Mare and the tide is fast coming in. He bats like batting is fun. He bowls like bowling is easy. He fields in the wrong positions – he even *stands* wrongly – but he catches everything. And worse, much worse... the populus down there, the common herd, see how *they* love him. They even leave the bars to watch him play: they stand around shop windows when they should be working. It is not right they cheer: our game, its heritage, is scientific, stately, ritualistic; it is not *frivolous*. As Macauley said of the Puritans – '[they] hated bear-baiting not because it gave pain to the bear, but because it gave *pleasure* to the spectators.'

There were other things, however, that tightened the starch on the Puritans' ruffs. Our Merrie Englander had intemperately primed the gossips' parish pump in other ways. The year began with a magistrates' court case on conviction for possessing illegal cannabis. On the field he had an altercation with an umpire. And another, later, with a traffic policeman. (Cricket being what it is to the English, most of the po-faced, horrified commentators took by far the dimmest view of the middle 'crime' of the three. Certainly it warranted most headlines.)

Botham also took to himself an agent. Not a pin-striped city-slicker, nor a narrow-eyed wheeler-dealer doused in after-shave – which most young sportsmen are urged to take, and with whom the media men and the sporting authorities feel at ease – but an unlikely charmer, way out and not 'in', a one-off, larkey hedonist, but nobody's fool for he had made his money and friends in pop music, fashion and property in the hottest school of all, in California, USA. He loved cricket too, and had once played for Lancashire's Second XI. Now he prodigaled home in a cowboy hat and a diamond earring to set up court in a Queen Anne mansion in the low, rolling Cheshire acres: he had his friend and onliest client highlight his flowing mane to set off his smile, and kitted him out in a collection of strikey, stripey old-tyme public schoolboy blazers that suited his cricket and lasered even more colours into the greyest of summers. On the side, he looked to strike bargains, and warming attitudes of pleasure and pizzaz; and always on the boil were preposterously appealing, sometimes potty, possibilities. Tim Hudson also sported a bootlace for a tie, and his own greying hair was swept back to a pigtail. His 'straight' partner was a charming businesslike wife who ran the 'office' with expert efficiency. There is no doubt that Botham blossomed as a Hudson Hero in 1985. Together, they enlivened the year. The establishment winced, So did the Press. So did some friends. Ian took off his fedora, went out and hit 80 sixes at just about 3 per innings – more than double the previous best

Right: **Hudson, his hero and their technicolour dreamcoats**

Opposite: **At times, Ian was simply bowled over by the nation's response to the walk**

hitters' average in history. He became England's most prolific wicket-taker of all time, as he and his pals won the Ashes as handsomely as they have been won in a century and more. And then he walked from John o' Groats to Land's End. Mrs Thatcher summoned him to tea – and the nation, catching the mood, thought to hum a few snatches of Gilbert and Sullivan . . .

> 'For he might have been a Roosian,
> A French or Turk or Proosian,
> Or perhaps Itali-an . .
> But it's greatly to his credit –
> He remains an Eng-lish- man . . .'

W.S. Gilbert would have approved of Botham. Mr Sullivan, perhaps less so, but for the sake of England, art and royalties, he would have merrily set any of the boy's rollicking, blunderbuss innings to the most martially rum-te-tiddly tune. And can you possibly imagine Dickens having the slightest doubt about Botham as hero? Or Chesterton, another rumbustious Merrie Englander? Indeed, shades of our cricketer, when the latter wrote, in his marvellous essay on the former, 'There is a great man who makes every man feel small. But the really great man is the one who makes every man feel great'. In 1985, Botham's capacity to make small men feel bigger by his presence on a cricket field was extended even to the

highways and byways right down the length of Scotland and England. His now famous walk took 35 successively excruciating days. He kept smiling and collected a staggering £750,000 for leukaemia research. Even Fleet Street could scarce forbear ... and someone in *The Guardian* nicely and spikily suggested the touching, triumphant trek had revived after centuries the once commonplace pilgrimage of previous mighty English Kings determined devoutly to expiate all their naughtier deeds by embarking on footslogs to distant shrines – like Henry II hoofing it to Walsingham after the Canterbury deed had been done.

And Ian, it must be said, often has cause for contrition. Sometimes he finds it in himself to give a sucker an even break, but more often than not he can't. He lacks charity to those he considers fools. He is brutally insolent if he sniffs the pompous or patronising. He can appear boorish, aggravating, aggressive, mulishly stubborn, and very short-fused. His appetites flirt with danger. He can lack tact, civility, and refinement. He can be gauche and coarse, and sometimes vulgar without being funny. Many friends have charged him thus ... by the same token they have never once hesitated to marvel at his loyalty, generosity, courage or sportsmanship; his championing of underdogs is legendary. He is movingly, almost bashfully brilliant with dogs, new-born babies, small children and old ladies. He is homely, patriotic, philanthropic, crusading and often very funny without being vulgar.

He drives too fast and, sometimes, drinks too fast. He can live very dangerously indeed. Warts an' all ... and quite right too. When moralists talk of the necessity for 'character' in a man these days, more often than not they mean *dull* character. Ian insists he has mightily toned down the famed and roguish roistering of his youth, the untamed, instinctive scrapes and japes and junketing. Increasingly, he enjoys supper with friends, chat and laughter and a good red wine. And, ah, perfection ... putting on a rollicking early evening video film and watching it from the floor, with Kath and the kids all around him. Not forgetting Tigger, the dog.

They have three children – the youngest, Beccy, born as Ian was halfway through his walk to Lands End. She will, as Sarah and Liam have, soon be introduced to the merry-go-round of Father's hectic circuit. To my mind, one of the most touching aspects of life with Botham is that, whenever possible, the family come too. In the contented clusters which circle the first-class cricket grounds of an English summer, you can be pretty certain there will be at least one member of the family watching their laddo play – whether it is Kath and the kids, Ian's parents from deepest Somerset or his in-laws from the broadest acres of Yorkshire,

January, Yeovil Town v Northwich Victoria ... a centre-forward finds space

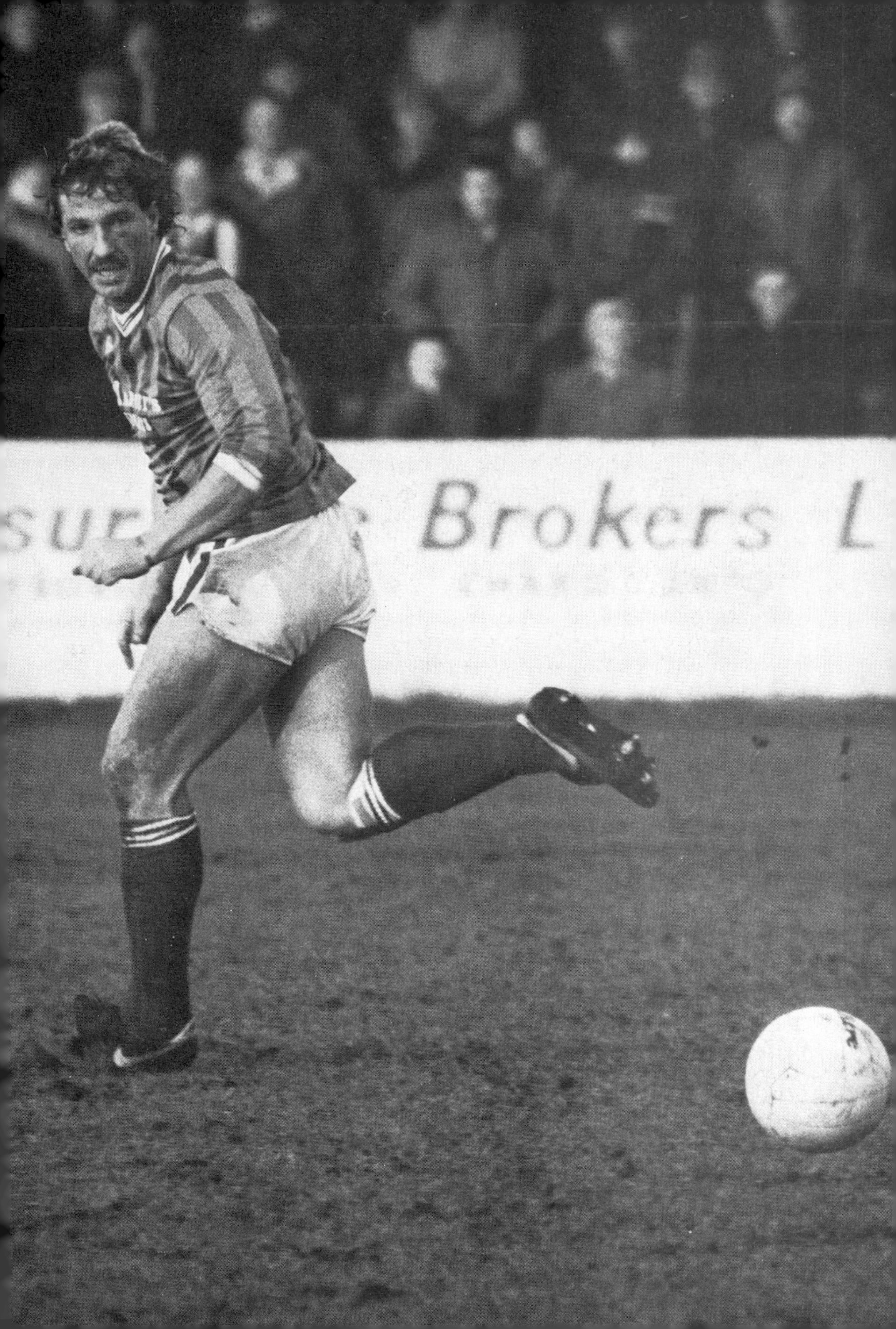
Brokers

plus it sometimes seems, any amount of sisters, cousins, aunts, uncles and pets. (Just as there might have been on the terraces during Ian's intermittent soccer career which now seems over: in early 1985 he left his beloved Scunthorpe, the Football League side, and played a few games for Yeovil, the Gola League club which he had first joined on leaving school.) 'The family help me keep my feet on the ground', says Ian. In the past it has been quite a job doing just that, as friends will testify.

The onset of a mellower period has been noticed by the Somerset all-rounder, Nigel Popplewell (son of the High Court judge whose melancholy duty in 1985 was to enquire into death and debauchery in British football), who retired in September after spending seven years in close affinity with Botham, at the wicket, in the dressing-rooms, in cars, bars, and hurrahs. Even in the last couple of years, says Popplewell, his friend has changed dramatically. 'He has recently acquired an interest in clothes, food and wine. This is nothing new – but it is the *quality* of such items that has changed. His clothes now exhibit a certain style – gone are the ragged T-shirts and holey jeans. Its leather trousers now, and blazers in strange colours. When proffered a menu at a restaurant, Ian will not just have a medium steak and chips, but peruse it with care (even if he does still need to have '*pommes frites*' translated for him!). As for wine, his ideal bottle of Burgundy three years ago was an empty one, suitable for some nefarious purpose. Now it is a 1978 Montrachet – to be enjoyed and savoured.'

At that *pommes frites* line, I interrupted to tell the yarn, courtesy John Arlott, of one young F.S. Trueman on the occasion of his first-ever game for Yorkshire, against Cambridge University in the late 1940s (Close was blooded on the same day). The county side stayed at the salubrious University Arms, across the hallowed Parker's Piece from Fenners. Fred had never seen even the outside of such a hotel before. At supper, the bow-tied waiter approached stiffly to take the first course orders. Fred, in a panic of incomprehension, considered it safest to go for the dish at the very top of the list. 'Ah'm going to start off with some o' that', he said to the waiter, pointing his great forefinger at the top line. It said, 'Samedi, le vingt trois avril'.

Popplewell continues on his friend's new drive for quality. 'In it, there is still, of course, the underlying fundamental Botham principle: "Everything to Excess". Wine, food, clothes, may all be of a higher quality – but they are not lessened in quantity. Ian is an extraordinarily generous man. He took us out for dinner several times last season just to see if his new Barclaycard worked! The last time he finished the best part of a bottle of 1939 brandy (with no apparent ill effects). He enjoyed it immensely, but was going to reserve judgment until he'd drunk a bottle of the '38 the following night.'

The very model of a
modern mannequin – but of
a future Hollywood career,
Ian says, 'I take life as
it comes'

One of Ian's most consummately brilliant Test match centuries, to my certain knowledge, followed a gloriously carousing night of revelry and good fellowship on the tiles. As the dark hours ticked on, everyone else collapsed into sleep where they dropped. Ian was left to join in, alone, with the dawn chorus. Thus, later that morning, his sumptuous innings was doubly awe-inspiring. All England was enthralled as the match was turned. They didn't know the half of it. Chesterton again:

'St George he was for England
And before he killed the dragon
He drank a pint of English ale
Out of an English flagon.'

Botham has yet to suffer as other mortals. He probably thinks Alka Seltzer is a pop group or something. 'Hangovers? What are they? Never had one in my life. Sure, I've had quite a few nights on the tiles over the years and then gone in next day and clocked up a hell of a lot of fast runs.' He adds, diplomatically, 'As long as it's once in a while, I think it doesn't do any harm.'

The most gorgeously dramatic case of what you might call drink-and-driving I have personally witnessed was when I covered England's tour to India in 1982. India is not what you'd call a drinking man's trip. For some reason we struck lucky at Indore – you know, friends of friends of a boozy

British resident or whatever. Ian and I were still on the barstools (me, just) long after the whole town, including our barman, were asleep on the floor. I managed an hour's sleep, if that, before having to grope for the team bus, Ian incredibly looking as if he'd slept like a baby. England batted. Indore's cricket field is a very big one. In no time three wickets were gone – Tavaré, Fletcher and Cook. Somerset's celebrant of swipe strode in, none too pleased, to join Gatting. He was still in his sandy-scuffed gym shoes and tracksuit bottoms when the call came. He played himself in with heavy menance, blocking the first 11 balls. In the next 44 balls he hit 16 fours, 7 sixes, 3 twos and 10 singles. When Ian arrived at the wicket, Gatting had not yet scored. When Ian was out – for a power-crazed 122 – Mike had reached 5. Ian strode back, garlanded with adoration by the awestruck Indian crowd, had a wash – and then went to the gym behind the pavilion to play three sets of badminton!

Good English drinking and good English cricketing have long enjoyed a partnership, for all that the Puritans blanch. The very founder of both feasts was 'the Doctor' himself. He too had a head for a hearty long session. His hundredth century was scored for Gloucestershire against Somerset in 1895 – 288 in fact, at 50 an hour and chanceless. That evening his supporters gave W.G. a celebration dinner. Somerset's champion, Sammy Woods, sat next to him and reported later – 'He drank something of everything, before and during dinner. And afterwards he sent for the whisky bottle. You just could not make the Old Man drunk. His nut was too large. About midnight, some of us thought we might start for home; but the Old Man said to me: "Shock'ead, get two others, and we'll play two rubbers of whist till two in the morning." So we did.' And next morning W.G. went batting again.

Woods himself must have been a stupendous fellow. We will meet this earlier Somerset captain on many occasions later in this book, for whenever I read of him I can sense his presence and gusto and grandeur to be in the very image of his successor, Master Botham. Sam would bowl like the wind, hit like the very devil, and then tell the tale of it all night to a tavern, usually Taunton's George Inn, where he lodged. He would sometimes, it is said, walk to 'away' matches in the county, refreshing himself through the journey with the contents of cider flagons, previously hidden in hedges or under hillocks by him or his friends for just such eventuality. Woods was, said the writer (and Somerset opening bowler) R.C. Robertson-Glasgow, 'convivial, some said too convivial. But drinking was just part of his life, and it made no difference to his kindness and

Sammy Woods . . . the man with most of Botham in him, still smiling – and swiping – into old age

humour. He made the younger players stick to beer and early hours – "Whisky and one o'clock in the morning won't suit you, my dears".' But in his prime, such combinations surely suited Sammy.

Oh, to have spent a consumingly cheery night in The George with Woods and Botham. And then watched them batting together next morning, hangover-free, just joyously bombarding the old pavilion in their roistering or, from the other end, seeing who could tonk the thing first into the Tone. Nigel Popplewell has watched one half of that heavenly partnership do it: 'Ian appears to be unaffected by the excesses off the field. He is an astonishing cricketer . . . and can be as good after a night on the razzle and two hours' sleep as he is after nine hours' sleep. I've seen him flat out in the dressing-room until he is in – then he just rubs the sleep out of his eyes, and hooks Malcolm Marshall off his eyebrows time and again. It really is extraordinary. In fact, perhaps he would not be half as good but for his extra-mural excesses. They all spring from the same well of his soul, and to restrict one might be to restrain the other and make him not only a lesser cricketer but a duller person altogether.'

My favourite story about Ian in this convivial context was the time Graham Gooch, England's charming and supremely talented opening batsman, took umbrage in Barbados when Ian was captain of England during the tour to the West Indies in 1981. After a sweltering day's batting at Bridgetown in which Graham had scored a long, big hundred the boys all repaired to the pub, the drinks on Ian, naturally. During the evening, the captain spotted Gooch's eyelids flickering, and his chin cupped comfortably in his palms. The big opening batsman was tired out after his perspiring, concentrating day in the field – especially as his daily habit through the tour had been to be up before breakfast for an invigorating run along the dawn-fresh beaches of the islands. Anyway, to see a friend and colleague showing signs of drowsiness when the night was just beginning was too much for Ian. He called an impromptu team meeting – to discuss whether Graham, because of his obvious lack of stamina, should be allowed to continue his early morning runs. The abstemious sportsman, Graham, blew his top – pointing out that sometimes of a morning, after eight hours' sleep, he had set off on his jog at the same time as his captain was downing his final rum punch of the party of the night before!

Cricket's legendary hitter was Gilbert Jessop. Might 'the Croucher' have liked a drink or two to fuel his furies at the crease? His most celebrated innings in a lifetime of batting pyrotechnics was at The Oval in 1902, when he turned the match for England with, till then, an unparalleled display of clean Test match hitting. But in his autobiography, *A Cricketer's Log*, Jessop just hints, demurely, that he might well have been on the razzle the night before at the Grand Central Hotel. Certainly, as the night wore on, he admits to gambling on the outcome of the morrow, and particularly on his own part in the coming proceedings – 'which was usually anathema to me... but was to assist in the laudable object of raising drooping spirits'. He then owns up to the fact that his 'first glass of Pommery produced that feeling which for want of a better word may be described as "more-ish"'. We have all had that feeling: these days the phrase is 'getting the taste'.

In 1938, at Madras, Joe Hardstaff, another heroic batsman of the long legend found himself, in the early hours, in a drinking contest – 'whisky, brandy, gin, the lot' – with a generous Maharajah. Earlier, a few other England tourists, including George Pope and Arthur Wellard, had dropped out of the running around midnight. At approximately 5 a.m., Joe suddenly gives in and goes out like a light. They carry him home to bed, thinking he's really done it this time: probably he will never wake up again. Next morning he goes out to bat against Madras – stays all day, makes 213 in five hours, hitting 24 fours and *Wisden* records that 'Hardstaff was never in any trouble'.

I crib that story from Harold Pinter's quite stunningly good little essay on his friend, Arthur Wellard – the same of Somerset and the 66 sixes. Before his death, in 1980, Arthur would umpire matches for the playwright's happy band of roving thespians, Gaieties CC. In the classic memoir, which I read after the old man's death, and have been lovingly carrying about with me ever since, Pinter wondered if Wellard's 5 sixes in an over off both Armstrong, of Derbyshire, in 1936 or Woolley, of Kent, two years later, represented his most memorable hitting. No, said Arthur, it was one hit above all that he remembered – off Amar Singh at Bombay on that same tour in 1938. 'He wasn't a bad bowler', said Wellard, 'he moved it about a bit. He dug it in. You had to watch yourself. Anyway, he suddenly let one go, it was well up and swinging. I could see it all the way and I hit it. Well, they've got those stands at Bombay, one on top of the other, and I saw this ball, she was still climbing when she hit the top of the top stand. I was aiming for that river they've got over there. The Ganges. If it hadn't been for that bloody top stand, I'd have had it in the Ganges. That wasn't a bad blow, that one.'

Good ol' Arthur! as they used to chortle when he launched another at Weston or Wells or Frome. When young Harold Gimblett hitch-hiked to Frome in May 1935 for his first ever county game (100 in 63 minutes), Arthur had loaned him the bat he did it with. Wellard was a hitter, pure and simple – about a quarter of the 12,000 runs he hit for Somerset were in sixes (508 in 633 innings: he scored just two centuries). By the autumn of 1985, Botham had hit 256 sixes for the County in 245 innings, plus some 80-odd in other first-class cricket for England, MCC, etc. (Vivian

Richards, by the way, has hit 202 sixes in 281 innings for Somerset – and more, of course, for Antigua and the West Indies.)

The record of Jessop, Gloucestershire's demon, remains the imponderable (and also that of his great hitting contempories such as Thornton and Ford and Bonner) because only in 1910 was the ruling introduced by which six was automatically awarded to a batsman who cleared the boundary 'rope' with a full pitch. Before that you only got six if the ball was hit right out of the ground. The cricket writer who has made a study of sixers is the south coast schoolmaster, the estimable Gerald Brodribb, whose intriguing researches led him to reckon that, had the 1910 ruling been in force throughout Jessop's career, conjecture can come up with a 'six average' of 35 per season. That is still a pretty phenomenal total over Jessop's 20-year career: only seven men since 1910 have hit over 40 in a summer – J.H. Edrich, A.W. Carr, H.T. Bartlett, and F. Barratt each managed it once, Viv Richards and Botham have passed the 40-mark twice; and Wellard did it five times in a career of 17 years.

Jessop, Wellard and Botham seem out on their own for *consistently* big hitting – but as Brodribb has pointed out in the *Wisden Cricket Monthly*, those who have reached 40 or more sixes in a summer needed an average of 42 innings to do so. In 1985, Botham's incredible 80 sixes came in only 27 innings – 'so if he had played as many innings as the others he could in theory have amassed as many as 124 sixes: even the great Jessop might have found that seasonal figure beyond him.'

Botham, meanwhile, had many more tunes to play, and at consistently higher levels. Jessop played only 18 Tests (batting average 21; 1 century; taking 10 wickets, and holding 11 catches). Wellard played thrice for England (47 runs, 7 wickets, 2 catches). Nicely, each described themselves as all-rounders, and they each played for western counties; all three had attitudes and interests that smacked of the land and the heritage of villagers. Jessop was a fine shot and horseman. His former new-ball buddy, Bill Andrews, once described Wellard, 'though originally from Kent, he was as much Somerset as farmhouse cider . . . he was as much at home on a farm as in a cricket net, I've seen him often with a gun in one hand and a fishing rod in the other.' You could readily say exactly the same of Ian Botham.

Having shown himself to be, arguably, the most explosive hitter the game has ever known, towards the end of 1985 (and by way of Land's End and John o'Groats) Ian Botham could take stock, if he was so inclined, on his chances of becoming the greatest *all-rounder* in cricket history. Mind

Arthur Wellard . . . sky-scorching Somerset hitter who also liked to bowl fast

The three other runners in the one-horse race: the outstanding all-rounders, from New Zealand Richard Hadlee (*opposite, above*), from India Kapil Dev (*opposite, below*) and for Pakistan Imran Khan (*above*)

you, even if he was not already the most successful English wicket-taking bowler of all time he has a very good claim to a place in the current England team as just a specialist batsman. His Test average is only a point or two behind those of Lamb (38.12), Gooch (37.83) and Gatting (37.43). He has reached 50 in 33 Test innings, and gone on to the century in 13 of these, just about 40 per cent. Compare this with Gatting, who has 'gone on' 4 times out of 17, and Gower (12 out of 37), to say nothing of the three other world-class all-rounders with whom Botham is most often compared: Hadlee (1 out of 11), Kapil Dev (3 out of 18) and Imran Khan (2 out of 9).

Pursuing the theme of longevity for a moment: Botham's 'century average', that is, the average of all his Test hundreds, making no distinction between outs and not-outs, is 128, the same as Boycott's. Keith Miller, a similar character to Botham, has a similar 'century-average' of 131. Botham has batted once for England at No. 4, 18 times at No. 5, and lower than that on all other occsions.

One of the remarkable turn-ups of the 1985 summer was the prolific (and top speed) scoring of the England upper order. Botham has not often been in a strong Test batting side: in 72 of his 125 innings, he has come in with the score at 150 or less. In only two of his 13 centuries could England be said to have been on top of the bowling when he came in, and these were marginal (185-3 against India in 1982, when he made 208, and 276-5 against Pakistan in 1978 – Botham 100). He has made centuries from such unpromising positions as 57-4; 58-4; 88-5; 92-4; 104-5; and 105-5, the last in the famous match at Leeds in 1981, when England were following on. Botham has made the highest score of the innings 21 times, a high proportion for a No. 6, and the best England aggregate of the match nine times.

But Ian loves his bowling. He ended the 1985 summer aware only that Dennis Lillee's all-time record of 355 Test wickets was sitting ready to be broken. For all that singular ambition, his bowling record looked at in tandem with his Test match batting is exceptional. He is the only Test cricketer to have scored 3,000 runs and taken 300 wickets; three others are approaching these targets – Hadlee, Kapil Dev and Imran Khan. He reached the simple double of 1,000 runs and 100 wickets in his 21st Test, beating the previous record of Vinoo Mankad, who got there in 23 Tests, and he reached the 'double double' in 42 Tests, overtaking Richie Benaud who had taken 60 Tests to achieve it. Derek Lodge's very simple means of assessing all-rounders is to divide the batting average by the bowling average, thus cancelling out any advantage conferred by the conditions. Botham comes very high on a list confined to those who have done the 'double' in Tests:

	Batting avge	Bowling avge	Batting & bowling
Sobers	57.98	34.03	1.70
Miller	36.97	22.97	1.61
Botham	**36.13**	**26.37**	**1.37**
Imran Khan	31.12	22.91	1.36
Goddard	34.46	26.22	1.31
Greig	40.43	32.20	1.26

It is worth pointing out, in admiring the figures, the sad absence of Mike Procter − courtesy white South Africa's wretched apartheid policies. I wonder where he would have figured after a full Test career of, say, a dozen years?

Apart from the *nonpareil* Sobers (and perhaps Procter, had he played more Test cricket), the Australian all-rounder, Miller, is often set against Botham when the romantics 'play' the statisticians around the hearth. To my knowledge, Sir Neville Cardus alas never saw Botham play. The grand old knight died in the winter of 1975 just after Ian's first sustained announcement of himself at Somerset. How Cardus would have approved of Botham. This, for instance, is what he wrote of Miller: 'He remains the greatest match-winner in cricket, capable of turning a game upside down in quick time, tossing his head and hair, swinging round rapidly and impatiently to bowl, a bold improviser, alive, inspiring, brilliant, naturally gifted. All reflex action of eye and nerve. And skills that might well take their source from the very bloodstream of this handsome cricketer.' There are less lyrical resemblances: Botham and Miller hit hard and were bowlers dependent very much on inspiration. But it is interesting to note that Miller, whose batting average (36.97) was much the same as Botham's, only scored over 50 in 20 of his 87 innings. He might have played on some poor wickets. And he was a much more defensive bowler than Botham, if figures are to be believed; his striking rate was 61.54 balls per wicket and he conceded only 37.24 runs per 100 balls.

A comparison with all the England all-rounders who have scored 1,000 runs and taken 50 wickets also puts Botham in an outstanding light, as is shown alphabetically, overleaf. Hammond's place at the head of this table is perhaps a little misleading: his batting was superlative, but he had few notable bowling performances in Tests, and his striking rate (95.98) was undistinguished. But add together the innings over 50 and the five-wicket performances of the above players and you will see that Botham emerges as a clear winner.

	Runs	Avge	Wkts	Avge	Batt. avge/ Bowl. avge	Ct	100	50	5w Inns	10w Inns
Bailey	2290	29.74	132	29.21	1.02	32	1	10	5	1
Dexter	4502	47.89	66	34.93	1.37	29	9	27	—	—
Greig	3599	40.43	141	32.20	1.26	87	8	20	6	2
Hammond	7249	58.45	83	37.80	1.55	110	22	24	2	—
Illingworth	1836	23.24	122	31.20	0.74	45	2	5	3	—
Rhodes	2325	30.19	127	26.96	1.12	60	2	11	6	1
Tate	1198	25.48	155	26.16	0.97	11	1	5	7	1
Titmus	1449	22.29	153	32.22	0.69	35	—	10	7	—
Woolley	3283	36.07	83	33.91	1.06	64	5	23	4	1
Botham	**4409**	**36.13**	**343**	**26.37**	**1.37**	**92**	**13**	**20**	**25**	**4**

World cricket in the 1980s has been honoured by the presence of three other galvanizing all-rounders, as well as Botham. At the time of writing, all four were preparing for Test tours which span 1985-86. Before they set off, their respective figures were:

BATTING & FIELDING:

	Tests	Inns	N.O.	H.S.	Runs	Avge	100	50	Ct
Botham	**79**	**125**	**3**	**208**	**4409**	**36.13**	**13**	**20**	**92**
Kapil Dev	68	101	9	126*	2788	30.30	3	15	26
Imran Khan	51	77	12	123	2023	31.12	2	7	16
Hadlee	57	96	12	103	2088	24.85	1	10	29

BOWLING:

	Balls	Runs	Wkts	Avge	5wInns	10wM	Balls/ wkt	Runs/ 100b
Botham	**18391**	**9046**	**343**	**26.37**	**25**	**4**	**53.62**	**49.19**
Kapil Dev	14522	7406	258	28.70	18	2	56.29	50.99
Imran Khan	12551	5316	232	22.91	16	4	54.10	42.36
Hadlee	14292	6341	266	23.83	19	4	53.73	44.37

I suspect Imran will no longer be the bowler he was, so this seems to make Hadlee the best bowler, Botham the best bat – with Botham's marvellous slip fielding bringing him out a clear winner. Or does it?

Let's apply one final litmus test. You will agree that any player who scores a century and takes five wickets in an innings in the same Test can consider himself a match-winner. It has only been done 22 times in over a thousand Tests. Thirteen players have done it once; two, Sobers and Mushtaq Mohammad, have done it twice. *Botham has done it five times.*

Christchurch, 1978	103,30	5-73, 3-38	3 catches
Lord's 1978	108	0-17, 8-34	2 catches
Bombay, 1980	114	6-58, 7-48	
Leeds, 1981	50,149	6-95, 1-14	2 catches
Wellington, 1984	138	5-59, 1-37	1 catch

Let the astonishing cricketing figures speak for themselves – remembering in *real* cricket and sport, no decimal figure or long-division table has ever produced an even half-decent piece of oratory. In this book, from here on in, we leave, as far as possible, the adjectival waffle behind, and also the dry and dusty decimal points. And we listen to the views of the men, and rivals, who live and work with Ian Botham, day in, day out. We talked to many cricketers – the 17 year old who battled with Botham on his county debut, the honest-to-goodness, highly skilled county pro, the oldest old hands in the business who have seen it all (they thought), and the onliest super-duper stars in the game. For instance, says Vivian Richards, 'I admire hugely the way Ian is honest and frank and down-to-earth in all that he does. He stands up for his rights and those of his colleagues. He is an all-round human being.' Thus reckons the captain of the West Indies.

There have been times – and in recent years – when England v Australia Test matches were played under a cloud of overwhelming antipathy between the two sides. Some of those you might call the ringleaders of those 'gangland' wars are now held in high esteem – and given high positions – by cricket's establishment. Ian Botham, all in the know would agree, is given little credit for his very singular part in restoring good fellowship and sportsmanship to every Ashes series he has played in since becoming the senior pro for England. A few years ago, an Australian captain would not deign to speak a civil word to, or about, an English player. Says the current Australian captain, Allan Border, of Botham: 'He can be a bit of a larrikin at times, but I find him to be a good fella. He's very straight. There are no dark secrets about the guy. No matter what he's done on the cricket field during the day, good or bad, he's always the first bloke to have a drink with you. I think he's misunderstood by the English cricket hierarchy. They don't like him because of his brash ways. But

'He's always the first to have a drink with you after the game' – the two adversaries off for a 'quiet night out' on the town

there's a lot of good things in his character they obviously can't see. Or don't want to. I class him as a good mate . . .'

Botham's long-standing team colleagues have long enjoyed his friendship as much as his cricket. Says Vic Marks: 'He can be grumpy and half asleep while waiting to bat, then all of a sudden he switches on as he walks out. He guffaws, jests and chatters at the crease, but when the bowler starts to run up, you can see the shutters come down over his eyes. He is a remarkable competitor. He loves a challenge. It's almost as if he needs adversity to bring out the best in him.' Nigel Popplewell concurs: 'It is a mark of his supreme ability that players who have played with him for ten years are *still* amazed at his talent. Ian will drag the most somnolent professional from the depths of the dressing-room to the pavilion balcony with some of his incredible displays of batting. There are no new superlatives to describe him. He is simply brilliant.'

Ian Botham's bowling, batsmanship – his very lifemanship – depends on daring dangerously. It seemed to his friends that he had embarked this new year under review most dangerously indeed when the very first headlines of January screamed out BOTHAM ON DRUGS CHARGE. (The winter previously, on tour with England in New Zealand, there had also been a plethora of headlines after a local woman freelance journalist had sold a story alleging Botham's use of drugs to the *Mail on Sunday*: Botham sued for libel and the High Court case is still to be heard at the time of writing.)

This new case turned out to have been quite preposterously proceeded with. On New Year's Eve, out of the blue, police found 2.19 grammes of cannabis in a bag in the bottom of a bedroom drawer at Ian's house in Epworth. The 'substance' was worth less than £4. Ian pleaded guilty and was fined £100. Police forces in most parts of the country no more than caution first offenders for possession of cannabis – certainly, as in this case, for such a tiny amount. Something still 'smells' about the whole episode, but it did not stop the establishment Puritans issuing righteous statements to all and sundry news agencies. Why is the nation so po about pot? A number of the most pious and 'horrified' statements came from self-proclaimed 'upright' citizens who, to my certain knowledge, have no qualms at all about driving a car dangerously when in a stupified drunken state. Drunken drivers have killed many more innocents than cannabis smokers. No matter, on they battered till the 'defence' organised itself to rout them – as just these three successive letters in the *Wisden Cricket Monthly* will testify:

> I DO hope Ian Botham does not play for England again. I have a young family – enough said?
>
> M.A. Grantham, Limpsfield Chart, Surrey.

> How I sympathise with Mr Grantham in his paternal desire to protect his offspring from Ian Botham. My own experience only serves to illustrate the harmful effects of succumbing to the dreadful weed. In May 1968 I smoked my first and last 'joint', and I am certain that therein lies the source of my subsequent misfortune. Although I have continually held myself in readiness to open the innings for my country, the call has never come. Thus in surrendering to one moment of sensual pleasure, I robbed my fellow Englishmen of the chance to witness the rebirth of English cricket, an event that was delayed until July 20, 1981.

Let me assure Mr Grantham that not only
does the occasional joint totally expunge
any natural cricketing ability one may
possess, but it also has another side effect,
which will soon become apparent to the
medical profession, viz. a feeling of
sudden and uncontrollable hostility
towards pompous sods.

Yours in Technicolour,
M.R. Frost, Swanley, Kent.

I am a poor man, but I would gladly give ten
shillings to know who told the officers of
the law about the contents of Ian Botham's
drawers.

Ian Greenwood, Edgware, Middx.

Ian himself thinks he was 'set up'. Sure, he has smoked the stuff. Are
there many young Englishmen of his age and lifestyle who haven't? 'But
I've never ever once had any marijuana in the house. Never. Ask anyone.
It was early evening, New Year's Eve. We were preparing for a little
family drinks party. Kath's grandfather, who's in his 90s, was coming so
we were all looking forward to it. About quarter to six, there was a knock
on the door. Four policemen I'd never seen before. Drugs Squad, they
said. Could they search the house? Sure, I've got nothing to hide, go
ahead. In court they said I'd demanded to see their search warrant. That
was simply untrue. They were in and out in no time at all. Straight
upstairs. Into the drawers. One of them said "What's this?" I said, "Well, I
know what it looks like." Kath and I then went down to the police station.
That was that.

'The following morning, New Year's Day, twenty-four hours before
anyone else had wind of it, a reporter from one certain Fleet Street paper
was outside my house. A hell of a coincidence, don't you think?'

In July, the Test and County Cricket Board asked all first-class players
in England to sign a declaration agreeing to submit to random dope tests.
With his Somerset colleagues, Richards and Garner, Ian took legal advice
before signing. 'I reckon that I had been stuffed once and did not want to
be "set up" again' – though in spite of the headlines it provoked, the
whole issue was the most pimply of molehills, for the TCCB expect every
player to sign each April, as a matter of course, an agreement that binds
them to existing Board disciplinary regulations – to include any amend-
ments and additions introduced during the season.

After his conviction, however, Ian had issued a statement of 'apology' to his supporters, especially if he had 'set a poor example to his young and impressionable admirers'. It was aimed, diplomatically and courteously, to a pretty hypocritical establishment. I doubt if the schoolboys of England gave a fig for it. They were just looking forward to the end of a beastly winter and the springtime start of a new cricket season. And schoolboys are very good judges: they think straight, they are bold, they are uncontriving; they understand that heroics are sponsored by daring, they are unapprenticed in prejudice. They also admire cricketers who hit the first ball of a Test match straight into the members' pavilion just to get their eye in. There is only one such man alive.

For now it was approaching the time when a seasonal cry was heard about the land. '*Is Botham in?*'

2 The whole town's too small

CRICKET seeps in; usually the operative verb. Shyly, in late-ish April, English cricket puts a toe in the water and then retires to the pavilion in a huddle of sweaters for a fortnight or so, almost pleased in a way not to have to take centre-stage after so much plotting, rehearsal and anticipation: it is enough for the time being to rejig, or rejoin in the jokes of last August, to tap in the new bat, to bet on cards or TV horses, and chivvy the umpires to forego their pointless next inspection and call the thing off for the day. Cricket shows itself with a blush, and early season cricketers themselves are coyly cuddled in long-johns and layers of steamy vests. Occasionally they might troop out for fielding practice with balls of soap and red-stained hands and guffaws. Content enough to be back together, they like to play in the summer softly, however soggily. It is enough in April to smell the blossom on the rain-drenched trees, and feel again the amiable, splintery scrunch of stud on the good, soft 'give' of pine or deal that floorboard pavilions. Some county players demand an April of regimented, cruel callisthenics for fitness; jigging and jogging and topped up with hours in the nets in front of a relentless bowling machine. Others lark about waiting for the rain to stop so they can bat and bowl themselves fit in the middle – and so within the month and in God's good time, it will seem as if cricket had never hibernated. Our hero is one of these.

There were other things, anyway, to fill the back pages in the third week of April 1985. It was a busy time. I conned for myself a pleasant few days in Spain, at La Manga sports resort where the previous September's Cupwinners, Middlesex (NatWest) and Lancashire (Benson & Hedges) were splurging their final prize with a week of pre-season training in the sun. They played a lot of golf and practised a little cricket, sometimes watched by blank and bewildered Bavarian holidaymakers who would lean on their golf trolleys and pull faces of incomprehension. On television in the evening we watched the Masters' golf from Angusta willing, with the Spanish waiters, a last-round charge from the dashing

Jack Simmons . . . old hand with the nicotined spinning finger

Ballesteros. We listened, through the World Service static, to the English FA Cup soccer semi-finals; and also saw, by satellite, beamed up through the jewel-starred ceiling of Nevada and down through the same in Spain, the stunningly brutal prizefight between the black boxers, Hagler and Hearns. But mostly the talk was of cricket. Half the Middlesex team – Gatting, Edmonds, Emburey, Downton and Cowans – had been on England's triumphant winter tour to India, and after they had told their tales with relish, they would cluster round to listen to Lancashire's veteran trencherman and off-break bowler, Jack Simmons. Having dined, as ever, well, Jack would plonk a shoe on the bar's foot-rail, cup a cigarette into his palm with his ochre-stained spinning finger, sup an ale, and tell the young men of the day he bowled out Sobers, or Cowdrey, or Graveney, or Barry Richards, or Boycott . . . or Botham.

Unlike some of the press-box preachers I was surrounded by at home, it was noticeable there in Spain that a fair-sized congregation of English cricket professionals were unable to envisage a Test team for the forthcoming Ashes series without Ian Botham in it. Only well past midnight, as conversation rambled into pleasantly slurring incoherence, might you have sensed just a passing flutter of uncertainty about the big boy's days being done. Well, he had already had a pretty long innings when you thought about it, especially living life at the pace that he did. Certainly, all agreed, one of the pleasures of the English spring was to be an assessment of Botham's form.

Simmons had to fly home early – to attend the select, annual, black-tied *Wisden* dinner in a London old gent's club. He had been named, at last, as one of the 'bible's' exclusive band of brothers, a Cricketer of the Year, to a general acclaim from every outpost of the game of, 'Well played, you 'ol bugger'. Jack, aged 44, was touchingly chuffed at this nod from the establishment, and he was seen off in style. I had to leave next day as well. A very sporty week was ending with one of any winter's most clamorous fixtures – the England versus Wales Rugby Union international in Cardiff. It had been postponed from frost-bound February. The British weather in late-ish April was scarcely any better, even though another little matter was getting under way that Saturday. Not that many realised it: it warranted two magnifying-glass lines in the national newspapers' fixture lists, and one news paragraph headlined 'Botham Leads'. On the very day England and Wales ended the rugger season, cricket was stirring: Essex were to play Cambridge University at Fenner's, and Somerset had assembled in the Parks to play Oxford University. I had planned to drive straight from Heathrow to Cardiff, stopping in mid-morning for a romantic half-hour or so for a first whiff of summer in the Parks. Some hopes. As I approached the old city from the East, I was overtaken by a fast flurry of snowflakes. I kept my head down and over the Cotswolds to Cardiff. A famously wretched winter was battering on with all barrels blazing.

They did play at Oxford on Monday. But it was winter still; thermal undies and a desolate scene. How now the poet at the Parks – 'the plane whispering love to the elm in the beautiful season of spring'? For a start, the famous old elms had been long diseased. It can be the world's most perfect cricketing ground. Now the slashing north-easterly came in over John o' Groats to rear up off a length at Oxford. So much for the dreamy, daisy-chaining, student lovers lolling on the grass watching Fry or Foster, Donnelly or Cowdrey. The Cherwell had baby ice-floes in it. Botham had won the toss, sent the undergraduates into the freezing field, dared his opening batsmen, Roebuck and Wyatt, to allow any team-mate an entrance, and bagged his captain's place nearest the pavilion radiator to watch the snooker on television. The county openers needed no second bidding: this one's for the averages: the old hand, Roebuck, resumed his meticulous vigil of the year before and warmed his own cockles at least by staying six hours for an undefeated 123. Wyatt made 145. They went even better in the corresponding icy panto of 1984 when the two of them put on a paltry 181 for the first wicket at Oxford. Then Somerset had declared at 365 for 1: this time Botham called in his batsmen 14 runs short of that. He had himself down at No. 5, but there was little chance of him batting even though the prospect had a few dons and undergraduates cycling up in their mufflers to enquire. Since he had first played in the fixture when he was 18 in 1974 (c Northcote-Green, b Stallibrass 2, to make their cricketing career for all three of them!), he had only turned out on two other occasions at the Parks (11 wkts and 130 runs for twice out in next to no time). As I say, no candy from kids.

Next day he stood, huge and swathed in sweaters at slip, like a snow-man sponsored by Michelin, cracking jokes and always being first to insist on signalling out the tea trolley for a warming brew – and, captain's prerogative, making sure it was laced with an appropriately spirited tingle. He bowled six overs of gentle off-breaks and Oxford's impressively crisp young captain, Carr, made a century. On the way home, even the fog was freezing.

For a county batsman, an April century against one of the University sides is a perfectly acceptable pipe-opener. But gluttony does not go down well in the freemasonry: they still talk with scorn of Trevor Jesty's greedy 248 against Cambridge a year or so before. Everyone at Somerset this time was pleased with young Julian Wyatt's hundred. Last season after good beginnings – notably a staunch knock against Malcolm Marshall and the West Indies – the farmer's son from Farrington Gurney had been increasingly found out by the knowing county bowlers as being, literally, a touch uncertain outside the off stump. Now, his first year's apprenticeship served, a steady advance was being expected of Wyatt – not least, as well, from such as Nigel Felton, a chunky Millfielder, Richard Ollis, long-legged Bristolian, and the bustling, bits-and-pieces competitor, Gary Palmer, son of Ken, the former Somerset all-rounder and now a leading umpire. The side was still in slight transition after the loss to retirement the year before of 'Dasher' Denning and the too-long promising Philip Slocombe. Now the all-rounder, Jeremy Lloyds, had moved north across the Avon to try for more luck with Gloucestershire. Young men like Stephen Booth, slow spin, and Mark Davis, nippy left-hand, could also fully establish a place of their own this summer. Not that Somerset had cause at all for anything but optimism as they gathered for their first Championship match in the spring of 1985. On the contrary, their two heavyweight champions from the West Indies would now be restored to the side following their country's tour through England of the year before: the emperor, Vivian Richards, quite simply, remained the present world of cricket's most awesomely lacerating batsman: as the bonny, beanpole Bajan, Joel Garner, was still, at the same time, the sunniest as well as sometimes the scariest of all opening bowlers. They were due back next month to join the established nucleus of Brian Rose, stalwart former captain, England Test batsman, and gardener; Colin Dredge, Frome workhorse, always galloping in against the wind; Nigel Popplewell, popular all-round tidy-upper; and the wicket-keeper, Trevor Gard, squat, stocky countryman, ferreter, pheasant-rearer with a warm appeal in every way.

Flanking Colonel Botham next to the Oxford radiator were the two Oxbridge Englishmen, Vic Marks and Peter Roebuck. They were now very much in their differing primes at cricket, and each was setting out this springtime after the handsomest of deeds the previous summer when the dogged, often heroic, sheet anchor of the innings, Roebuck, had scored prolifically enough to have been called to England's colours in quite a few other eras, and the amiable and often underrated all-rounder Marks had finished 1984 with over 1,000 runs and 86 wickets with his lulling off-spinners to win himself another England tour to India in

Vic Marks . . . Oxbridge, author, and chief lieutenant: 'Ian can be utterly infuriating, but he's impossible to dislike and never boring'

the winter. Both these close friends had taken to authorship. In recent seasons, Roebuck had published a series of beautifully observed essays on cricket – spiky sharp and speckled with casual insights that us behind the ropes could never be privy to. Marks followed fast to the inkwell, producing a popular, potted history of Somerset CCC in 1984, and now, after India in the winter, one of the most readable, unghosted tour books by any cricketer.

Back in February, the *Daily Mirror* had reported from India – under the extravagant headline BOTHAM BUST-UP – that two of England's senior touring players (not, it goes without saying, being named) were claiming that the side was 'better off without Botham'. One, apparently, said: 'I would rather have been paid £12,000 to tour without Botham than to have received another £5,000 to come with him.' Now, in the spring, some serious cricket writers were assessing Botham's position. In the April edition of *The Cricketer*, the former Warwickshire bowler, Jack Bannister, asked, 'Colossus at the Crossroads: will England need him this summer?' Wrote the well-respected Bannister: 'England can win without him … there *should* be no problem about slotting Botham back into the side, always assuming that his form and fitness in the first six weeks of the season warrant it. But the borderline between his powers to create and destroy have become too blurred not to be re-defined before his re-entry into orbit is even considered. All too often before this winter's tour, it has been Botham's finger on the self-destruct button. This summer the selectors must ensure he is treated in exactly the same way as every other England player. If he delivers with the ball, fine. If not, then the decision to play him, regardless of performance, is no longer valid. Botham still has a part to play for England. Perhaps even a big part. How successfully he does that is far from straightforward, and a realignment of attitude by everyone in the next few weeks is essential. In the end it is down to the player himself.'

Meanwhile, Vic Marks had returned from India to check the proofs of his book. The chief lieutenant had begun and ended it with an affectionate appraisal of his county captain: 'Ian had toured every winter since 1977 and needed a break if he was to remain the lynchpin of England's cricket throughout the eighties. Inevitably, his absence would create an enormous vacuum both on the field and in the team room. We all know that only he can change the course of a Test within a session, but who is going to fill our Yorkshire opening batsman's shoes with shaving foam, deafen us with Toyah or lift the depression of colleagues by sheer exuberance? Occasionally he can be utterly infuriating, but he's impossible to dislike and never boring. I shall miss him and so will millions of Indian cricket lovers … The fascinating question this new summer will be whether Gower can harness the awesome talent of Botham to effect. Ian, too, certainly respects David Gower and will support him, but will Gower have the strength to wrench the ball from Ian's hands in a Lord's Test match against Australia if he believes a change of bowling to be beneficial – or will he shrug his shoulders? Botham himself will experience a new kind of pressure. Though there is still a gaping hole in the England side for him to fill, the Indian tour will have shown him that he's not indispensable; it is possible for England to win without him. I guess that he will have been slightly surprised by our success and particularly since this winter has not proved quite as peaceful as he would have hoped, he'll be anxious to make the headlines in June – for his cricketing prowess. Despite his prodigious Test record, he'll still have plenty to prove and that's when he's at his most dangerous as a cricketer.'

We shall see what will come to pass.

For now it was the real thing. And could it have been a fluke that Mike Gear, the Test and County Cricket Board's assistant secretary and fixtures' planner at Lord's, had brought Nottinghamshire back to Taunton for the first Championship match of 1985? (It was: he works at least 18 months in advance.) For seven months earlier, when the September leaves were turning as sharply as the off-breaks after a heatwave summer, it was at Taunton that Nottinghamshire had lost the County Championship title to Essex on the very last afternoon of the season. Some chivalrous, knife-edge captaincy by Botham had set Nottingham to score 297 in 60 overs: they had responded dramatically, failing to win only when an heroic hit had been held in the outfield off the penultimate ball so Essex, sweating on the radio commentary in Chelmsford, pocketed the prizes and the pennant. Now Nottingham's captain, the astute and organized South African, Clive Rice, was back at Taunton at the first time of asking. Richard Hadlee, the oustandingly sharp New Zealand all-rounder, was waiting till the may was in bloom, but Derek Randall was, as ever, bristling keen to be led out once more by Rice – as was England's new 'find' from the tour of India, the composed young coolhand, Tim Robinson.

Alas, the weather had shown no improvement on Oxford from four days before. Out of the milky-white sky the same Arctic wind lanced the very marrow of the cricketers as, up yonder, it had clumps of leaden clouds careering crazily across the long quiff of the Quantocks. For all that, Taunton is a better place than most to begin at the beginning. With its spanking new, modern bricked and tiered pavilion, the old ground has popped proudly into the second half of the century only in the last two years: yet on the other side, once the 'business' end, the familiar old paint-peeled clutter of woodworm and woodwork and staircases, tearooms and viewing decks, have all remained intact. It is like a relic of an Edwardian Channel ferry moored forever and for memory on the banks of the River Tone. Like Newcastle United's football ground, or Ipswich Town's, or Cardiff Arms Park, or the Scarborough and Hastings cricket pitches, Somerset's cricket headquarters are plonked at the very core of its bustling old town's urban heart. There is something rather warming about coming out of Marks & Spencer's and, on the busy pavement still, hearing the smatter of applause for a boundary struck, or the ooh or aah for a wicket. At the cricket, you are part of the life of the town: the river, two churches, the coal depot, the cattle market, the pubs, the schools and the car parks. The high altar's outside wall of St James's parish church has been pock-marked and peppered for ten years now by hits from Botham and Richards, just as it has weathered a whole succession of Somerset's scientific smiters – plus one or two sloggers, I agree – in the eight decades before then. In that time, on this field, W.G. Grace toasted himself in champagne at the wicket after hitting his hundredth hundred in 1895. By coincidence, it was also at Taunton 30 years later that Jack Hobbs surpassed the Doctor's centuries' record: he toasted himself in ginger ale. Also in 1895 – Archie MacLaren scored 424 at Taunton, still an English-

Taunton's county ground: top right is the new pavilion on the riverbank; bottom centre, the endearing paint-peeling clutter of Edwardiana

man's record innings: there is no mention I can find of Archie's celebration beverage, but he did dedicate his innings to Miss Maud Power, a
rich Australian beauty he had met on tour the winter before. This was
conveyed to the colonial news agencies – and might have helped the
settlement of their marriage the following March.

Such memories must be logged in languid, midsummer days. Now in
reality, a new Championship was starting before a smattering of teeth-
chattering Eskimo-clad enthusiasts, a couple of hundred folk huddled
round their hipflask or Thermos. On the stroke of 11 they lean forward in
anticipation. This is New Year's Day to them. A middle-aged man in a
white coat bends low his nutbrown face out there and quietly commands,
'Play!' – and the big-boned Newark farmer, Kevin Saxelby, eases in
to bowl to Wyatt, who lifts his bat high and pores peeringly over the
trajectory of the whizzing thing to study how the pitch – and the wind –
will react to it. It smacks into the gloves of Bruce French, the close field
stand easy, the huddled 200 reach for the Thermos, and up there in
the billiard room, Ian Botham puts his feet up and contemplates the
camaraderie of cricket and his next six months or so.

It was, to be sure, a more comfortable place for contemplation. 'The old
pavilion was simply an embarassment. It was impossible to entertain any
visiting team there without blushing and apologising. Any senior player
from any county knows there was one side of the dressing-room they just
couldn't change at: if it rained, floods simply poured in, and the junior
pros would have their bags covered in towels, basins and buckets. It was a
disgrace. Then at a stroke, we strolled across the field a couple of years
ago and went from the ridiculous to the sublime. The new pav must be
just about the best on the circuit: other teams love coming to play here
now.'

After Middlesex and Essex, who have been pre-eminent in the
Championship through the past decade, the bookmakers had Somerset
and Nottinghamshire possibly together on the shortest odds to win at
least one of the three trophies on offer each domestic summer. Though
never having quite the consistency to make a prolonged route march
towards the Championship, Somerset's panache had won them five one-
day titles inside the past half dozen seasons. Inspired by the crack
commandos, Richards, Garner and Botham, the nucleus of the corps was
built and cherished by a rum old commandant-exile from Yorkshire,
Brian Close, who laid down the house rules for competitive vigour, first to
Rose, of the heavy plodding gait and sharply plotting mind, and then to
Botham, who led the county to their last victory at Lord's in the 1983 Nat-
West Trophy final. In the first century of their existence Somerset did not
win a thing. In the 1950s they were bottom of the Championship four

Brian Close . . . the rum old commandant

years running. Since Close left, having bullied and badgered some self-belief into his young team, they have not only won a full sideboard of trophies but, in the Championship, they have been in the top four on three occasions, the top eight five times, and never once been in the bottom four.

Mind you, Somerset have always been pretty hot stuff on captains. The very first, when the club was formed in 1875, was the Rev. Stirling Cookesley Vowles, son of the vicar of Middle Chinnock, near Crewkerne, who was known to conduct funerals in his cricket flannels. When the county were allowed entry to the Championship in 1891, the captain was an old Harrovian, Herbie Hewitt, from Norton Manor, near Taunton; he was known far and wide as 'the Colonel' and I imagine he resembled Hugh Griffiths playing the squire in a Fielding film, rumbustiously going in first and tally-ho-ing the poor bowlers to all points. He was a left-handed cutter and puller and once at Taunton put on 346 with the scholarly Lionel Palairet (against Yorkshire, of all people), which confirmed the county's senior status.

The Colonel gave way to Sam. Of all the gusty cricketers that so smack of the land and the westermost shire, I fancy Sammy Woods had the most

SOMERSET COUNTY ELEVEN.

of Botham in him. Large-nosed, six foot and fearless, both twice as handsome when they smile: both want to bowl fast and ever-experimental all the day long, field in the most daringly silly positions, bat with a lusty, unlaboured belting simplicity, and devote most spare time to the age-old countryman's crafts of huntin', fishin' and sittin' in pubs surrounded by tankards and friends and neighbours. Sammy captained the county with a chivalrous brio for 13 seasons. He was Australian by birth (how many times have we heard that Botham is a 'natural' Aussie?) but pure Somerset by absorption. Sam also played rugger for England at wing-forward (what a mayhem-causing flanker Ian might have made at Twickenham, come to think of it), as did his successor as county captain, John Daniell. He was a hitter, too, always aiming for the cattle market, to knock a noisy auctioneer off his perch with his 360-degree dervish golfer's swish. In the field he would stand unconcerned at suicide-point in a Homberg hat and take some fiendishly courageous catches – mostly off Farmer Jack White, a veritable Verity of left-armers with the lulling deadliness of Underwood and the laconic leer of Lock. White succeeded Daniell as captain in 1927: the 'Varmer' was a frugal bowler and a feudal squire when it came to encouraging the worker pros. Two local legal eagles followed as captain, Reggie Ingle, a Bath solicitor, and the splendid Bunty Longrigg, who could bat with distinction and always with humour. At the end of his first match for the county, a fellow player, only five years his senior, said to Bunty: 'You know nothing at all about cricket, but don't let that worry you'. It was unlikely to do so in a county that remembered Sam Woods's words to a new cricketer on his first day at Bradford against Yorkshire: 'Hello, my dear, I don't remember seeing you on the team. What's your weakness? Batting? or Bowling?'

Pure Somerset of the legend that; a text taken from the county's predecessor to Roebuck, the Oxbright essayist, Raymond Robertson-Glasgow, who swung the new ball on and off for 15 pre-war seasons, producing some fizz-full opening spells and a voluminous logbook of quite captivating writings. Of the batting style of R.J.O. Meyer, who succeeded Longrigg as leader, Robertson-Glasgow reflected on a 'pleasant inclination to drive balls of good length into the deep, and to cut yorkers past backward point'. Meyer later founded Millfield School. Reports show him as a marvellous cove. Once, so they tell, when the bar was closed on the Manchester Express, he pulled the communication cord at Crewe so the team could nip out to stock up from the station buffet. Another time, when playing fortunes were low, he thought to enliven the

Somerset at the turn of the century under the captaincy of Mr S.M.J. Woods

Maurice Tremlett ... fresh faced man with the film star looks – and artillery man's straight drive

dressing-room with the occasional sing-song. He went to a reputable second-hand salesman in Bath and asked, 'May I have a piano for my team?' Replied the ivory dealer, 'A fair swap, guv, a fair swap.'

The upturn in Somerset's Championship fortunes after those successive humiliations in the early 1950s came with the appointment of Maurice Tremlett as the county's first professional captain. He was a strong-shouldered, kestrel-eyed fresh-faced man with a film star's looks, and a much undervalued tactical flair. He liked to bowl fast – and did so a few times for England on tour – till, unaccountably, he 'lost it' and rhythm and action collapsed in a discordant jangle. So he concentrated on a batting style which, on carefree days, was garlanded with the most spectacular of straight drives – a dangerous, clean-struck hit that would look to part the cringing umpire's hair before carrying on, still rising, to become a distant speck over the town. An artilleryman's shot. When Tremlett had taken Somerset by storm on his first dashing appearance in 1947, the county side included two of the most renowned hitters the game has known. It must have been a riveting apprenticeship for the young man. Harold Gimblett was a scientific hitter, a stroke-making opening bat nervelessly unafraid of clobbering the first ball of a crucial match for six. And then the next. His timing was matchless. Any innings

42

**Harold Gimblett . . .
a carefree hitter yet
wracked with self-doubts
and uncertainties**

by Gimblett crackled with an uncomplicated, carefree, countryman's zest – alas, it only seemed so, for the poor man was wracked with self-doubts, uncertainties and bouts of manic depression that, later, killed him. Much more at ease with the world was Arthur Wellard, who arrived, jaunty in his loud metropolitan jacket, from Kent in 1927, immediately took charge of the players' card school, and then proceeded to bowl fast away-swingers off the highest of actions till 1950. And hit like fury. He had nothing of the fully-fashioned artistry of Gimblett; his mighty swish would clock the ball crazily up and over either long-on or long-off or, mostly, over the excitedly humming crowd. Then his face, varnished mahogany by the sun, would crease into laugh lines, till he would settle again over his, seemingly, child's-toy bat, and attempt to repeat the medicine – only a little bit higher this time. Twice Wellard hit 5 sixes in a six-ball over. One time, at Wells, it is said that the umpire ordered him to take it easy on the final delivery because there were no spare balls left. In 1935 Arthur hit his phenomenal 66 sixes in the single summer – the all-time record which had now stood for exactly half a century. Boundary sixers, remember, had been allowed only since 1910 if the ball cleared the confines of the whole ground. When MacLaren, for instance, scored his 424, he hit only one six – and 64 fours.

43

The biting wind of April, in this event, must freeze any continued reverie of summertime sixers. The Nottinghamshire bowlers had warmed their spirits at best. Without their champion, Hadlee, the old fox of a captain, Rice, had manipulated his attack with shifty *nous* – and he himself had come on to winkle out the middle of the Somerset order just as Ollis and Rose had almost cemented a stout partnership. The ball was swerving. The advantage was poised. Botham made his first entrance of the summer, in mid-afternoon, at 121 for 4. Kevin Cooper (nicknamed, naturally, ''Enery') had been bowling well and carefully from the River end – one for 22 off 11 overs so far. Botham began with almost exaggerated, dead-bat calm, crouching over the ball in his white helmet. Then he took off the crash-hat, changed his bat – and sprang at Cooper. In eight overs from Botham's arrival, Cooper conceded 74 runs – 61 of them to the Somerset captain.

Says Ian: 'My nature is just to go out and play. I say "Mornin'" to everyone, then if the ball's in the slot, well, you hit it. Sure, you aim at the shortest boundary. I've mis-hit many a shot that's cleared Taunton's old press-box. Sometimes, yes, I have thought it might be nice to deposit a ball on to the end of someone's nose in that press-box. I might try to psych out one of the too keen younger players when I get out there – but with the older players, well, we just look at each other and grin: they know what I'm out there for, they know what I've come for. One or two of the younger ones might tend to strut around – but they're really just expecting you to put them in their place.'

Including that careful start, he reached his half-century off 36 balls. His 5 sixes came off Cooper. He shared out the 11 fours and, after the break for tea, he top-edged a hook, having hit 90 in 77 balls and re-arranged the scoreboard from 121 for 4 to 243 for 7. Poor, persevering Cooper's figures were also in a mess. From 1 for 22 in 11 overs, they now read 1 for 119 in 25. Afterwards 'Enery – a long-serving pro with 400 county wickets in his bag – made for the bar, feeling a touch punch-drunk but, as ever, generous. 'I suppose I copped it because one of our seamers had to bowl into a gale force wind. As the most experienced guy, I drew the short straw. He just hit me through the 'V', with the wind doing the rest. When he hit me for 18 in that one over, they all went straight over the top into the executive boxes. In that wind, all I was hoping for was that he'd get a top edge. What a very fine player he looks after his winter's rest: it has obviously done him a power of good.'

Clive Rice, the 36-year-old who has seen it all, and then some more, just shakes his head and grins. 'You can't do much about Both when he's in that kind of mood. The only way to be certain of getting him caught is to have two fielders standing in the crowd 100 yards behind the bowler.'

Rice reckoned Cooper had been bowling beautifully when Botham came in. The ball had been swinging a lot, and seaming. Suddenly it wasn't any more. 'When this mood is on him all you can hope to do is give Ian singles to stem the flow of sixes. At least he gives you plenty of time to organize your fielders because the ball keeps sailing out of the ground and you have a five-minute wait for it to return! I agree that Taunton is a small ground, but the whole town is too small for Both, never mind the playing area! I have never seen a better hitter of the cricket ball: he goes straight through the line, which is the one good chance of hitting it if it seams around a little. He looked a lot more refreshed out there, somehow. And he's learned about technique now and narrowed his batting down, so that he plays his best shots, not that old slogging across the line. He is so good off the front foot, so devastating off the back foot (the hook and the cut especially) that he leaves very little margin for error among bowlers. Another crucial factor – that he hits the ball so hard – serves not only to demoralize the bowler, but it makes the ball get soft so very quickly. He smashes the life out of the ball, so the seamers can't get it to bounce. The spinners are equally neutured by this systematic assault so that eventually good bowlers don't want to bowl at him with an old, soft ball.'

Next day, Robinson scored a century for Nottingham by way of introduction to a likely Test match colleague. Ian was very impressed – but was only able to bowl seven overs before leaving for treatment on a badly bruised calf. But Marks and Davis bowled well and Notts were all out 26 runs short of Somerset's first innings total of 314. The doctors suggested Ian rest his injury – but, of a sudden, on the last morning, Somerset's batting folded up to Cooper and the young Scots-born spinner, Peter Such. Botham limped in at a calamitous 77 for 6. Second ball from Such splintered the first-tiered press-box. The next went over square leg. Such boldly kept the ball up. So did Botham. Such won in the end – after conceding 5 sixes and being hit for 44 of Botham's explosive half-century. Such's 3 for 23 in 12 overs became 5 for 72 in only 33 more balls that Botham faced. He limped back – and by teatime Nottinghamshire had won at their ease by nine wickets, their first Championship victory over Somerset for 17 years. Kevin Cooper was fast to console and then congratulate young Such. 'Peter bowled so intelligently. He could have been overawed. We dared him to keep the ball up, and although the assault was devastating, he got Both in the end. Again he only hit one way – with the wind. He's not daft, he works it all out quicker than people realize. You must always keep the ball up to him if you're a spinner because he does take a chance. But that bat is so heavy, and his timing is so wonderful, that he just seems to lean into those sixes. He is the longest hitter in the game and I know every single bowler thinks at some stage, "How the hell can I

bowl at him?" He will hit it where he wants – block one ball then smash exactly the same delivery out of sight next ball. If you beat him, he'll nod respectfully and share a joke. He's a real good sport and a great competitor. You can bowl at Gooch, but not at Beefy, because he'll take on anything at any time now. He dosen't bother a fig if he plays and misses the first ball. It must be nice to have a temperament like that.'

Clive Rice packed. First blood. First points in the bag. A performance like that at Taunton last September and he'd be captaining champions now. Ah well, it had been Notts' game, but Botham's match. No, not a bad start for the lad – 'he's a cricketer who will be talked about in the same way as W.G. Grace. At times he's silly, but aren't we all? What astonishes me is the English Press – you just don't appreciate him: you build him up one day and knock him down the next, because it gives two stories, rather than just one, I suppose. And it's pretty ruthless the ways you do it as well.'

On the way home I read the new May issue of the *Wisden Cricket Monthly*. Its columnist, E.J. Brack, was in full spate: 'I am reminded of my father's words 20 years ago when I extolled to him the virtues of the youthful George Best. "He'll never last", he said, "he has an unforgivable indifference to God-given talent." Sadly, there appears to be every sign that Botham, like Best and other sporting geniuses before him, possesses that instinct for self-destruction which leads to prominence in the front pages of the tabloid newspapers but is anathema to success at the highest level of professional sport . . . Still, a few months short of his 30th birthday, Botham should now be at the peak of his physical and cricketing powers. Yet the question marks abound. Can his bowling be taken seriously any longer? The occasional inspired spell hints that the old ability to combine hostility with movement remains, but too often these days Botham tries to buy wickets with a series of ill-directed long-hops. The control which is so essential to successful bowling at Test level is frequently lacking, and the ball which once seemed to swing to order now follows a straight course more often than not. Botham's batting has not changed much, although some might say that it should have done.'

Shame the magazine had not asked Clive Rice for an article. Or Kevin Cooper. Incidentally, within the month Ian was to meet up with his Nottinghamshire pals again – in a Sunday League match at Trent Bridge. He hit 20 off the last five deliveries to win the match. Cooper again was the bowler, and this is how he remembers it: 'Just before I bowled that last over, I said to Richard Hadlee that I fancied he was going to try to finish it off in that over. I was right. The last ball was an ideal "dot" ball – just short

Clive Rice . . . the 36-year-old who had seen it all, and then some more

of a length, and on the off stump. He just launched into it and whacked it over mid-wicket. Hadlee and I just exchanged rueful smiles and, yet again, it was game-set-and-match to Botham. It takes an amazing talent to decide where you're going to deposit a delivery before it's even been bowled. I just knew deep down that was what he was doing to me in that final over.'

Hadlee, the richly-gifted New Zealander, is often considered the equal of Botham as a Test match all-rounder. As a bowler, Hadlee has a supreme talent of varieties. As a batsman, he knows his challenge offers no contest. After that Sunday assault on Kevin Cooper, Hadlee shook his head, smiled, ran his fingers across his moustache, and spoke in awe: 'I hate bowling to Ian. He's down the pitch at you, waving that massive bat, determined to knock you off a length. Give me someone like Boycott every time – a batsman who can be beaten by a piece of skilful bowling, despite his talents. Botham, on the other hand, just makes things happen – his approach is so unorthodox, even though his technique is strictly textbook. He is unquestionably the most remarkable hitter in my time, his efforts are astonishing, considering that he is never out of the papers or the public gaze. You would imagine that life would be one big hassle for him, but he's overcome all that goldfish bowl stuff and continued to do it out there on the pitch. In many ways, that has been his greatest achievement – to get his mind right at last and to channel his wonderful ability into the right areas.'

The umpire that Sunday at Trent Bridge, by the way, was the former England batsman and captain of Yorkshire, John Hampshire. He, too, has seen a few dramatic finishes in his time. 'This was unbelievable, as if Ian had suddenly decided it was time we all went home. Cooper couldn't bowl at him because Ian has a nasty habit of plonking it out of the ground. It was pure strokeplay, not slogging. The winning hit was amazing – he was batting at the Radcliffe Road end and he hit the thing went over square leg, out of the ground, over the car park and into Hound Road. All with no effort at all – and Cooper's a ruddy good bowler!'

The Taunton weather had perked up only somewhat for May Day, when Ian and his boyhood friend, Rodney Ontong, set forth to toss for innings. The sun shone weakly and the wind was sharp. Botham's calf injury was still a drag but when Glamorgan batted, he gave himself a longish spell to, as he grinned, 'disperse the blood'. It seemed to work. He bowled with hostility for 18 overs, taking the wicket of Wales's sharp young fast-bowling prospect, Greg Thomas. But with Ontong stoking up the innings after some fiery play by Javed, Holmes and Younis, Somerset's top-order reply was limp in the extreme and, on the second morning, Botham was at the wicket with his side in disarray at 89 for 5 – a

48

mountainous 298 behind. There might just have been something else to spark him besides his team's spineless start. On the Saturday previously, at Lord's for Worcestershire, the carefree Indian all-rounder, Kapil Dev, had made 100 in 76 balls – a very fast rate of knots, and those who saw it were still passing the word round with enthusiasm. By the way Botham began his innings against Glamorgan, you felt he might just have heard the buzz. He says he hadn't. Kapil, like Hadlee, is considered by some to be an all-rounder at the top of the world's short-list. Ian took guard – and launched at once into young John Derrick, hitting him for 23 off his first two overs, sixes chasing fours.

He lunched at 45 not out, went immediately to his 50 (off 35 balls) and then paced himself to a century in another 39 – thus outdoing Kapil by two balls. Wily old John Steele came on: first ball Ian smithereened for six, next one, a fierce blow, was wonderfully held at deep long-on – by John Derrick. The 112 took just 91 minutes – exactly the time the poor Oxford University team were taking to be all out for 24 against Leicestershire in the Parks. Botham had hit 8 sixes. Suddenly, in just three first-class innings, his season's tally of sixes was 18. He had hit 252 runs so far in only 33 overs. A rate of almost 8 runs an over.

Young John Derrick charmingly enjoyed the occasion. 'It was a great experience to bowl to him. We are just like the crowd when he comes on to the field; there's a little buzz among us fielders – and the bowlers as well. When I bowled my first ball at him, I thought I had got through him. I half-appealed, but at the very last instant, he whipped me away through mid-wicket for four. As he followed through on the shot, I stood there, with my hands in the air, cursing the fates. Botham grinned and said, "Off the middle of the bat, son, off the middle." I thought I bowled well at him – so did my captain – but still a couple of very good balls went straight back over my head for six. Rodney suggested I bowl him a bouncer and I nearly got him caught at deep fine leg with a surprise one. At my pace (medium) it was worth trying once, but not again – he'd have been ready and it would have gone for twelve! I suppose I'm just the sort of pace for him. But it was a pleasure to witness such an innings, to be close to such a player. My main impression is one of immense power and confidence. No one else I have seen can rival Ian Botham for that. Yes, I look forward to bowling at him again. Well, he is a great player. I would love to get him out one of these days.'

Greg Thomas, honey-haired, broad-shouldered and the likeliest Welsh fast bowler since Jeff Jones played his 15 tests for England, also enjoyed the encounter. Many in Wales were pining for the day when Thomas might open England's bowling with Botham. Or share a thunderous century partnership, perhaps. For the present, the challenge was short but sharp. Reflected Greg: 'When I batted, I hit him for a couple of fours in a row, so then when he got me, I was told in no uncertain terms by him to get back to the pavilion. I liked that – to me it seemed he was showing me some respect. Well, at least he had noticed me. When I bowled, too, I thought there was some respect. I almost got him out off one lofted drive, and then again after a top-edged hook. Oh, sure, from the moment he comes in, we feel the extra surge of adrenalin; the whole game feels it. He can be an intimidating prospect, but I loved the challenge. He must be the best batsman I have bowled against – and many bowlers up and down the land will be saying that if he continues this sort of form.'

Says Ian: 'I hit Greg at once, high over the square leg boundary and said to him: "C'mon, son, you're not quick enough to drop it short t'me" – he actually *is* quick enough but you don't tell these young fellows that! Actually, he responded well and that's when I thought "I like this guy". He didn't go into his shell, or any sort of sulk. He looked round at me as he walked back as if to say, "You wait, I'll show you". I liked that. In fact, he's bowled two or three ruddy good spells to me. He's quick too: I really hope

Rodney Ontong . . . fellow apprentice when Ian did things his way. 'Nothing's changed, has it?'

the selectors might take a gamble on him soon: though I'd be shocked if they did – too much to expect of conservative selectors.'

John Derrick (who answers to the name 'Bo', of course) seemed pleased to be out there for another reason. From Blaengwawr Comprehensive, he had worked three years on the Lord's groundstaff – the same apprentice-ship that was served a dozen years earlier by both his present county captain, Ontong, and Botham. Indeed, when they went 'up' in the spring of 1972, Ian and the delightful Johannesburg-born coloured all-rounder, had rumbustiously shared a flat together. They did the traditional dogs-body things, just as Derrick was to do – mowing, pushing, cleaning, netting, bowling, fielding, and being awfully subservient to snooty MCC members. Wages – £12 a week. At first, Ian had been best regarded among this Dotheboys cadre of hopefuls for his genial, galumphing tearaway's 'presence' more than for his promise at cricketing. Most thought he had been unwise not to have taken up the apprenticeship that the League soccer club, Crystal Palace, had offered him while he was still at school in Yeovil. At Lord's, popular as he was, it was thought that he would need a deal of luck, as well as more application, if he was going to make even a reasonable bread-and-butter county cricket professional. Two knowing old ex-pros, Len Muncer and Harry Sharp, were the ground-staff coaches at Lord's. Neither were too smitten with Ian's promise at the time. Muncer's perpetual cry was, 'You should have stuck to soccer, lad'. He was later to admit, 'Frankly, I never thought he would become the player he did. He had enthusiasm all right, so I reckoned he would make only a good, average county player.' Muncer, who had been a Glamorgan stalwart through many summers, thought Ian far too raw, not to say raucous. At batting, wildly wilful slogging ruined all his hard work in the nets; at bowling, well there were at least half a dozen lads on the staff who were better. Man and boy glowered at each other for a year – and so it came to pass that the flame began to flicker, for when Ian had done his time and left for Somerset, his father received this final report from Lord's: 'A very outstanding cricketer who shows a great deal of promise but does everything his own way. He still needs a lot of guidance and is proving better with the bat than the ball, possibly because he has not had a great deal of opportunity, although in the course of time, he will prove to be a very useful bowler.'

Recalls Ian: 'Len Muncer never liked me. But I got on well with Harry. Muncer liked grovellers; he simply said I couldn't bowl: I tried to prove him wrong, but he would never let me bowl. He didn't like my batting either. Harry used to stand behind the net when I was batting, and every ball he'd say, "Pisshole shot that, Botham, pisshole shot – but as long as they keeps working, keep playing 'em". I could relate to Harry: we could go and have a pint with him in the evenings.'

A dozen years on at Taunton, where the king is in his castle, Ontong remembers those early 'battles' Muncer had with Ian, who had seemed at the time a very ordinary player. 'But I was always impressed then how Ian did things his own way. Nothing's changed, has it? In this innings he hit me straight back with a crack like a rifle shot. The ball hit the leg stump and careered past John Hopkins at wide mid-wicket, and went on for four. Hopkins was completely wrong-footed. The presiding umpire would have had a leg broken if it had hit him. We were all astonished at such power. I really do feel he is stronger now than at any time. He is certainly more correct technically. It's difficult to dream up a plan to get him out; you have to accept you'll get stick if it's his day – and realise that he's done the same against better bowlers than you. Yet I love bowling at him – he and Viv are the biggest challenges today to any bowler. But at least Both gives you a chance, doesn't he? Did you see how I brought on John Steele? The old pro against the brash extrovert. A great contest. Steele aimed to tie him down, tuck him up a little, frustrate Both and get him out – just as he did.'

Ian retorts by telling the truth about the flat he and his friend shared as apprentices: 'It was at Hamilton Place, just down the road from Lord's. We were only, what, 15 or 16? In actual fact, Onty wouldn't tell you, but we got thrown out of that flat – you know, arrears in rent, broken windows, in fact for just about everything that 15 or 16 year olds can do. We only got about £12 a week. So, homeless, we slept at Lord's for a few weeks: just dossed in the dressing-room at the Nursery end. Nobody knew. We could have been thrown out, I suppose, if anyone had found out.'

In the meantime Somerset's second innings crumpled disastrously around Popplewell's brave and chirpy 81 (the captain lbw Holmes 3) and in no time another loss was logged, again by nine wickets. The season's start had been bleak in more ways than the weather.

3 Opening Border skirmish

NOW the Aussies are here. The traditional enemy. Certainly Ian Botham's favourite foe – and by a fluke to relish they are coming to Taunton for their first county match. English cricket wonders – not to say worries about – what sort of mob they have sent over this time. The April defection – bribed by South African *rand* – of three players chosen originally has scarcely weakened the party. The substitutes for McCurdy and Rixon, who would have been hard-pressed to make the Test side, are Gilbert and Phillips; and the experienced bowler, Alderman, is replaced by the even more knowing Thomson, Lillee's old mucker. The captain is Allan Border, a well organised limpet of a bat, a battler capable of narrow-eyed counter-attack, who is not often inclined to let a smile soften the pointedly-cultivated 'Desperate Dan' bristle on his chin. Border is going to be a formidable competitor. His style of leadership, we sensed, had an affinity with Ian Chappell's of a decade ago. Both men have all the combative, spiky abrasiveness of a gangland boss. We expect nothing less from Australians. The Ashes mean a lot to them. When they were regained a few years ago in Sydney, I'll never forget the wicket-keeper, Rodney Marsh, joyfully hurtling across to embrace Chappell and exclaim, 'We've got the bastards back . . .!'

By the way, I met Ian Chappell last summer. He now works as a front-man for Kerry Packer's TV station and was on a flying visit to Europe with his camera crew. He had a day at Lord's; then an afternoon at Wimbledon filming an interview with Lew Hoad, an Australian sportsman from a gentler, more laconic, laid-back age. Lew now lives and laughs in Spain. After the interview, Ian excused himself, saying he was in a rush to catch the flight to Barcelona; he was being filmed next morning running the bulls through the streets at the great festival in Pamplona. 'Had he been there before', asked Lew? 'No, I've never even been to Spain before.' Yet he was really being filmed running the bulls at Pamplona? 'Sure. Got any advice?' Lew cocked an eyebrow, looked down at his compatriot, and drawled, 'Yeah, make sure you have one real good crap beforehand!'

HIGH WIDE AND HANDSOME

Border's team of tyros has a dozen making their first official tour to England. There is no Bruce in the party, but at Lord's this week England supporters were running the rule over Craig, Dirk, Greg, Wayne, Graeme (without an 'h', of course), and not forgetting good ol' Kepler, one of sport's increasing number of South African loophole-threaders; he returns to England with a new passport by way of Orange Free State, Transvaal, Western Province, Sussex and Queensland. The gypsy, Wessels, and Graeme Wood, the two senior, solemn, stubbly-chinned, Wrigley-munching, opening batsmen will be heavily relied upon by Border to start all voyages with their crabby caution and care – though Wood, who scored a century in the doomed Lord's Centenary Test, is bound to display some magnificent aberrations in his running between the wickets. *Yes! No! Wait! Yes! No! Sorry!* are Wood's regular squeals that are bound to encourage England's pre-lunch labours. Goodness knows how the nerves of his partner, Wessels, stand up to such 22-yard panic. Wessels is a different kettle of crab altogether. An introspective concentrator, with an almost monastic devotion about occupying the crease, Wessels speaks to few men, except to suggest someone might care to have a sparring session. Literally, his hobby is the noble art and his cricket bag always carries a couple of big chestnut-red pairs of championship gloves. When he is dismissed at cricket, he will sit for hours alone in his car, cursing the fates or his folly. He is a devilish difficult man to get out.

AUSTRALIAN CRICKET TOUR 1985
Official Sponsors - CASTLEMAINE XXXX

Mind you, it is by no means certain Wessels will open with Wood. He may yet be a stronger sheet anchor at No. 3. It all depends on where the captain sees himself in the order. The rest of the Test match batting places are up for grabs, more or less, between Andrew Hilditch (also an opener, no slouch, and the solicitor son-in-law of Bobby Simpson), Dirk Welham, who has faded since his enterprising but ultimately tortuous debutant's century at The Oval last time; the too-long promising Greg Ritchie, so far just a powerful looking 'nearly-man'; David Boon, a pugnacious Tasmanian with a bandit's moustache; and the attractive stroke-making wicket-keeper, Wayne Phillips. Simon O'Donnell, strong and handsome, with the ability to smile, has the makings of a genuine Test all-rounder. He will probably take third bite at the new ball after the snarling, aggressive, straight-backed Geoff Lawson, and Lillee's 'pupil', the swift, hostile, 20-year-old apprentice, Craig McDermott. Mind you, the wicked old 'javelin hurler', Jeff Thomson, could yet have one last, hot summer in him; already he glowers and glows like his new peroxide hair-do.

Anyway, pace bowling should be the least of Border's worries. I may be terribly wrong, but once they have them in their sights, I reckon even the most modest county No. 5s will reap a fair bit of hay from the trundling turners of the bespectacled Murray Bennett (orthodox left-arm), and 'Dutchy' Holland, venerable and untested, and a romantic choice as a leg-spinner. Botham, especially, might enjoy facing these two. I think the shires at least will take to young Greg Matthews, the off-spinning bits-and-pieces man. His every ball is a fizzing wicket-taker, judging by his *oohs* and *aahs* and supplicating antics after every delivery. You know the type – every village opposition side has one; even if you dispatch him for miles, or at least to the next field: *Phew!* he grimaces and tells you in sign language how lucky you were even to lay a bat on the thing. The young man has not yet learned to bowl more than five good balls an over – but when he does he could be very, very useful, especially if his batting comes on in tandem. In craggy response, his profile looks not unlike a gritty, youthful Doug Walters: when the sixes sail over the hedge, and after the defiant *oohs* and *aahs*, he turns back to his mark as simpering sad as Stan Laurel. Matthews is built like a junior light-welterweight, and he has had his Sydney barber crown him with a jutting-prowed, punky-

The 1985 beer-sponsored Australians: left to right (standing) E. Alcott (scorer), R.G. Holland, R.B. Phillips, K.C. Wessels, D.R. Gilbert, S.P. O'Donnell, C. McDermott, M.J. Bennett, G.M. Ritchie, G.R.J. Matthews, G. Dymock (assistant manager); (sitting) D.C. Boon, W.E. Phillips, G.F. Lawson, A.R. Border (capt), B. Merriman (manager), A.M.J. Hilditch, J.R. Thomson, G.M. Wood, D.M. Wellham proud crew-cut. When he was introduced to the Press at Heathrow, one sage reckoned he looked as though he was about to be deported *to* the Colonies, rather than having just transported himself *from* them.

It reminded me of cricket's favourite Etonian, Henry Blofeld, whose description of his arrival at Sydney Airport one time has itself circumnavigated the globe. A drawling, revolver-holstered Ocker customs cop apprehended Henry at the barrier and demanded he fill in his forms correctly. First question was, 'Have you a criminal record?' Henry looked the fellow up and down, 'My dear old thing', he gushingly apologised, 'I didn't realize it was *still* obligatory!'

So here they are, the Gregs and the Dirks, the Waynes and the Craigs and the Keplers. It is, as it ever was, intriguing to wonder which one will make it big – and which one will have completely vanished from recollection even by October. Somebody always does one or the other. Look at any tour party team-photo of history, home or away, and see some bright-eyed, blazered bod in the back row and say, 'Blimey! Who the hell was he?' For instance, who remembers Graeme Beard? (He was the last Aussie tour's back-row all-rounder make-weight.) There is an excellent trick question that confounds even the most diligently academic cricket buff, when asked to name the finest ever touring party to these shores – Bradman's 1948 Australians. It should be a cinch. Fifteen names are rattled off merrily. One from the last two always draws a blank. It is either Colin McCool, biffing bat and round-arm leg-breaker, or – more usually – Ron Hamence, who was a squat and stocky back-foot batsman. Neither got a game in the big time, while the hitherto unconsidered 'baby' of the side, Neil Harvey, became a 'great' between May and September. Which will be which this time? Who will be lost – or found?

Dear old Colin McCool, by the by, came back to England and played some sterling seasons for Somerset. But he could not quite come to terms with the warm, but always wettish, West Country, as his garrulous, gregariously glorious compatriot, Sammy Woods, had done long before, and the knowing baldie, Bill Alley, was to do later. As that summertime treasure of *The Times*, Alan Gibson, put it once – 'His five years up, McCool went back to Australia. He missed the sunshine. "There's no winter", he said, "and the beer's better. And the effing off-spinners don't turn!"'

Much, of course, was going to depend on the new captain. We all knew of Allan Border, defiant and gritty mid-order bat. What sort of fist would he make of leading from the front? In the late winter I had travelled to Sharjah, in the United Arab Emirates, to cover the four-cornered tournament of one-day matches between India, Pakistan, Australia and England. It could have been jokey stuff in the most unlikely of settings, but the teams took it seriously and it was an interesting week. I spent some time with the Australians and was much impressed by Border. There seemed no doubt that he was in charge. Now the time had come to see if he would be leading by example. Taunton, nicely, represented the first opportunity to find out. On the plane coming over to England, apparently, the chief airline steward had congratulated Border on the behaviour of his team – parties of Australian sportsmen have been known, once or twice, to become just occasionally rowdy on such long hauls. Anyway, at the steward's congratulations, the old hand from the Chappell era, Jeff Thomson, jocularly remarked, 'That means we've got off to a really bad start'. The new captain simply withered him with an icy look. Before setting off for Taunton, the team had practised at Lord's. After his net, one session, the young batsman, Ritchie, had flopped down and lit a cigarette. Sharply, Border told him to extinguish the weed and get working. Ritchie shamefacedly complied. The team had got the message.

Benaud, Australia's best, bravest and most imaginative leader, once said captaincy at cricket was ninety per cent luck and ten per cent skill – but he also added, in musing on the ten per cent, that the man who sees

Allan Border . . . footwork and a beady eye – and suddenly he's shouldering his bat to salute the surprised applause for his fifty

the opening and goes straight for the jugular is the one who enjoys his champagne cocktail at sundown. The one who dithers for an over or two, 'is the fellow who reads about the next Test series from the comfort of his own living room, sipping a cold can of beer'.

By coincidence, as Border brought his team to meet Botham's, I had been charged by *The Guardian* to spend the week selecting some passages for serialization from Mike Brearley's new book *The Art of Captaincy*, which seemed certain to be the standard work on the subject. In it, England's former guru explained: 'Top-class captaincy, like top-class sport, calls for combinations of qualities that do not always lie easily together. Yet each in his own way, men like Bradman and Benaud, Illingworth and Close, the Chappells, Fletcher and Greig, have known intuitively when to intervene and when to leave alone; when to insist on well tried methods being relentlessly repeated, and when to experiment. They are tough *and* considerate; they can run a strict ship *and* allow leeway.'

Now at Taunton we can begin to watch the development of the waddling, stubby-legged, competitive Border. I fancy he could yet have greatness in him. Of his batsmanship there is no doubt. Unobtrusively, he has already made well over 4,000 Test runs – steering, nudging, sometimes carving, while we have had eyes only for the guy at the other end. Steady-as-she-goes and undemonstrative – only the relentlessly rolling jaws giving hint of fierce concentration as they chomp away at the chewing gum – Border has shored up the middle of an Australian innings on countless occasions. In the winter, he was shoved centre-stage, almost as an after-thought, when Kim Hughes ran sobbing from the scout hut after handing in his badges, unable to cope with the Press and the pressure. (He was soon to be managing both pretty well again: amazing how a large bundle of South African booty can calm neurosis.)

Border has always been an awkward cuss to bowl at. His reputation was founded on a barn-door defiance at the crease. His method is built around the simple first principle of scarcely lifting his bat from the blockhole as the bowler delivers, rather like those boring schoolboy stonewallers who were apprenticed in French cricket. But the genuine stonewaller spares bad balls. Border doesn't. He has footwork, a beady eye for anything fractionally wayward, and the wrists and forearms of a blacksmith. The little fellow has just come in – and suddenly he's shouldering his bat to salute the surprised applause for his fifty. He is in his early thirties, but as Robertson-Glasgow remarked about Border's compatriot, Grimmett, 'You cannot say that he is old or young, or in any known state of age at all. He and the calendar have never reached any proper understanding.' To continue the theme, just as Mr Pickwick was obviously born in tights and gaiters, so Border surely began with a large-peaked, dark-green cap and ripe views on the status of the top-spinner – and the despatch thereof. It may come as a surprise that, after an apprenticeship in Sydney, Border served his articles in Gloucestershire, a county famed for the graces of batsmanship, from the Doctor himself through Hammond to Graveney. Eleven years ago, Border played a season for Gloucestershire's Second XI.

Kerry Packer's cheek and chequebook had topsy-turveyed Australian cricket. Suddenly, there were vacancies for players in grade and state cricket. Allan had been a keen and fairly good player at North Sydney High School – Graeme Hole, lovely bat, and Ian Craig, brief boy wonder, were also former pupils. He began work as a clerk in the film library of an oil corporation. Weekends consisted of a lot of surfing and a bit of backyard cricket with his brothers, John and Brett. He joined the Mosman club and, suddenly, cricket became the obsession. The coach there was that stringy, weatherbeaten old enthusiast, Barry Knight, who had emigrated after umpteen seasons on the English county circuit with Essex and Leicester. By the week, Barry was increasingly of the opinion that the stocky, stubborn little gum-chewer with the superfluous backlift was a genuine 'find'. Certainly, it was very hard to prise him from the nets.

Mr Packer's palaver left spare places in many a first-class batting order. In 1977, Border played his first game for New South Wales, and two seasons later, on the strength of a doughty century against Western Australia at Perth, he was given the prized green cap against Brearley's team at Melbourne. He made 29 and 0 – but he was off and running. At the end of that initial, modest, bit-part state season, the young man had vowed to 'give cricket a real go'. Word filtered over on the grapevine that Gloucestershire were in need of decent players. Knight urged Border into the adventure. It was a soggy introduction to the comparative big time. Just like this book. Same month, same place. In the Spring of 1977, Gloucester thought to see what he was made of and picked him at No. 5 against Oxford University at the Parks. It rained all day. And all the second day. On the third, the county made 126 for 3 (Stovold, as ever, crackling busily) in the couple of hours in which play was possible, and when the final blanket of rain came down, the 21-year-old Australian was left high and not very dry with 15 not out.

Through the rest of that summer he played twelve innings for the county second XI, averaging 39, and all the time learning to play low and slow and cannily. At the weekends, he played for the Downend Club, which he carried to the top of the local Bristol league. It was all craft and graft and learning – and hitting bad balls into the next parish – a process he continued in the following English summer when he returned to the land of showers and sunny periods to match himself against the best of the Lancashire League. He played for East Lancs, following such illustrious 'pro' compatriots as Bruce Dooland, Colin McCool, Neil Hawke, Bob Cowper and Kerry O'Keeffe. He hit 1,137 runs and took 55 wickets – and up there, they still shake their heads and whisper about his power-crazed 179 against Rawtenstall which was dotted with 13 sixes and 15 fours. How's that for a stonewaller!

Now the gritty, fidgeting, box-adjusting, four-square little warrior is back as captain of his country and, in batting terms, very much the king of the pack. The tableau is set: I reckon we might gaze upon it an awful lot this summer – as Australia's captain, barrel-chested, still and nerveless, settles himself, unsmiling, at the crease, stubbly chin sweating, NCO's moustache pouting with defiant trim, jaws relentlessly rotating in concentration, elbow up, wrists cocked, his bottom jutting out towards square leg... the very perfect personification of the Pommie-basher. Botham was ready at Taunton.

He was delighted to see Border again. The night before the match Ian and Tim (Hudson) launched their new collection of sportswear – the blazers and boaters and full works that were to add a dash of colour to the summer. It was, in effect, Tim's own launch into the public consciousness. 'I first met Tim in '79 in LA on a benefit tour with Norman Gifford. I thought, "Who's this weird guy?" and he felt the same about me. He's a really good friend now, and a family friend, as well as agent and manager. The thing with Tim is that he in no way jumped on any bandwagon when things were going well: he came and saw me when things were at their lowest. He was almost the first to ring when I was feeling so rotten about the drugs' case. My former agent, Reg (Hayter), will always be a friend; he did a lot for me; but going to Tim seemed just to be a natural progression. Certainly I hope to have many a drink yet with Reg in El Vinos, his Fleet Street hideout.'

Ian sent word to the Australians' hotel to come to the clothes launch. It delighted him that they arrived en masse. 'Thommo took to the blazer and hat at once. It might not have suited Allan quite as well – but it was lovely to see him again. We started our Test careers at roughly the same time. I know this season there is going to be even more slagging me off for consorting too much with players on the other side. It's bad enough when we play the West Indies – guys I really like off the field. It's going to be much worse now Allan is captain of Australia. This criticism, "Botham too friendly with the opposition", strikes me as pretty rich when sport is meant to be an activity which encourages the making of friendships. Isn't that what sportsmanship's all about? I reckon it is a charge made by people who haven't got any real friends at all themselves. Do you know, I heard it on good authority that Ian Chappell had warned Allan to steer clear of me this trip – socially, that is – saying my friendship wasn't good for the Aussie team? Typical of that man, I'd say. I'm told Allan replied simply, "You can't chop and change such a thing as friendship. If you have a good friend, then he's a good friend: end of story." Their door is always open to me – especially in Australia, I must say – and my front door is always open to them, as everyone knows. And when you're out in the middle, no one plays it harder than friends do. Botham versus Border has always been a rattling good ding-dong, I'm telling you.'

Border against Botham. Australians versus Englishmen. The saga has been going on for well over a century now. For this latest beginning, the golden day was as benign as smiles of the Somerset crowd were broad. More like the Golden Age, someone said, as Australia's batsmanship beggared belief. Tradition demands that new tourists start uncertain on their land-legs, and prod and potter as they play themselves in. These latest Australians came to Taunton and were 197 for 2 at lunch, and it looked as if they might even make the 721 runs scored in a day against Essex by Bradman's team of 1948. Like then, I suppose the local throng of 5,000 basked unbiased; they burred with pleasure. Border himself came out of the traps like it was three weeks on, and Derby Day. Agreed, Somerset were nothing like at full strength. Dredge had badly injured a knee, Wyatt had measles, Richards had not yet returned from the Tests in the West Indies, and Garner, too, was still at home. Border might have been pleased enough at the latter's absence. Before the match the Australian captain had been ruminating on his early days – and how proud he was to have been picked for the first 'combined' Test side his country selected after the schism had been healed with Australian cricket's establishment and Mr Packer's World Series: 'But being introduced by batting at No. 3 against the West Indies came as a real shock to the system. Garner soon made me feel totally out of my depth – I just couldn't middle the ball, and Richards, fielding in the slips, was chuckling and laughing at my discomfort. It wasn't pleasant at the time, but it really did spur me on to succeed in Test cricket. Between my teeth I was saying "I'll show you, you mug!"'

Now here he was showing Somerset at least. At one time it looked likely even that he would outpace Botham's 76-ball fastest century of this brand new season – but the Somerset captain himself calmed the tempo with a short, bounding spell after lunch. In his earlier morning overs, Botham had bowled fast and well on the docile pitch; he had baited and hooked Hilditch with the old one-two and a resulting dolly to fine-leg, and then sprawlingly caught Wessels at slip. In the end, alongside trenchant knocks by Welham, Boon and Phillips, Border's century came in 100 balls, and then he declared at 356 for 7. 'I had said to Allan, "If you don't declare, mate, then we'll bat all day tomorrow." Looking at the Somerset line-up, I could see him thinking we just possibly might, too. Anyway, Allan has always looked for a real game of cricket. What's ruined these county games against tourists in recent years is that they've increasingly used them for pre-Test batting practice.

'Sure, I was chatting to him all through his innings. It was a ruddy good one, too. He was totally relaxed. Between every ball we were rabbiting on about this and that, about old times, "How's old so-and-so?" you know, that sort of thing, "What's been happening here? What's been happening there?" Nothing about cricket. Then I put Vic [Marks] on, and Allan shouts down, "OK, let's see how short this boundary really is. C'mon Marksey, throw it up!" and I thought, aye, aye, I've watched him bat from close up for years and always rated his batting, but this is a new Allan Border, totally relaxed, and confident in his ability.

'Yes, a lot of talking goes on out there. It's the same when Viv's playing for the West Indies: out there I might curse Viv; he curses me: you know, I call him a "spawny, lucky bugger!" and he might glare – or grin at me with all his teeth. He might whip me over mid-wicket for six from outside off stump and I'll seethe, "What bloody sort of shot was that? Haven't you ever read a textbook on batting?" Then we both grin. Oh no, not really seething. With Viv, he and I can count even the slightest little passing niggles on one hand: we've never fallen out and I don't think we ever will. We're too alike, too much the best of friends. And I hope we always will be. Same with Allan Border.'

Jeff Thomson . . . old pal with the peroxide hair-do and the wicked old 'javelin hurl'

Border, in the most unfriendly way, now let off the leash his three fast bowlers, the long-running, lugubrious Lawson; the precocious and cocky young bull, McDermott; and the once fearsome, now ageing swinger, Thomson, whose peroxide hair-do matched that of his longtime friend and foe, Botham. Thomson is 34 now and his unique, elasticated boomerang-thrower's action can no longer engender the awesome pace that had one former England opening batsman, Mike Brearley, saying: 'Broken marriages, conflicts of loyalty, the problems of everyday life – all fall away as one prepares to face up to an over from Jeff Thomson.' He had not played Test cricket for two years but still nursed an ambition to log 50 Tests and 200 Test wickets – he needed one more match and three more wickets. His Queensland buddy and the Aussies' reserve wicket-keeper, Ray Phillips, had been quoted last weekend in *The Observer*: 'Thommo's completely misunderstood. He is his own man and very set in his ways, but he is also a family man with the kindest heart I know. He never gives up or complains, except maybe about a pitch, which everyone does, and you could never accuse him of being a hypochondriac or a prima donna like some fast bowlers. He has been operating into the wind more often than not for the past two seasons, so he doesn't bowl flat out, perhaps a couple of effort balls an over. Instead, it's guile, using the crease, swinging the ball away, cutting it in and out – he's got a genuine leg-cutter going now.'

First Lawson worked up a fair lick in his sombre way; then young McDermott charged in, breathing brimstone and glowering fiercely at the end of his run as his mentor Lillee had doubtless instructed; then Thomson catapulted in and dug in a few sharpish rib-ticklers. Roebuck and Popplewell did all the hard work, then succumbed, and suddenly Somerset were 65 for 4 with 40 difficult minutes of the day to go: they still needed 143 runs to avoid the follow-on. Botham entered massively, white knight in a new helmet; he windmilled each arm, and consulted with Rose in mid-pitch: 'Let's see first what this lad is really made of.' McDermott was, as lads do, pawing earth near the sightscreen and, from the distance, signalling his cordon of slips to retreat even another foot or two. It so happened that England's own (and venerable) once earth-moving fast bowler and captain, Bob Willis, had driven south down the M5 with his look-alike brother, David, to see the fun. In the end it was no contest. McDermott galloped in full pelt, grunted out the expected bouncer – and Botham, a half-smile to his scowl, swatted it off his eyebrows, first bounce, for a sumptuous four. In his next 27 balls, McDermott was laid to waste. Rose started driving with a calm ruthlessness; Botham just swashbuckled, hooking and pulling and grinning. The youngster conceded 43 runs before he was taken off, resorting at the last – more in flustered accident than design – to a skull-high beamer that had

The white knight's helmet for McDermott... and, first ball, Botham, a half-smile to his scowl, swats it off his eyebrows for a sumptuous four

Ian dropping to the ground like it was an air raid. From being the brash young world-beater 27 balls before, now he looked like a village bowler whose belt had snapped.

Ian was momentarily relieved he had taken out a helmet. Most first-class cricketers now wore them – with Botham, Richards and Gavaskar three of the shining exceptions. In the 1930s Hendren had experimented with a home-made helmet, but the hard hat had not caught on till the habit was resumed by Amiss and Brearley in the 1970s – though they were being worn in the last century at Cambridge as this verse about the furious Botham-like Victorian would testify:

> 'There was a young fresher named Jessop,
> Who was pitching 'em less and less up
> Until one of the pro's
> Got a blow on the nose
> Said "In a helmet of brass – I'll dress up".'

Craig McDermott ...
breathing brimstone and
glowering fiercely like
Lillee instructed

Ian would rather bat bare-headed. Not so much bravado as 'freedom' – 'I only wear one when someone might look intent on hitting me. I don't think this beamer was deliberate, it just slipped out. It was very close, though. I didn't see it. Well, you don't expect it. You're looking down at the deck. McDermott is quite sharp with his blood up and I hadn't faced him before, remember. He looked very promising indeed, I thought. And young "Billy-Craig" showed me later in the evening that he was prepared to learn, and to listen and watch. We talked quite a bit about the partnership with Brian Rose and he realized that he had done it all wrong – he bowled up to Brian, who smashed him through the covers and all over the shop, and he bowled short to me and I hooked and cut him all over the place. I was pleased we had seen him off, but it was good to get a first look at him.'

The evening's play, of course, had also revived Ian's long-established joust with Australia's senior strike bowler, Lawson, a solemn, cunning, and often dangerous operator with over 100 Test wickets in his locker. He emphasised to his strapping new apprentice the need to concentrate when bowling to Botham: 'He is one of the few players in the world with the ability to hit any ball you bowl to the boundary. Try to give him absolutely nothing to cut – that's definitely a non-percentage area. Try to bowl reasonably full at off stump, and as quickly as you can. Anything else at a slower pace will get smashed. If you bowl leg stump he'll hit it over mid-wicket, high and hard. He's a pretty good hooker; usually he hits them out of the park. When he slashes they usually go over the slips. But he always makes you feel as if you have a real chance to get him next ball. The first time I bowled to him was in England in 1981. I got him lbw for nought in the second Test. He was playing across the line. It was a pretty awful shot. He seemed to play a lot of similar shots next Test at Headingley. I kept thinking, "I'm going to get him any moment". But he made 149 and won the Test!' Lawson's final advice was 'set a cover on the fence and a deep mid-off as soon as Ian comes in: that can tend to upset him a bit, so always remember it. Also, I don't think he actually relishes the real bouncer as much as he thinks he does.' Ian smiles back at the wry grin from his long-time foe – 'Henry's a great guy', he says, 'some fellows think he's a bit, you know, sulky and sultry. But I have always enjoyed his humour and his dry wit!'

Geoff Lawson . . . a solemn, cunning and often dangerous operator with over 100 Test wickets in his locker

Meanwhile, just before the close the leg-spinner, Holland, came on. Botham at once hit him savagely through mid-wicket, cover-point and long-on. As they were retrieving the ball, Ian noticed his friends, the long, busby-haired Willis brothers, standing on the boundary. David Willis recalls the cameo: 'Bob and I had strolled round the ground and we were standing next to the sightscreen underneath the old pavilion chatting to Alan McGilvray, the veteran Australian broadcaster, about the lousy exchange rate for Aussie dollars and the exorbitant price of cancer-sticks in the UK. Beefy saw us, stepped back from the wicket and waved. Broad grin. The next ball from Holland pitched about middle stump. Beefy came down the wicket and hit it straight between our heads, splintering a piece off the sightscreen. Honestly. We ran for cover. More Botham laughter. Holland rubbed the paint chips off the ball and made vague and rather hopeless gestures at fielders to move a little this way and that. They seemed to react by saying that they weren't allowed to field in the members bar so they'd just stay put. Sadly play ended for the day just after that and the Aussies were saved.'

It had been a clinking day's cricket, but Border too was somewhat relieved at the end. He reflected on his long-time mate and rival: 'The thing about the guy is that he's so aggressive and he really believes in his own ability. He has a permanent positive mental approach to everything he does. That's where his success comes from. Right from the very first Test match we played together I've seen how his presence on a cricket field generates excitement. You feel this buzz around the ground when he comes into bat. And when he's bowling there is always a feeling something is going to happen, whether it be a flood of runs or a couple of quick wickets.

'His batting is exactly the same. He's willing to have a bash at anyone and take on any size boundary. When you are the opposing captain you live in fear of his cutting loose. At the close today, you could see the relief in every player's eyes. He plays his better innings when his team is in trouble. He has always regarded attack as his best method of defence, and he is so positive in his mind about his capabilities that it comes off so many more times than it fails.'

Botham had scored 53 in 30 balls. With Rose he had added 86 in 10 overs. He had re-introduced himself to his old Australian friends. And particularly to two new ones, young McDermott and the 38-year-old Holland, a direct descendant in the long line of Australian leg-spinners established by the likes of Mailey, Grimmett, O'Reilly and Benaud. The two would remember this curt and over-cheery welcome to England by Botham. That worthy showered and shampooed, and took Jeff Thomson out to sample the night life of Somerset. In the crisp evening of one of the merriest May days in my memory, I meandered the half-mile or so to St Mary's churchyard – not to the nearer St James's where, on another May day in 1978, the hymns at Harold Gimblett's memorial service were accompanied so appositely by the regular smattering of applause for Viv Richard's sixes in the field next door. Here at St Mary's cemetery, Sammy Woods was buried in this same first week in May 1931. Fifty-four years ago, half the cricketing population of England, it seemed, joined a whole county to line the streets of Taunton as Sammy's cortege passed. Now St Mary's churchyard was empty and serenely still. In C.B. Fry's essays *Cricketers With Whom I have Played*, he wrote of Woods: 'The power of his huge thighs, long back and knotted shoulders is colossal. He keeps his bat straight and hits with several horsepower. He is the Ajax of the cricket field and would defy any lightning. If he stays an over or two he makes complete hay of the bowling... it is always a solemn moment when "Greatheart", swelling with courage and pursing his lips into that child-like smile, comes from the pavilion to set right the failure of half his side. There is no better man than he to go in when the wicket is bad or things are going wrong. He has boundless enthusiasm, and the power of infusing a strong sense of it into others. What is more, he tries every ounce and makes others try also.'

Would old C.B. have needed to change a word if he had been looking down on Taunton today – perhaps penning a piece for the *Celestial Times*? He probably was. With Sammy alongside him, sipping cider still – and contributing the column of colour.

After the Lord Mayor's Show of that first day, the match came down to earth. Next morning, Botham hooked and cut Thomson's first two balls for boundaries, then scythed too dramaticlly at Holland and was stumped. Rose had his right forearm broken by a vengeful riser from McDermott. Somerset were fast running out of players and the captain spent much of the day attempting to raise Vivian Richards by telephone in the Caribbean. Wessels eked out a worthily painstaking century, and Australia invited Somerset to score 359 in the final five-and-a-half hours. Roebuck defiantly carried his bat, Marks fought jauntily while the rest were mown down by a venomously charged spell from Thomson (14-1-44-6), including Botham, caught behind for four.

Border's Australians, well pleased, moved northwards to continue their preparations at Worcester. Somerset's collective start in the three-day games had left them pondering on their Championship challenge, to say the least. The earlier of the one-day tournaments, the Benson & Hedges, would surely be more to their traditional liking. It was not to be – Roebuck's grit, Marks's savvy, Popplewell's vim and Botham's contin-uing rampant vigour was attracting little support from the rest of

Somerset's injury-wracked 'extras'. Asked to score 293 against Kent, they managed a paltry 191 – only the briefly dramatic sub-plot of Botham versus Chris Cowdrey giving the Taunton crowd any warmth. On the Indian tour, Cowdrey had taken Botham's place as all-rounder in the Test matches: he was still, for obvious – and unfair – reasons the establishment's favourite. Botham strode out, hit Cowdrey dismissively to the boundary through long-off, then long-on. He pulled him for another four, then lifted him over mid-wicket for six. He made 45 in 30 balls before Cowdrey, relieved, had him caught off a wide half-volley.

In the next B & H challenge, at Southampton, Botham was at the wicket at a parlous 39 for 3, with Malcolm Marshall, probably the most hostile and feared fast bowler in the world, snarling in his lair. Botham hit 48 in 56 balls before he was bowled. Hampshire knocked off the 168 needed with a yawn and the loss of just three wickets. Somerset were out of the competition and the defeat by Glamorgan on the following Saturday made no difference. Forlornly chasing 237, Somerset managed only 144 – Botham caught by Miandad, off the bowling of his smiling old London flatmate, Rodney Ontong.

4 Showing a certain youthful style

THROUGH the month, it goes without saying, Botham's Sunday sixes continued to scatter the picknickers at the John Player League grounds – yet for the Somerset captain and his team the first four weeks of the season had represented the very best of times and the very worst of times. At least Richards and Garner were back for the Championship match with Hampshire at Taunton. Mind you, the weather had had a relapse and found itself unable to greet the two dark princes of summer with the same warm enthusiasm as all Somerset did – not least the county's cricketers. The golden-wonder crispness of that first day against Australia semed an age ago as the morning woke with a chill, damp mist in the air. It was no day for batting – though you could see the long, black, tree-bobbled fringe of the Quantocks, the age-old sign for Taunton that the rain, at least, would hold off. Alas, even the coin conspired, and Botham cursed as he lost the toss. Somerset were told to pad up and face the music on a glisteningly moist pitch that found a reflecting glint in the eyes of the pacy quartet of visiting bowlers: Hampshire fielded Marshall, in his very prime and probably the fastest, certainly the most dangerous, bowler in the game; his high-bouncing and hostile raw apprentice, Connor; the awkward, left-armer, James; and the skilful, skidding, highly considered Tremlett. The latter was very much at home: Tim, born, bred, and schooled in Somerset, is the son of Maurice, the aforementioned county captain, and has the same handsome, open, countryman's face and lithe athleticism. In fact, Tim is more 'Zummerzet' than his father was – or, to be sure, than Ian Botham is. Oddly, both Tremlett and Botham were born in Cheshire – Maurice at Stockport in 1923, Ian at Heswall in 1955, where his parents kept home when his father, Chief Petty Officer Les, was in the Fleet Air Arm, stationed across the water from Liverpool, at Londonderry. When Ian was three, they moved to Somerset, Les having left the Navy to be a type-test engineer at Westland Helicopters in Yeovil, which made even more headlines through 1985 than his son did.

Vivian Richards, now happily back in the family, signed his adoption papers as a son of Somerset far later than Ian – but as soon as he did, aged 21, a close family was made the warmer by his presence. It was now eleven springtimes ago that the two men, of such differing character and from such distant cultures, arrived together at the County Ground for pre-season training. Vivian had been to England on one occasion before he came to Somerset. It was a brief trip. He will never forget it. Richards is the son of an Antigua prison officer, who was a fair island cricketer himself. The boy did well enough to win the scholarship to the grammar school, but then, to all intents, the bookwork stopped. His cricket was riveting already. A voluntary coaching body sent him and Andy Roberts, a fisherman's son, to London for a few weeks, to Alf Gover's indoor cricket school at Wandsworth. They had never been coached before. Mr Gover got him to keep his bat nearer his pad when he drove. It was bitterly cold. They were lonely and frightened and their landlady had not heard of hot water bottles. If he didn't have a pile of shillings for the gas fire alongside him at night, Vivvy thought he might truly freeze to death in his sleep. They went to the cinema a lot, and the high spot of the trip was watching Arsenal play Leeds United at Highbury. They were mighty pleased to get back to their sun-blessed coral island. Vivian thought about going to New York, where relatives had settled, or even training as a garage mechanic. He became a waiter at Darcy's, a 'city centre' café on one of St Johns' two streets. At batting he was already the risen star for the Rising Sun CC, for whom the demon shock bowler was Master Roberts.

In 1973, an ageing cricket-nut bookmaker from Bath had accompanied a club tour by the Mendip Acorns to the Caribbean. In his wallet he carried a dog-eared cutting from *The Cricketer* in which Colin Cowdrey had mentioned 'a chap in Antigua called Richards was quite promising'. The bookmaker was Len Creed, later to become the Somerset CCC chairman. Len was always – indeed, sometimes both boringly and boobingly – on the lookout for recruits. The airport taxi took him straight to the Blue Waters Hotel, where he told the taxi driver to go and fetch the island's favourite batsman from his bar. Next day, Len Creed saw the waiter bat. Viv should have been out – indeed *was* out – first ball, stumped. The umpire knew the gentleman from England was watching and let him stay. Viv scored only another 30-odd, but it was enough for Mr Creed to buy him a ticket to Taunton that night. He would 'qualify' for Somerset as groundsman-helper at Mr Creed's lovely Landsdowne Club in Bath. Some of the Somerset committee laughed when Creed brought back his black batsman. Creed paid – and prayed.

All that while Ian was still limbering up and laughingly ladding it up at Lord's. The two young men came together for training at Taunton in cold and early April, 1974. They were told to share a club flat with the chirpy, whistle-happy, beautifully named spin-bowler, Dennis Breakwell. Fun ensued, reports the legend – which was soon to be busy logging the cricket by day. Richard's first innings for the county was on April 27: his undefeated 81 won the Benson & Hedges tie against Glamorgan at Swansea. When Tom Cartwright, venerable former England player and county coach, was injured, Botham was blooded in the Championship against Lancashire on May 8 (c David Lloyd b Hughes 13, and 0-15 in three overs). At Hove against Sussex, captained by England's aggressive, stringbean totem, Tony Greig, and fired by England's hottest fast bowler in over a decade, John Snow, the two greenhorns 'made' the quality cricket press together for the first time. The era's doyen of sports reporting, E.W. Swanton, was there for the *Daily Telegraph*:

> May 22 1974. 'Seeing the fondness of Richards, the young Antiguan, for the hook Snow now posted a second long-leg to him. Richards's answer was to hit him for 14 in an over, including two of the sweetest hooks you ever saw, bisecting the space between the two. One was reminded of Rowe dealing thus with Willis in the Barbados Test. Richards has already evoked the warm admiration of as good a judge as C.J. Barnett, and I must say that first impressions are highly favourble. He sees the ball very early, and hits it mighty hard – in other words very much as Charlie Barnett used to do.'

> May 23 1974. 'For the uncommitted spectator arriving sharp at eleven o'clock there was disappointment in the early demise of Richards who drove his first ball for four, edged another and then skied to Greig a ball that may have stopped a bit. There had been a little rain before the start. So Somerset were obliged to postpone the celebration of his first county hundred. I expect, though, that they will not have to

wait long for the pleasure, and that this
mature-looking 22 year old, if he can curb
himself just a little, will soon be wearing the
plum cap of the West Indies. He came over
last year at the instigation of Len Creed,
vice-chairman of Somerset, without
commitment on either side, and scored
2,600 runs for the ancient Lansdowne Club
of Bath, playing just on Saturdays and
Sundays. Taylor was out as soon as in, but
Botham, a youthful all-rounder from
Yeovil, showed a certain style in making a
brisk 26. Botham is taking Cartwright as his
mentor – a sensible decision to be
recommended to other teenagers who have
as admirable a model to imitate.'

The show was on the road. Charlie Barnett, the former England and
Gloucestershire opening bat from the 1930s, who would splat the first
ball of a match for six, *thwack*! with just the same venom as he would slap
a piece of plaice on to the slab of his fishmonger's shops in Cheltenham
or Cirencester, was also to make the match award at Taunton when
Hampshire arrived for the final B & H qualifier on June 12. Botham had
played four first-class innings, that 26 at Hove his highest score, and
taken one wicket for 144 in 50 expensive overs. In the West Country sun
after breakfast that morning there was a touching reunion in front of
Taunton's rickety, wood-creaking old pavilion. As Richards had taken
Somerset by storm so, with less affection because of the hurtful nature of
his job, had his boyhood friend from Antigua, Andy Roberts, exploded
that early summer into the consciousness of all the Championship's
batsmen. Word had already gone round how he was very, very good
and very, very quick; and the deadpan, almost sombre, mien above his
assassin's goatee beard helped not at all when even international county
batsmen found themselves coweringly unable to read the awesome three-
speed gears of his quite scary bouncer. No helmets then. The two young
friends – and, suddenly, rivals – embraced before the game and talked of
this and that, familiar things, and family, and the old fraternity they had
left behind at Rising Sun CC in Antigua. They parted to change. 'I'll get
you today, Viv', was Roberts's parting shot.

I was in London that summer. I remember June 12 well. I was on the
sports desk rota at *The Guardian*, in charge of the mundanely math-

ematical job of sub-editing the county cricket scores. It was a pleasant enough summer's task: you could have a longish, laughing lunch, drift in to chat up the odd secretary, and then work like fury at the teleprinter's teatime scores, collating a million snips of paper, so as to get across for a *Blue Lion* quickie at opening time. Then, around 6.30's cricket close, amble back to scissors-and-paste the remaining bits and pieces, write a few corny headlines to fit, and go help the printers put them into the page that the sports editor had planned. Thus I remember the second Wednesday of June 1974. 'What strength Somerset-Hants?' asked the boss around 5.25, just over a 4-minute mile away from opening time. 'It's all over', I said, 'Hants 182, Zum already 113 for 8. That new guy, Richards, is out for one, and Roberts is getting nasty; he's just knocked three teeth out of the mouth of some poor unknown geezer called Bow-tham or Bottam or something.' So Henry Blofeld's expected report from Taunton was relegated downpage and the matches at Canterbury – where Dudleston and Davison had dramatically collared Underwood – and Worcester – where *The Guardian*'s favourite Lancashire was being inspired by Wood and Lloyd – were given pride of place for the morrow. It was clear to slip out to the pub.

In an hour we strolled back. All hell! Henry's amazing accent was strangulating the wires from Taunton as he demanded to dictate intros for the *Wizard, Rover* and *Boys' Own Paper* at one and the same time. The 18 year old tail-ender who had gone in at 113, with an impossible 70 needed

74

Opposite: Roberts and Richards . . . freezing to death on their first trip to London a dozen years ago

Left: June 12, 1974 . . . walking off the field and into the headlines for the first time. This was the first picture the photographer, Patrick Eagar, a passionate Hampshire man, could take since young Botham's amazing blitz had begun

off 15 overs, had done it. The boy with three teeth suddenly missing – he put them in his pocket – at twenty past five had stood up, dusted himself down, gingerly fingered his Mick Jagger lips, nursed the rabbits away from Roberts and laid about him with such controlled abandon as to win the day with an over to spare and one wicket standing. 'We will hear a lot more of this astonishing young man', wrote Henry. In front of the pavilion, Charlie Barnett (just as he had the month before at Swansea) handed over the envelope and said, 'I think we are going to hear a lot more of Ian Botham.' The young man himself said, 'When I was hit in the mouth it, sort of, relaxed me. It made me more aware, keener, less nervous. The lads brought me out a drink of water. I knew I would get a yorker next ball. I tiptoed back and clipped it for three.' A couple of overs later and Roberts bounced wickedly again. Ian swivelled and hit it venomously over the white hoarding and into the faraway car park. Another reporter there was Chris Ducker, who has deservedly won a prize as Sportswriter of the Year. 'In 20 years of watching Somerset', he wrote, 'I have never been more exhilarated by a single shot.' Another young man, still making his way in journalism, was there to take photographs. He was older, but far less professional than the young No. 9 batsman. Patrick Eagar – son of Desmond, the secretary and eminence of Hampshire – admits he was so stultified with partisan annoyance at Botham's crashing, continuous nerve that between the time Roberts hit him in the mouth and Botham hit the winning run, he was so seethingly fuming at Hampshire blowing it that he could not take a snap. Certainly he missed the shot that brought tears to Ducker's eye and decibels to Blofeld's dictation. Botham's batting, at almost the first time of proper, measurable asking, had measured up to Chesterton's definition: 'Courage is almost a contradiction in terms. It means a strong desire to live, taking the form of a readiness to die.'

And now, eleven summers on, it happens that Hampshire are back at Taunton with another West Indian fast bowler who has set the counties on the floor. Malcolm Marshall, from Barbados, was in his full pomp now. At once, this mist-smudged May morning in 1985, he had Somerset rocking back, whey faced. The former England captain, Mike Brearley, faced scarifying overs from both Roberts and Marshall at their most legitimately sadistic. On sale at Taunton this morning was Hampshire's centenary book of celebration, in which the splendid Brearley had written of the traumatic, masochist's satisfaction of squaring up to Roberts and Marshall: 'Andy was very fast and straight, with a ruthless out-swinger... Marshall seems to me to be a very similar bowler. Skiddy with a horrid, dangerous bouncer... the natural successor to Roberts is Marshall and he seems to be every bit as good. I think I had become more confident by the time I played against Malcolm and was more aware of my own responses. Andy always had that evil glare which made me less natural with him, that air of menace. Malcolm looks a little more boyish, more whole-hearted perhaps – not that Andy wasn't whole-hearted – but Malcolm is getting better and faster, and with five or six years to go as a top world-class fast bowler...'

Marshall paced out his short, dramatic run and slithered in, coiled to strike. Young Wyatt went; then, in the fifth over, Roebuck took a fearful blow. He examined a finger minutely, then wound back his glove and with staunch courage settled again over his bat. Tremlett came on – and relieved the physical pain at least by at once bowling the gritty opener. Back in the pavilion a broken finger was confirmed – by which time a jet-lagged Richards was back indoors as well, tamely caught for a duck in the gully after three balls from the waspish seamer, Tremlett. Silently cursing consternation and concentration pervaded the home dressing-room. Popplewell had posted the half-century with Roebuck still there; now, of a sudden, with Ollis quickly gone, Tremlett had taken three for six, and Botham picked up his bat at a parlous 58 for 4. Marshall and Tremlett each raised a level of adrenalin. This would be the decisive champions' joust. Says Ian: 'Malcolm and I are good friends. We've had many a contest. Always enjoyable – and keen. He's a magnificent bowler – and cricketer and athlete. It always amazes me how a skinny little bloke like him – "the skinny wimp" I call him – can generate such 100 mph stuff. He is unquestionably the quickest in the world; and he can swing it too. We

**Malcolm Marshall...
'skiddy, with a horrid,
dangerous bouncer'**

always play it hard – and have a laugh and a joke afterwards. As for Tim, everyone rates him on the circuit. He really is becoming the nearest thing to Tom Cartwright: accurate, lifting, intelligent, knowing, cunning, and always relishing the challenge.'

At once Tremlett had Ian dropped at third slip by Cowley. The batsman, poring massively over each ball, was by his standards relatively circumspect till lunch, indulging himself with only a handful fo tasty *aperitifs*. He especially enjoyed one glorious, skimming 2-iron six off the bounding Tremlett. For all his caution, Botham hoisted his 50 in 43 minutes – off just 17 scoring shots: 2×6, 7×4, 2×2, 6×1 – and in the hazy afternoon sun he set about his haymaking. Connor started in: he went for 15 in the over and repaired, bewildered, into the country. Cowley lolled up with his spinners: he went for 19 in the over. Tremlett sealed an end, as he can, and after Popplewell, Marks and Mark Davis hung in there. Botham had to take on Marshall, refusing a few singles to do so. It was championship stuff: the lithe black demon snorting in, the blond boy counter-punching with a thrilling, almost too daring venom. Every time Marshall began an over, Botham pulled on his white knight's helmet and waited, tensed and still. Crack! If the West Indian dropped short, Botham would pull him; if shorter, he would hook; at full-length, he would drive with the fully arced follow-through of a carefree golfer. Into the river or into the graveyard. It was measured brutality. He passed his century in 76 balls – exactly the same as against Glamorgan – and was finally out, b Marshall, for 149 out of 193 in 106 balls. He hit 6 sixes and 20 fours, and next day Richard Streeton of *The Times*, who has seen it all at home and abroad for 30 years and never resorted to hyperbole, called it 'an astonishing display of controlled hitting; a counter-attack memorable even by his own highest standards ... it is hard to imagine anyone has ever hit a ball harder.'

Another old trouper with an even better view was the umpire, Sam Cook, Gloucester's left-arm spinner through three decades, who was playing in a Test match 28 years ago this month. Even a long beer could not quench Sam's enthusiasm for the day he had witnessed: 'I've never seen anyone play Marshall so well. The shorter he bowled, the further Both hooked and pulled. He made him look a slow medium-pacer. I know that Marshall admired Both for the way he took him on. Yet he also plays so sensibly when necessary – shielding his lesser players from the strike. I played a lot against Arthur Wellard and he and Both both hit straight just as hard. But Arthur didn't hook. Both is a far better player, sharing Arthur's inclinations to hit the ball miles in the air. As a hitter, he's on a par with Arthur. He's a grand lad, is Both: he wanders in, has a laugh and a joke and seems to have no nerves. He is definitely one of the great entertainers of my time.'

In his stand of 85 for the seventh wicket, Mark Davis had scored only the last two runs! Vic Marks had also been a 22-yard witness: 'It was an absolutely brilliant knock, riveting to watch. I added 30-odd with him and it was simply a different game when he was on strike. His pulling and driving was majestic against one of the best fast bowlers in the world, with his tail up, and in favourable conditions.'

The buzz over such batting was still about at the weekend when Peter Roebuck, before setting off to nurse his smashed finger in the less clamorous climes of Greece, logged this note for the *Sunday Times* sports pages: 'We have all been astounded by Botham's batting this May. He has corned timidity, blasting away with awesome power. His leg-side shots have tended to go square of the wicket – this season they're going through mid-on. Against Hampshire, within an hour he had forced Marshall to defend the boundaries with five men. A bumper reared up at his chin – he swivelled and cracked the ball over square leg. Marshall peppered Botham with short-pitched deliveries; lesser mortals would've blocked them, but he pulled them to mid-wicket for four. To a yorker from Marshall he dropped his bat down and sent the ball scuttling past umpire

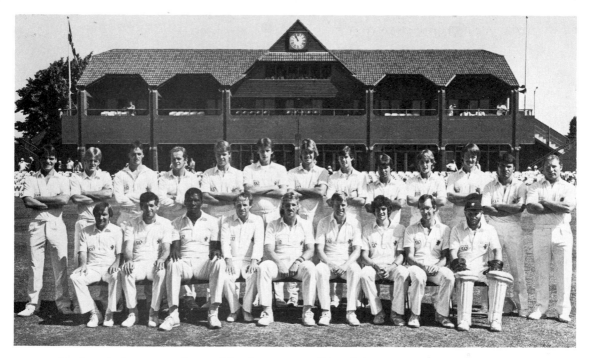

Botham's Somerset, framed by the new pavilion: left to right (standing)
R.J. Horden, P.A.C. Bail, R.L. Ollis, M.R. Davis, S.J. Turner, M.S. Turner,
A.P. Jones, G.V. Palmer, S.C. Booth, J.G. Wyatt, R.E. Hayward, N.A. Felton,
D. Waight (trainer); (sitting) P.J. Robinson, C.H. Dredge, J. Garner, V.J. Marks,
I.T. Botham (capt), B.C. Rose, N.F.M. Popplewell, P.M. Roebuck, T. Gard.
(I.V.A. Richards was missing)

Cook. Twice he missed his shot; a drive which eluded point – and an edged hook which struck a spectator on the head!'

By then, however, Somerset had lost another match. After the first day's one-man display of pyrotechnics, it was an unlikely result – especially as Hampshire looked to be still in a dazed degree of shellshock when their reply stood at 107 for 7. Botham had at once got rid of the ever-menacing Greenidge, Garner and Richards had taken their first wickets of the northern summer, and, behind the stumps, the livewire little ferret, Gard, had snapped his traps shut on three victims. Then Tremlett and James heroically broke Hampshire's 60-year-old eighth-wicket partnership of 227 to turn the match. And it stayed turned – just – in spite of a blazing and fraternal answer to his captain by Richards who hit 10 sixes and 19 fours in his 186. Botham kept his friend company for only ten balls, scoring 19, including 2 sixes into the wide, blue yonder.

Rose was back at home, thinking about doing some gardening with a broken arm. Now Roebuck's splintered finger would keep him off the field till July. But it was very good to have Vivian back. It had become an

Viv...'his friendship means the world to me: one of the most beautiful of men'

endearing and enduring friendship. It had crackled, Ian remembers, with a smiling fellowship, since that very first day. 'Bath. Somerset Under-25s v Glamorgan. I came down from Lord's, he was qualifying at Lansdowne. I'd heard all about this amazing new batsman. He'd heard about this new all-rounder. We met in the dressing-room. I actually settled down to watch him bat. I don't usually, but I was told it could be interesting! He was out first ball, clean bowled by a grubber. We were in real trouble. I went in and got 90. We went out to field. I didn't bowl well. Viv got 6 for 25 bowling doddly off-spinners – or, anyway, those doddly some-things-or-others of his. We decided then – OK, he'd get the wickets for Somerset and I'd do the batting. We laughed, and that was the start of one of the closest relationships in sport, I suppose. Viv's friendship means the world to me.'

Throughout the decade, and before, cricket had been beset by quandary over South Africa. If the white people there were not allowed by federal law to play games, even in school playgrounds, with fellow black South Africans, well, should the rest of the sporting world play with them? On most political issues, Ian is trenchantly right-wing. On South Africa, friendship with Vivian opened and closed the case. 'I became aware of the awfulness of apartheid by travelling with Viv in those early days. It opened my eyes to what it must be like to be black over there. Not now, because now he's Viv Richards, "the great cricketer". But when we were younger you could actually see resentment in some people's eyes when we knocked about together – you know, "Who's that black man with Botham?" How awful – especially as Viv is one of the most beautiful of men, a meticulous dresser, clean and smart, well educated, very intelligent, good brain. But as a youngster I suddenly realized some perverted people were not accepting him just because he's black – and they wouldn't even talk to him. I just could not understand it.'

It goes without saying the white cricket administration of South Africa – pariahs of world sport, in one sense, but with money in large enough wads to set up a string of so-called 'rebel tours' to their country – would know they had bought themselves back into undisputed business if the world's two black and white champions graced their playing fields together. Ian is aware of that. 'These two South African guys came over to talk Viv and me into taking a multi-national side over there. It was a *hell* of a lot of money. We would have both been millionaires overnight. Honestly. I said, "What happens if Viv and I want to travel together? Or drive together? Or stay in the same hotel?" One of the guys said, "Oh, no problem there at all, we'll make Viv an *honorary white man*." That was it. End of conversation. Honorary white man! So if I go to Barbados or want to play cricket in Antigua, am I made an honorary black man? It's balls, the whole thing's total bollocks.'

It is not only South Africa that gets the blood up. There are a great deal more exclamations of 'absolute total bollocks!' batted about in the Somerset dressing-room than sponsored by that blighted Republic. Sometimes, you feel there is more yahoo-ing in this corner of Taunton than on the most virulently noisy Radio 4 morning at 'Yesterday in Parliament'. After the Oxbridge public school trio of Roebuck (Millfield), Marks (Blundell's) and Popplewell (Radley) air their various tutorial-taught theories, the House buzzes with interjections from the likes of such Hon. Members as Mr Gard (Huish Episcopi Comprehensive), Mr Garner (Foundation School, Barbados), and Mr Ollis (Wellsway Comprehensive School, Keynsham). The Hon. Captain (Bucklers Mead Secondary Modern, Yeovil) sums up: 'We are such a collection of individuals. In a political sense we go from the most militant of left to the most far-out right. There is always some debate raging – usually, mind you, with the West Indies boys sleeping right through it all. Roebey and me just argue for the sake of arguing: even if we are basically in agreement we will still go hammer-and-tongs. Anything, from the tiniest news item

Nigel Popplewell . . . eating or running or doing 3,000 press-ups before lunch

about milk bottles or rates to disarmament or hanging. Marksey will sit back and listen with a grin playing across his face, and then, in just a couple of sentences, perfectly summarize what Roebey and me have been spluttering over for the previous hour. Pops will then dive in – and Roebey'll attack him and his upper-crust background. It can get hilarious. Then Gardey will nudge me and say in his great broad accent, "Which way be you votin', Rook?" And I tell him, and he just says, "Okay, that'll do for I." It's always been so rewarding, stimulating and bloody good fun.'

The delightful Popplewell once boxed for Cambridge University at middleweight. In Philosophy, Politics, Economics or Natural Sciences he will not readily move up a weight division or two, even for a title fight. Says Pops: 'Firstly, Ian is a great deal bigger and stronger than I am. I will not, therefore, argue with him if I have a logically superior point, since I am likely to end up either covered in whitewash, or in a bath fully clothed – or both. Ian's politics are a little to the right of Atilla the Hun, and a suggestion that Mrs T does not always walk on water will result in an unpleasantness involving bats, pads, helmets and anything else not screwed down at the time. And it must be said that his enormous physical strength is combined with a hot temper that can sometimes act to his detriment. Yet while this temper will rage violently, it will vanish as

Trevor Gard ... 'I say, Rook, me spuds aren't coming through'

quickly as it has come. Out there, for instance, he will bowl bouncer after bouncer at a batsman, trying to knock his 'effing' head off. Swear at him, insult him, and ostensibly hate him – and five minutes later, he will be gently chiding the luckless individual from his position at second slip.'

In his turn, the captain stops stuffing the qualities of Mrs T down the throats of his team and, with his best and most benign of smiles, surveys the floor of the House: 'Popplewell could be doing anything: he could be eating apples or buns, he could be running, he could be doing 3,000 press-ups before lunch, he could be having a bath... and cursing who's whipped his talc. Roebey would be reading *The Times*, or a vast tome without a picture on the cover, or squinting over a book or an article. He yawns a lot because he always gets in early to have a knock in the nets to get his juices flowing. He feels the nets are home from home. His friend, Marksey, is a bit like me. Nothing much must happen of importance too early in the morning. I reckon we both look slovenly, lazy and dozy before the day has really woken up. Only after midday are Marks and I ready for anything...'

Botham would not, one fancies, be ready for much unless he'd been cadging a light (or vice versa) from Trevor Gard for the captain's tiny little twig-like Henri Wintermann 'Café Crème' cheroots. Their dressing-room

Colin Dredge . . . 'a million miles from Frome' to bowl all day

Joel Garner . . . '200 miles for a beer'. The shirt reads 'Guess who's Back?'

clutter of towels and talc, bats and boxes invariably merges into the same shared territory. 'It wouldn't be the same', says Ian, 'if Trevor wasn't next to me, cup of tea steaming, his trusty old pipe billowing smoke as he chews over the phrasing of his latest – and usually useless – words of wisdom. I love him. He calls me "Rook" for some long-forgotten reason. We can be sitting there. Dead silence. When, suddenly, for no rhyme or reason, he'll nudge me like a fellow conspirator, and come out with some deeply philosophical point in his great, broad, West Countryman's accent. "You know", puff, puff of pipe, nudge, nudge of elbow – "See, y'ere, Rook, I've been thinking: There was an ol' owl who lived in an oak/The more 'ee 'eard, the less 'ee spoke/The less 'ee spoke, the more 'ee 'eard/Why aren't people more like that ol' bird?" Beg pardon, Gardey, I'll say. "I just remembered that", he'll say, "an' thought it worth telling you. I dunno, says something about those Press boys of yours, p'raps?" Or any little country saying that he might deem appropriate to the day. Nudge, nudge – "Two moons in May, means no 'ay." Or at, say, a crucial point in a match, he'll suddenly look at me, all earnest like, and say, "I'm having real trouble with my chrysanthemums", or "My spuds aren't coming through." What the heck are you meant to say to that?'

The two pace bowlers look down on the rest from their great height.

The 'Demon of Frome', Colin Dredge, at 6ft 5in, is still 3in shorter than Garner. 'I guarantee, to the extent of betting a thousand quid on it, that Dredgy will announce his presence at the dressing-room door by kicking it a sharp crack with his toe as he opens it – then make out he's hit with his head. *Arghh!* Every single morning. What a good lad! Salt of the earth, people like Colin. Bowl for you all day long, work hard at his cricket. We're all so pleased he's at last moved into the Taunton area to live. Frome was a million miles away, there's nowhere worse in Somerset to get to or get from – especially the routes he took!'

Unlike Joel. The 'Big Bird' likes to fly in his car. It does not necessarily alter his mood. 'It all depends', says his captain, 'how he's feeling that morning. If his knees are giving him gyp, or it's cold and wet, it's all one long m-o-o-a-n, man. We call him "the taxi driver". He adores driving. He thinks nothing – honestly – of driving a round trip of 200 miles just to have a beer with someone. Just loves being behind the wheel. An amazing guy. I don't think he ever sleeps. A beer at Littleborough tonight? No problem. Taunton to Littleborough and back. Think nothing of it. No sleep. Honestly. Just a catnap here, an hour's siesta there. What a good team man, and good friend. But when I'm batting against him in a Test match, if the day is cold and his knees are feeling it, I can guarantee the first three balls will hiss past my lughole. But he's marvellous to field to, Joel. Quick, sure, but a lot of bounce. So you don't drop much off him. You daren't, anyway.'

What of the captain himself? He was now having to leave his so far unsuccessful team to flex once more his spirits against the Australians in the three one-day carnivals, the public preface to the serious Ashes business.

5 One of my tamer dismissals

BEFORE he left for Old Trafford he checked, for once, his cricket bag. Now Viv was back, Ian's favourite bat was never safe. His West Indian friend had a habit of borrowing it. With Ian re-introducing himself to England, Richards took in a new bat of his own next day and went quite gloriously potty at Taunton, laying Warwickshire to waste with 322 in just 258 balls, beating the previous highest for the county, 310 by Gimblett in 1948. Vivian hit 42 fours and 8 sixes – and one fancied he would be using that bat for quite some time. Such withering use of a piece of wood reminded me of that marvellous definition by the playwright Tom Stoppard, that a thing which looks like a wooden club can only take on a different aspect in certain, very special hands – 'If you get it right, the cricket ball will travel 200 yards in four seconds, and all you've done is give it a knock like knocking the top off a bottle of stout, and it makes a noise like a trout taking a fly . . .' Other mortals attempt the same – 'and the ball will travel about ten feet and you will drop the bat and dance around shouting "Ouch" with your hands stuck under your armpits.'

Botham and Richards have their bats custom-built by Duncan Fearnley, old first-class cricketer turned cottage-craftsman and entrepreneur. Each man preferred, just about, the heaviest bats in the game, over three and a quarter pounds, with Botham's fractionally heavier. Each spring, Fearnley would send Ian down three or four to Taunton, by train or van. This year, so far he had only used two – one in the middle, one for practice. The 'net' bat develops different characteristics – 'because you usually practice in the mornings when there's dew around, which can make a cricket ball very heavy: it can affect a bat tremendously.'

Richards is far more restless in his search for the perfect blade than Botham, who has gone through whole summers taking just one out to the middle. Unless, that is, Viv starts to covet it. 'I should think he's whipped about six bats of mine in the last three seasons. "Lend us this", he says. Out he goes with it. If he doesn't get any runs he gives it back; if he gets 30-

odd or more, or hits a couple of good shots with it, or especially, a really good six, I never get it back. Mind you, nobody else would do it to either of us; with us, it's just a question of "what's mine's his, and vice versa".'

This summer, it so happened the game's purists were taking this trend in heavy bats very seriously indeed. No matter that the world's best batsman and perhaps history's finest all-rounder preferred to use a heavy bat. They were not consulted, of course. Old men debated the cons between themselves, midst the musty aromas of sacrilege. No less a pundit than the editor of *Wisden*, John Woodcock, had opened for the prosecution in his editorial in the new almanack, and no matter that Richards and Botham, indisputably the two most exciting strikers of the ball in modern times, each played with bats weighing well over three pounds. Wrote the editor: 'The weight of the modern bat has also led to a change in batting styles, the cut and the hook being the strokes to have suffered most. In 1956, when Gunn and Moore supplied the Australian touring team with bats, the order was for sixteen between 2lb 2oz and 2lb 4oz and one of 2lb 6oz. This last one was for Mackay, who had a method all his own, involving no detectable pick-up of the bat. Today's average weight is nearer 2lb 10oz, not a few being of 3lb and more. Is it surprising, therefore, that it has become fashionable to stand with the bat already raised above the shoulder? No less an authority than Bradman sees this as a "negative and regressive idea" and one which "detracts greatly from the style and flow of batsmanship". Bradmans's own bats weighted 2lb 2oz. So did Compton's. Using a modern mallet they could never have played with such marvellous dexterity.'

Wisden Cricket Monthly was not slow to take up the cudgel on behalf of the lightweight rapier and in its June issue another trenchant defender of the olde-tyme faith, E.M. Wellings, blazed away from his retirement bunker in Basingstoke. Weighty bats, he wrote, cannot even be 'picked up'; they have, alas, to be 'hoisted'. Oh, the lack of romance in the modern champion. '[these bats] must similarly render the batsman's reactions slower, and with the other modern body and arm pads restrict freedom of movement. A good player using a bat of 2lb 2oz should have the speed of footwork to render helmets and those other pads redundant.' Wellings said the heaviest bat he himself had ever used had weighed in at 2lb 7oz. 'It felt like a log, and did not pick up smoothly. I got busy with a spokeshave, carving slabs off the back. The weight was much reduced, but I never achieved the right balance, and it did not enjoy service outside the nets. It was with one of the lightweight bats that Richie Benaud emulated C.I. Thornton at Scarborough by driving the ball high over the houses and into Trafalgar Square. When such mighty hits are possible, there seems no sense in burdening oneself with extra poundage.'

W.G. . . . 'could have benefitted from a heavier bat; he could send the ball a mighty distance when he opened his shoulders'

Ian sighs and puts the two old buffers in their place. Modern techniques have quite radically changed bat-making, he says. 'In a way it might be less of a craft, less a romantic cottage industry – but there's much more "science" in it now. For one thing, they can kiln the wood nowadays with far more precision – that's what gives far more "bulk" to the bat, but without the density. My bats may be heavy, but they pick up so beautifully you'd never know. I "discovered" the heavy bat about six years ago. In 1981, I remember, Sir Leonard Hutton lifted one of them and described it as "a railway sleeper". I wonder how many runs Leonard would have got with my "railway sleeper". It's all a question of balance now: so it doesn't *feel* heavy. And the grips are crucial too: I've got big hands, so I like a big thick handle, and on top of that I'll have Duncan wind on three or four extra grips – not quite in Clive Lloyd's league: he has about eight! Nowadays, of course, you can get very thick rubbers, as opposed to the old standard "thinnies". Everything about the art has changed.'

Bradman, for all his genius, was a tot of a fellow; Hutton in his prime was wiry slim. Light bats suited them and their style. Richards and Botham are immensely strong men; power-players. I daresay W.G. Grace would have used a far heavier bat had Fearnley been in business in Victorian times. In his *Hints for Young Cricketers*, published eighty-six years ago, W.G. Grace wrote: 'As boys grow up they should be provided with bats according to their style of play. It stands to reason, for instance, that a hard hitter will want a heavy bat, or, at all events, a heavier bat than a batsman who plays quietly. Driving, or hitting straight forward, can be best done with a heavy bat, while, of course, it is easier to cut with a light one. I never saw a good cutter use a heavy bat. Personally, I play with a bat weighing about 2lb 5oz, which, I think, is heavy enough for anybody; but, as I have said before, a few ounces make very little difference if the bat is really well balanced. Of course perfectly balanced bats are hard to secure, and a batsman who possesses one regards it as a treasure.'

W.J. Ford, that big-hitting contemporary of 'the Doctor', reckoned Grace would have benefited from an even heavier bat – 'for, with his huge frame and splendid physique, he would have made an extraordinary hitter if his splendid patience had not restricted him to "the game". When he chose to open his shoulders and give the ball the full benefit of his assault, he could send it to a mighty distance, especially on the on-side rather square.'

Ford must have been a splendid chap. Physically, he out-Bothamed our Beefy. He played for Repton, Cambridge University and Middlesex through the 1870s and '80s as a trenchant all-rounder. He stood 6ft 3in and, in 1886, weighed in at 17 stone. He was also a journalist and author. Of himself, he remarked, '...a big man with a big bat, I excelled in drives... the story of a spectator who shouted out, "Take him a tree", when I once called for a new bat, is historical, but I wound up my first-class cricket by straining my arm over a monster hit off Pougher into the members' enclosure at Lord's.' Discussing his contemporaries, Ford stood firm on 'the premise that you can't hit sixers with a two-pound bat – Bean, a desperate driver for so small a man, uses a bat of 2lb 9oz, as did Lyons and Bonnor. Fowler had a specially long handle, which certainly adds to the swing for a drive though it must be inconvenient for other strokes. Bonnor's and Thornton's bats ran to about 2lb 7oz, and it is doubtful whether huge hits as opposed to hard hits could be made with a much lighter "implement".' (Thornton, of course, was the big hitter of the day; Bonnor and Lyons were the legendary Australian clouters; Bean played for Notts and Sussex; Fowler scored 900-odd runs for Somerset in the very earliest days of their first-class existence, once hitting a ball from W.G. on the Spa Ground, Gloucester, for a paced-out 150 yards, and, against the Club & Ground at Lord's, clearing the lower part of the old pavilion roof with, as Ford himself reported, 'the grandest hit, bar none, that I ever saw... the ball hummed over the slates as if it had left the mouth of a gun.')

Meanwhile, 101 summers on, grand-hitting Somerset's grandest of all hitters was travelling north to take on the Australians again, his three and a quarter pounder bunged in the back of the boot. Ian's early season form through the continuingly miserable May had dispelled even the most jaundiced calls for his non-selection for England and the fact his return might jar the close-knit team spirit that had been built up during the winter tour of India without him. In fact his two 'rivals' for the job, the Kent players, Cowdrey and Ellison, were no threat at the time – Cowdrey, after a breezy start, had lost form; Ellison was still treading gingerly on an injured ankle. Botham, anyway, had dismissed any idea of rivalry – 'There was no "edge" between us at all. We knew it was yet again something dreamed up by the Press. Richard and Chris are very good friends of mine, have been for a long time. They wish me well, and I wish them well, of course I do. And it's not meant to be the least immodest, but Chris and Richard, I know, would both tell you who was the most *proven* Test all-rounder of the three of us.'

For the most part now, however, the flak was stilled from the English Press and all the speculative buzz on Botham's international future, which many had enjoyed when the victorious team arrived home from India, was silent. A few snipers let fly from defensive positions – in, for instance, the correspondence columns of *The Cricketer*: 'Although there is no ready-made replacement for Botham, I believe that it is time to say thank you for his past services and to pack him off to Somerset. As far as Test cricket is concerned, with his diminishing all-round ability, I believe it is not a case of "Colossus at the Crossroads" but of "Fallen Hero at the End of the Road".'

But such shots as that, from a Mr Paul Thomson, were answered in the same pages by volleys of support for the unquestioned 'People's Choice'. Why, asked Mr D. Webster, of Redcar, had the 'antis' given 'no consideration at all to the batting or bowling averages turned in by the so-called all-rounders who had toured India? Had Botham returned such figures, the Press would be having a field day.' And Mr J. Lamb, of Tonbridge, was also disgusted: 'Of course Botham is domineering and unselectively aggressive. These are the very characteristics which play a large part in making him the most extraordinary cricketer of his generation. Botham "bashers" should accept that to omit this player from an England team on the grounds of his detrimental effect on other players would be an

Heavy bats, say the purists, detract from 'the style and flow of old time batmanship'. Oh yeah? This one, off Holland, landed somewhere near Manchester's Warwick Road railway station

admission of weak captaincy. The best way of evaluating Botham's overall worth to England would be to ask Allan Border's Australians whether they would rather play an England side with or without him in it.'

The worthy Border, by the way, had arrived in Manchester with, since the pipe-opener at Taunton, a further trio of hundreds under his belt. It had been an overture round the shires to match Donald Bradman's. Indeed, apart from the Don, only C.B. Fry, Everton Weekes, and Mike Proctor have bettered this opening promenade of four successive first-class centuries by Border. The spiky little Australian captain announced himself pleased to be back in Lancashire. He recalled his spell in the League, as a boy with East Lancs: 'It got my batting sorted out and what I learnt in Lancashire was the hard grind of being an honest-to-goodness working pro. They expected me to score all the runs, take all the wickets, if the ball was in the air someone would shout "pro" and I was expected to run and catch it. Then, even before a game, they would have been expecting me to roll the pitch and put the scoreboard numbers in order.' The Australian also spoke fondly of Botham, and put the final exclamation mark to the already discredited and contrived 'debate' about Ian's return to the England side. 'We Aussies find it incredible to behold. When we were here last you knocked him down, only to build him up again. Now you're knocking him down before a Test match has even been played. I sometimes think your Press batter him just *because* he's the greatest cricketer in the world.'

However, sad to tell, on the morning of the first of the three one-day international matches for the Texaco Trophy, the Press of the world were battering on about a sport suddenly far more apocalyptic than cricket. In Brussels the night before, at the final of the European soccer cup, a small batch of 'supporters' of Liverpool FC had inspired such monstrous mayhem against rivals from Italy's Juventus that when the dust rose from the ensuing riot and collapse of masonry, 39 people lay dead.

Italy shrieked in the throes of grief; Britain woke up next morning, stunned and humiliated and wretched. The city of Liverpool was cowed in abject contrition – and less than 40 miles away, by fluke of the calendar, it fell upon the cricketers of England and Australia to attempt at least a public service to prove that a spectator sport with the capacity to attract a vast throng could conduct itself in an embracing spirit of warm comradeship, endeavour and chivalry. And they did just that at Old Trafford – under a blue-blessed, almost mocking, cloudless sky.

England batted, and at once lost Fowler, Gower and Lamb. Botham came in at 27 for 3 to join Graham Gooch, the returning prodigal. Ian has always enjoyed batting with the imperturbable Essex opener who can, when the mood is upon him, equal Botham in the grievous bodily harm that can be done to a leather cricket ball. 'It was so good to have Goochie back.He was just coming into his own as a truly world-class operator when he imposed the ban on himself for going to South Africa. The thing that makes Goochie so difficult to bowl at is his "forceful defence". He can even block fours as they say W.G. used to do. He's worked out his own technique. He knows exactly what he's about. He's a tremendous player and man.'

On his own admission, Gooch was very nervous. His three-year ban from Test cricket had lopped off, just like that, perhaps a quarter of his international career. From the ropes, however, he showed not a flicker of frailty as he dropped anchor to give Botham his head. They added 116 in 28 overs on a dreary pitch that made uninhibited batsmanship as laborious as scything a field of wet thistles. The leg-spinner, Holland, pushing the ball through with the warm cross-breeze, accounted for Gooch at 143. Botham went out to meet Holland – and hit him two thundering blows over the mid-wicket fence, and then with a merry chassé down the pitch, an even more thrilling skimmer that was still rising as it cleared the sightscreen.

Gatting had bustled in, intent on acceleration, and played two reverse sweeps – that is, suddenly crossing hands as the ball approaches from a spinner and impudently sweeping it, 'left-handed' through the slip area to third man. Or imprudently, as the purists would have it. But in one-day games, when a fielding captain is stifling all orthodox scoring strokes with defensive placements, modern batsmen find it an occasionally useful ploy: it unsettles the bowler for one thing, and it is unlikely he has bothered with a deep third-man.

The young off-spinner Matthews had come on. Ian hit him over long-on for six by way of a greeting, then after the second of Gatting's reverse-sweep twiddles had gone for three, Botham hit Matthews over mid-wicket for his fifth six. Next ball, bravely tossed up, Ian waited, genu-flected, and teasingly attempted his own reverse sweep. He missed and was bowled.

There was a collective groan of sadness at such a glorious innings – 72 in 82 balls – being cut off in its prime by, as it were, his own hand, as well as an accompanying titter of apprehension that their reckless boy would return to the pav and surely be hauled in front of the beak for so cheekily flouting convention, and being found out. And so it appeared, for the chairman of selectors, Peter May, was at once quoted as having ordered Botham never to play the shot again. May, in fact, had been nowhere near as dogmatically magisterial as that. Probably England's most classic amateur batsman of post-war days told the Press that the stroke was never

Gower and Botham –
partners again in the One-
Day Internationals . . . you
put your short-leg in, your
long-leg out, your fine-leg
squarer, and you shake
them all about

95

used in his era – when, of course, there had been no serious or necessarily frenetic one-day, limited-overs cricket. 'I have thumbed through the MCC coaching manual and found that no such stroke exists', said May, with rather schoolmasterly dismissiveness: 'I told Ian he is a great player and with his strength he has no need to use it. It involves a great element of risk though Ian said it had been very profitable for him. Like Botham, Gatting has enough strokes to score runs without employing it. He used it for the first time when he was on 193 in the Madras Test during the winter and I didn't think that was the right time to use it. Certainly I would not have considered using such a stroke when I was batting; nor would Weekes, Worrell, or Bradman.'

Ian was narked with himself. But, as ever, it soon passed. He shrugged, and smiled, as if to say, 'there's no business like show business': 'The reverse sweep has been in my repertoire for one-day cricket for a long time. I've probably got 200 runs with it for, what, three times out. The hoo-ha about Peter May "banning" it was not true, just another thing got up by the Press. There is no way, for one minute, that Peter May would – or could – tell me how to play. Anyway, when all's said and done, this was one of my tamer dismissals. I've got myself out in far more macabre ways over the years, I'm telling you. An interesting statistic might be to tot up every time I've been got out as opposed to getting myself out, trying to force it too much. Anyway, in this game, batsmen forget to give bowlers the credit as well. So, good for Greg Matthews. I'd charged him the previous ball, and it had cleared mid-wicket for six. So I expected a flatter delivery: ninety-nine per cent of the world's spinners wouldn't have tossed up the next one. So jolly good luck to Greg. He is already a good, thinking cricketer: this proved it, didn't it? A bubbly personality, too. I think he's going to be really useful for Australia in the not-too-distant future. He's enthusiastic, a real individual, and his own man – he goes for it in his own way.'

Which is pretty much what his captain said about Botham. 'At the time', said David Gower, 'I thought, "Bloody hell, what's he played that shot for"'. But always with Ian, you have to realize quickly that the Man is the Style, warts and all. He had played so superbly anyway – and all credit to Matthews, who had just been hammered for six. He dared to float up the next and it did Ian. Anyway it is not that outrageous a shot, and Ian usually plays it well. In India in 1981-82, he played it against the medium-pacers, which was reckless even by Both's standards. But he is usually in credit with it against the spinners. P.B.H. had a word with him

'I've got myself out in far more macabre ways over the years, I'm telling you . . . anyway good luck to Greg Matthews'

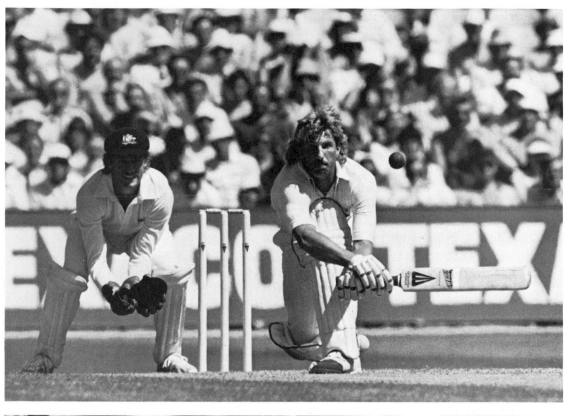

along the lines of, "Do you need to play it?" but it was ridiculous to suggest that the chairman would attempt to ban it with a player of Both's experience and class. Yet again, because Ian's concerned, it's another case of complete overkill by you media blokes.'

The dig did not stifle the media. Woodcock in *The Times* called the stroke 'a poor, not to say childish piece of cricket . . . He can make his hair what colour he likes, grow it as long as he wants, claim special privileges for his "minder" and in some respects be larger than life. But to gamble a hard-won advantage on a reverse sweep against Australia, even in a one-day game, has nothing to be said for it.'

BOTHAM SWEEPS TO DISASTER echoed the tabloids – indeed Matthew Engel, in *The Guardian*, said the stroke might have been 'specifically designed to bring out the bile in those cricket sages who prefer to observe the cracks in the Botham canvas rather than the masterful brushstrokes. When he bats like this, I think everyone should be prepared to accept Botham's judgment.' The shot might have been that of a sacrilegious heretic to Mr May, but it was nothing new to a more recently serving England captain, Tony Lewis, who told readers of the *Sunday Telegraph* how the tactic genuinely upset fielding captains. The three Pakistani wizards, Hanif, Mushtaq and Javed Miandad, had played the shot to huge advantage: 'For Mushtaq, the master, it was no risk. There were always a set of circumstances leading to it. He would note the vacant field behind the stumps on the off side, watch a spinner set about the business of bowling defensively, perhaps pushing the ball through and getting in a groove of containment, and out would come the reverse sweep to confuse the bowler and the captain, and bring about a re-arrangement of field placing. It is a stroke that has to be decided upon early, but you have to wait until you can be sure that it will pitch well up, on or near the half volley. The front leg must be in the line of flight – the exact rules appling to the orthodox sweep. Unfortunately for England, Botham picked the wrong ball. If Botham had been bowled around his legs, trying an orthodox sweep to hit the ball to the populated area of the field, he would have been excused. Limited-overs cricket is regimented enough. If you believe in preserving wild life, then let Botham and his reverse sweep live.'

The most mischievous of Botham's supporters – 'He has been chosen by the Gods and for him to be shamed and shackled in public by a mortal chairman of selectors is a disgraceful thing', said Brian Bearshaw in the *Manchester Evening News* – wanted to ask Mr May about a certain England captain 24 years ago being bowled round his legs on this very same ground for an ignoble duck when he airily essayed a sort of upright, swatting sweep to a leg-break delivered into the bowlers' rough from round the wicket. May was that batsman; Benaud the Australian bowler that day who couldn't believe his luck. England then had needed only 106 runs to win at a run a minute with eight wickets left. It was not in a one-day knockabout, and some still said that one stroke lost and won the Ashes series of 1961. But, in the end, no one dared mention it at Mr May's press conference in 1985.

Mind you, the reverse sweep has, in actual fact, its roots in the game's long legend. Mr May may not have come across it, but W.G. himself did. Some ten years or so ago I remember sub-editing a piece on the very subject which the late and still much-loved Ian Peebles had submitted to *The Guardian*: 'Middlesex being in a strong position, "W.G." sought to delay their progress by bowling very wide to the off at that spirited Irish Baronet, Sir Timothy O'Brien. A couple of wides were enough to raise the Bart's pressure to bursting point and the next one he thrashed back-handed through the slips, doubtless to the accompaniment of a blood-curdling Hibernian oath. Indeed blood was nearly spilt when the ball whistled past the ears of Brother E.M. Grace, who happened to be standing at slip. What fraternal alarm this caused W.G. is a matter for conjecture but, seeing his tactics foiled, he managed a fine show of shocked outrage. "I'll tell you what it is, Tim", he said, "You'll kill my brother." To this he received the obvious reply. "And a bloody good thing too" retorted the Bart.

'Baulked in the verbal as well, W.G. dropped the lofty hauteur and proceeded to straightforward threats, "If you do that again", he said, "I'll take my men off the field." Of course the Bart did it again and immediately found himself, except for a scared young partner, alone and monarch of all he surveyed, at which he relieved his feelings by thrashing the stumps many a mile into the air. In the prevailing atmosphere this could have proved a costly gesture; for the Brothers, seeing the umpires unnerved, might well have lodged an appeal for hit-wicket.'

Of course, this time, when all was said and done, Botham's crime had been to play his shot – pictures of which were already winging round the world and bouncing off satellites – at the comfortable enough position of 160 for four wickets. It was no fault of Botham's that England's tail collapsed to leave Gatting high and dry – and that Australia knocked off the runs with five balls and three wickets to spare. The visitors also won at Edgbaston in the second game – Gooch a century, Botham next on 29 – thanks to Border's irrepressible 85 not out. England won at Lord's – Gooch and Gower each scoring hundreds to out-do Wood's challenging century – but there was no doubt that Australia had drawn first blood. When the Ashes series began for real at Headingley in ten day's time, Border's men would probably start as favourites. Ian was particularly pleased that his bowling was beginning to fire on all cylinders. And there was mutual pleasure at his being back in the big time.

On either side of the one-day internationals, Somerset had played their western rivals, Gloucestershire, who had started the season in the most unlikely trim. Indeed Gloucester, the Championship wooden-spoonists of the year before, had cowered in the shadow of their neighbour's colourful successes for a number of seasons. The first game, at Bristol, was wretchedly waterlogged: two whole days were lost after Somerset, inserted, had made 211 for 9. Botham made 5, caught at slip off Gloucester's raw young tearaway, Lawrence. Ian was suffering bad stomach cramps – indeed he had sent out for a potion from the nearest chemist before he went in. Anyway, the England v Scotland soccer international was live on television and it was no day for cricket – a damply miserable three-sweater job. And to think, next week would be flaming June. Flaming hell.

Inside the fortnight Gloucester came to Bath. Botham put them in on a pitch which alternated in patches between lush-green and biscuity-bare. Garner and the captain immediately had them 15 for 3 and then an ironic passage was played out for Somerset to rub in the fact of their injury problems – for Jeremy Lloyds carried his bat through the remainder of the innings for an heroically played 93. Lloyds had left Somerset the year before, crossing the Avon for more opportunities. Some say Lloyds had left to get out of Botham's shadow. The innings meant a lot to Lloyds – but also to his former captain: 'I was really sorry Jeremy had left us: I always rated him very highly as a top-notch bits-and-pieces player – and I mean that in a high-grade way. He's a great improviser, and will do any job for you: stick him in as opener and he'll do it, just as if he's down at No. 7. A great man – and a good bowler and fine fielder. I didn't want him to go. He went – and obviously with our injuries he would have been playing far more for us this year than he has been for Gloucester.'

When Somerset batted, Popplewell took on young Lawrence in a fury, hitting 9 fours in 38 balls, but wickets fell on the worsening pitch and when Botham came in at 147 for 5, 36 were still needed to avoid the follow-on – and with Gard in hospital with concussion to compound the wretchedly long sick-list. It worried Botham not a jot – the follow-on was saved almost with derision, and by the time the tedious drizzle ruined the match he had scored 76 not out off 47 balls – 5 sixes and 7 fours – and had seemed on course for yet another record-breaking century. His batting was now becoming quite riveting and afterwards the Gloucester captain, David Graveney, who has been in on his friend and rival's development through the years, was more than happy to discuss it. 'What can you do? In he walks with a cheery "hello" to one and all. His first ball from Walsh

David Graveney ... 'for any normal mortal it would have been a struggle'

is thrashed past me at gully for four at catchable height; the second, a bouncer, is deposited over square leg for six, and the third is straight-driven, first bounce for four. For any normal mortal it would have been a struggle, especially with the follow-on looming. To Both, it was a doddle.'

In over a dozen years, Graveney – son of Ken and nephew of Tom – has taken around 600 inexpensive first-class wickets with his devious left-arm, lobbed little hand grenades. He admits being on the wrong side of some spectacular campaigns with Ian: 'Now and again he's been caught at long-on, but usually I've come off second best. This was no exception. Although he showed me some respect, I suppose, he decided to go for at least one "out of the ground" shot per over. I bowled one good length ball that was a little quicker – and he hit it back at me at catchable height, but at such velocity that I got out of the way, and so did the umpire, David Constant; it screeched past us for four. Petrified, my follow-through then got shorter and shorter – and poor Connie was hopping around anxiously for the rest of the innings. I had a long-on, a long-off, and a deep extra-cover (Davison) on the fence in front of that row of seats. As I saw him come down the wicket, I decided to throw it up wider and slower. It dis-

101

appeared over Davo's head, over the seats, and vanished out of the ground – 100 yards, I reckon. He was not really at the pitch of the ball, so I had stuffed him slightly because he was just a touch out of position – but that sort of thing makes no difference to Ian when he makes up his mind to attack.'

Graveney reckoned Botham was playing 'straighter' than he has ever seen him – as well as adding a variety of disconcerting – to the bowler – little nurdlers and 'earners' that keep runs ticking over. But the heavy artillery was more awesome than ever. 'He always keeps his head so still and his eyes level. He is not afraid to hit through the line of the ball. It takes guts, you know, to swing when your left foot is some distance away from the pitch of the ball. Most batsmen defend against the good length ball – Ian blasts it with great power. If I wasn't a player, I'd queue to watch him bat ahead of anyone else. He empties the bars. Those who go to cricket to drink, for the social chit-chat and not to watch every ball, stop talking and concentrate when Both is batting.'

'As a left-armer, I must say his work around the leg stump is quite superb – that lovely pick-up and then the lap. He's also developed another shot, the late cut, which he plays delicately even to the good-length ball. He loves it when you think you've got everyone correctly positioned up on the ground, i.e. behind the bowler or covering the drives. That means he's got many more options in other vacant parts of the field. That's when he smiles – that's when he knows he's got you completely buggered. He is quite the longest hitter I've ever seen and, to my mind, the complete model for an attacking, dominant batsman. More so even than Viv – because Both is very orthodox, 90 per cent of his shots are precisely correct.'

That dramatic announcement of himself in this innings at Bath might have had one umpire taking cover. The other, John Hampshire, himself no slouch in his England days, watched from square leg – unbiased, of course, but purring with pleasure: 'He scored 12 off his first three balls from Walsh – 4,2 then a pull through mid-wicket for six. It was never more than ten feet from the ground and it landed smack against the top of the sponsor's tent like a shell exploding. He hit another six off Walsh that was just as impressive – straight back over his head, over the sightscreen, over the tall trees and into the garages behind the ground. A colossal hit – over 100 yards I reckon – and Walsh is not a man to be tampered with, especially on a wicket like this.'

This time Alan Gibson was there for *The Times*. He summed up the innings in a Somerset sentence: 'He hits them here, he hits them there, he hits those Turmuts everywhere.'

6 Why not sit back and enjoy it?

AT least the rain had relented in the North. Mind you, there was still a wintry chill about Headingley when the teams assembled for the first Test match of another Ashes summer. The poor Australians had a pallid look, having scarcely felt the sun on their backs since arriving six weeks ago. Border apart, all the batsmen could have done with more runs around the shires; the cold complaining bowlers were in even sorrier nick, cupping hands in armpits for warmth and, on approach, gingerly treading in their own muddy, stepping-stone footprints. It might have been March; the way the winds howled through the rafters of the football stand, it should have surprised no one in the large crowd if two Rugby League sides had trotted out. In these conditions, Headingley can be a bleak place, and almost barren of atmosphere and romance, even on the first day of an historic series (for what England v Australia series isn't?). On a languid, heatwave day of midsummer, Headingley can set a perfect stage for cricket – yet it remains logged in the game's canon more for memories of men, moments, and matches than for an intrinsic 'mood' or tranquil recollection. The longtime and celebrated cricket correspondent of the *Yorkshire Post*, Jim Kilburn, must have spent more time than anyone at Headingley. Even he is low-key about its charms: 'The touch of sentiment so strongly impressed upon other great grounds has seldom fallen significantly upon the Headingley atmosphere. It gives no obvious cause for either affection or dislike. It is efficiently designed and administered for the presentation of cricket but it contains no treasures of picture or memento, no plaque or memorial gate.' It has the commercial rather than the domestic appeal. Time perhaps will bring its heart to be worn on its sleeve. And yet... and yet, what men, and moments, and matches. Rhodes and Sutcliffe, sure; Leyland and Trueman; Verity and Hutton and Hampshire. Don Bradman scored just 30-odd less than 1,000 runs here in just six Test innings (average 192.6). Macartney, the 'Governor General', scored a century before lunch at Headingley. Boycott, the rum emperor, scored his hundredth hundred in a Test match

Headingley '81 . . . Hoorays for possibly the most remarkable of any Test hundred

and had his cap stolen for his pains, after which he gave cricket's most famous imperial salute. Sweatbands ahoy! Peter May, pale and slim as a schoolgirl, made a century in his first Test match here. And Ian Botham won the Ashes on his own – with a little help from Bob Willis and his friends.

So here, at the first time of asking, the Australians were being given an opportunity to purge their spirits of Botham's incredible victory in 1981 when England had come from so far behind as to have started the penultimate day with bookmakers' odds against them winning being chalked up at a pretty conservative 500-1.

This time Australia started well on a disappointing pitch. The bounce may have been uneven, but there was very little of it, tirelessly as Botham and Cowans dropped it short. Australia's vice-captain, Hilditch, who had so elementarily fallen for Ian's old one-two – Short! Hook! Fine-leg's! Thanks! – at Taunton did not oblige this time, and set Australia doughtily on course with a measured and unfancy 119. The critics, to a man, thought little of Botham's short-pitched ploys. Some you win, some you lose, shrugged Ian, still convinced of the Hilditch blind spot: 'Andrew is a fighter alright, but he is a limited player in as much as he scores the huge bulk of his runs to third-man or fine-leg. Okay, he won today's battle, but one day doesn't disprove a theory in this game. But look at all these cuttings – "Hilditch hooks Botham's string of long-hops at will: why does he persist in bowling this rubbish to a great Australian hooker?" As usual, it is all complete and utter drivel. Do you guys really think about what you write up there? Why can't the great British media ever give us any credit for actually thinking about our cricket. Okay, it might not work all the time – it would be a pretty stupid game if it did – but, believe it or not, we do think out there when we're bowling. We're thinking all the time.'

Hilditch unwound the sweatband-bandage he wears under his visored helmet. Someone said he looked like a wounded infantryman invalided home from the Somme. He seemed just as relieved to have survived, and there was the blush of triumph on his perspiring face: 'From his very first over it became obvious to me that Botham doesn't care one little bit if you get runs off him. He's strictly a wicket-taking bowler. If you, say, cut him for four, he's just as likely to bowl the very next ball in exactly the same spot. He doesn't care if it goes to the boundary again. He does it in the hope you will play it wrongly. He's always trying something, which means that he bowls a fair few wicket-taking deliveries – but in between that, with respect to him and because of his "experimental" style, there's a fair few balls you can score off. He "goads" you: you wait which is a little bit different to some of the other great bowlers I've faced. Like Lillee: as well as bowling a lot of wicket-taking deliveries, Dennis never offered much to score off. With him, it was very much a matter of trying to survive six or seven overs until he came off. With Ian, it is a totally different thing going on out there. You don't often see a front-line batsman just desperate to survive against him. It is less frightening, more cat-and-mouse. He gives you lots of chances, but you know he wants you to be too greedy. He is a wicket-taker, pure and simple. It seems all part of his pattern to let you score a few off him, so you might be lulled. I got away with it today, because I went after him but kept concentrating, I suppose. But I know this was only the first skirmish in the battle: it's going to be a long and intriguing war, I guess.'

In spite of Hilditch's pugnacious, perspiring innings, Australia were all out for 331. At second slip, Ian had taken two lightening-flash catches to send back Wessels and Border, and he had been generally pleased with the zip of his bowling: 29-8-86-3. Gently, through the soggy spring, he had been stoking up a fair head of steam in Somerset. In the minor sub-plot, he had taken Simon O'Donnell's wicket, first ball in the young man's first ever Test. In the one-day internationals a fortnight before, Ian had clean bowled the highly promising Australian all-rounder in each of his innings. Thus had it been a salutory start for O'Donnell, who was being built up and billed by his own Press as a genuine contender to the Pommie champion. So far it had been no contest, man against boy, and the boy looked bewildered. The handsome Australian seemed over-awed by Botham's psychological bounce and aggression. He told friends he did not like Botham at all.

Then Tim Robinson, calm as you like, strolled out and won the match for England. The revelation of the India tour took up at home where he left off. It had been a bitter-sweet story. Robinson's Nottinghamshire opening partner, Chris Broad, had gamely and unflinchingly gone in first for England against the savagely wicked venom of the West Indians the summer before, doing more than enough to presume his place on the hot, dusty but far less skull-lethal tour of the sub-continent. In the event, the selectors had decided in their wisdom that Broad could not play spin-bowling as well as Robinson. So Tim toured and Chris, wretchedly disappointed, took over his friend's winter job of stirring up support for cricket at Trent Bridge. With no disrespect to Robinson, the rest of the England team felt rotten about Broad's treatment. Says Ian: 'For quite a while, most guys on the circuit felt Tim was a really good player. Mind you, we all thought Chris was a bit mistreated, rather like David Steele a few years ago. They picked them both to try to defy the might of the West Indies, then turned round and said, "You can't play spin, thanks and goodbye". Well, how do they know you can't play Indian spin till you go there? Chris deserved the chance to prove them wrong, though certainly, many of us thought Tim might have been picked before Chris in the first place.'

Robinson made a quite classically composed and unhurried 175 – an introduction of himself to home that could not possibly have been bettered. Particularly as England had started with a couple of alarums and notable exits. Gooch and, again, Gower, had no sooner come than gone. Gatting and Lamb chipped on, but briefly for a five-day Test. The Saturday sun came out to warm the knowing packed house at Heading-ley. They had enjoyed their lunchtime picnics. And now Botham came out to join Robinson. He clopped lightly down the pavilion staircase, and into the sharp light which winked on the cascading highlights of his pop star's hair-style. It was the first time much of the nation can have seen it. Somehow it augured panache and gallantry for England, though the traditional Yorkshire cricket buff – all short-back-and-sides and 'business' strokes and earnest, worried brow – might have winced, not only at how brightly the Taunton barber's girls had done their stuff, but with what bravado Ian windmilled his great three and a quarter pounder,

O'Donnell, tyro
contender, sent on his
way first ball . . .
then slapped, bullyingly
cruel, for four.
The young Australian
had some revenge of
sorts during the rest of
the series – and found
a new friend

first with the left arm, then the right. Botham, they knew, was 'alf a Yorkie 'isself, but they were never quite at, well, ease with their madcap boy, having learned his cricket down there at unserious Somerset. They respected him, however, almost in spite of themselves; though it wasn't quite right to turn *real* cricket into a ruddy carnival. ('Ere comes t'clown', Mike Brearley heard someone say.) Yet surely he had to graft today? This was a Test match against Australia, the cream of the batsmen had gone, bar this neat lad, Robinson, and England were still 67 behind. It was not long after lunch. England should surely pinch and scrape and eke their way to a cautious lead by close of play. Nothing less was expected. If these two got their heads down, mind. Botham nodded to the necessity and played himself in, massively certain and restrained, barn-door close to pad, eyelashes lowered, eyes kestrel-sharp, wary, concentrated and keen.

Of a sudden, he launched the bombardment as Lawson avoided a shattered kneecap only thanks to his adding a startled Russian dance step to his follow-through routine. The screamer rebounded from the sight-screen some 30 yards. He was off and away, and a serenely savage cover drive to the pavilion encored the fact. Hutton could not have played that – his classic stroke – with such dismissive venom. Then an on-drive to a balanced, poised perfection that only Peter May might have matched. Then, even, a sliver of an exquisitely timed late-cut that rippled past third-man's stretching left hand like it might have been played by Ranji. His treatment of O'Donnell in particular was almost bullyingly cruel. In between there were two colossal, heroic blows. Having hit Thomson, bowling fast, back over his head for a stirring, one-bounce boundary, he then picked him up quite superbly and hoisted the thing into the faraway, furthest seats of the excited throng. Twenty minutes before, Australia had needed but one wicket and they would have had both hands round England's throat. Now, almost ludicrously, Border had five men pinioned on the fence between mid-wicket and long-off – each praying, I fancy, that even a mis-hit would not single them out. In fact, Botham played no false stroke in the 51 balls he faced. The fifth wicket partnership was worth 80 in 13 overs. Border put himself on, as if acknowledging that a leader must at least be seen to go down, saluting, with his ship when all hope of rescue had gone. Botham chasséd out to the Australian captain and let fly with a wondrous, soaring six which exploded on the topmost deck of the football stand like a hand grenade. It gave England the lead, and the innings had turned the match. A few runs later, when the persevering Thomson slanted one in from the edge of the return crease and Botham played on, the celebrating applause at Headingley can only have been equalled when the same young man walked back after his historic 149 in the same match four years before.

Robinson and England sustained the momentum to the extent that Australia, 202 behind on first innings, had to battle to leave England any sort of target. Hilditch again batted stubbornly, Phillips counter-attacked valiantly, and Botham again dismissed O'Donnell – though when England set about the 123 needed to win, O'Donnell clean-bowled Botham for 12 which delighted the younger man no end. For the first, time, Botham grinned at his 'rival' as he left the wicket. England won by five wickets.

It had been Robinson's match. Only R.E. Foster, eighty-one years ago, had bettered the Nottinghamshire opener's 175 on an Ashes debut. Yet as the teams had a final beer together on Tuesday afternoon, the buzz was still of Botham's Saturday. Border described it as 'awesome'. So did Robinson. Botham's good friend, 'Thommo', who has seen it all in a dozen years round the cricket fields of the world, had simply 'enjoyed it'. No, he didn't mind bowling to Ian, 'because everything is just much more interesting when Beefy's around. There is no normality, no groove. Anything can happen – and usually does.' He did confess to becoming a touch 'tighter' when he had to bowl to Botham – 'though I don't know why 'cos a bad ball is as likely to get him out as a good one. I've known him to get out to a full toss, and a long-hop. You just have to put him out of

Tim Robinson ... dramatic homecoming after the revelations of India

your mind and bowl. And just don't try too many things at him. Reduce all his options if you can. Yet he breaks all the rules, so planning against him is pretty impossible. We always mention him at team meetings – but mostly because we think we should, rather than plotting any theories to counter him. Like his bowling, you never know what's coming next. Sometimes, when he bats, I hope and pray that he is going to go early – but there is a sneaking little feeling at the back of my brain that keeps saying, "Okay, he's in the mood, why not settle back and enjoy it?"'

Somerset, meanwhile, had at least won their first Championship match of the season and Ian travelled to London to meet them for their next game against Surrey and to congratulate particularly his vice-captain, Marks, who had taken 8 for 17 against Lancashire at Taunton – the best bowling figures for the county since Brian Langford's 9 for 26, also against the north-western side, in 1958.

The Oval is not one of Ian's favourite grounds. Well, for a start, it is famous round the circuit for its menus. Like any office or factory workers, don't forget, first-class cricketers also have a lunch hour. It is especially important for Botham, who wakes up only to a cup of hot tea. 'I never eat breakfast. Sometimes, on the circuit, I don't even have lunch. On some grounds, lunches are so abysmal that you *can't* eat them: I won't name names, else I'll have club secretaries after me: they know who they are though. Mind you, Taunton used to be one of the very worst of the lot at that old pavilion of ours; now it's very good. Choice of salads and much more: I don't even mind taking Kath and the kids in there for lunch now. But some of the other places, dearie me: Hampshire can be a bit dodgy at times, especially at Bournemouth; in fact Mark Nicholas [the Hampshire captain] has apologised for the standard of meals they have dished up.

'You take the rough with the smooth, I suppose. Leicester food is pretty ropey. And there was one place this year so bad that I had to send some-one out for a burger. The Oval used to be diabolical but I hear they are really planning to try hard this year, for the Test anyway. One time at an Oval Test we all threatened to do a deal with Wimpy or McDonalds unless the food improved. Anyway, if it is edible, my eating's still a bit funny: if we're batting, I'll probably have a full lunch: if we're bowling I'll just have a few slices of meat. At the Tests, Nancy at Lord's for instance, always knows what to send me if we're bowling – a nice plate of roast beef or perhaps a couple of steaks, and a dish of veg. In the evenings, too, I'm odd: sometimes I can have a slap-up meal, sometimes I don't need or want anything at all. I don't eat half the amount I used to. I've always reckoned you only need eat when you're hungry. I'm not great on stews, or things with lashings of spuds like opening bowlers through history are meant to have thrived on. I eat very few spuds. I like seafood particularly; and chicken, or any game. And only fresh vegetables. I used to eat twice as much when I was 20 or so. Now, I sometimes turn down steaks – for one thing now I'm not quite sure what they put in them these days. On the whole, it's a real myth about my 'great appetite' – another thing the Press totally invented, and then have to keep repeating so they think it will come true.'

Even The Oval's food looked more palatable than the weather. Evil black clouds scudded low across London's city skyline all day during which only 53 overs were bowled before the rain swept in. Roebuck was back with a Greek suntan and a mended finger, and he held firm for a painstaking 45 overs against Tony Gray, the new long lank from the Caribbean who had suddenly become the talk of the circuit. At 154 for 6, Botham was 24 not out when the rains came down, having set about the 6ft 7in beanpole and clocked him for three boundaries in his last over. It was Ian's first ever sight of Gray: 'He's big and tall and gets a lot of bounce. He's nothing like as quick as he is going to be – and has got quite a bit to learn yet. He's Joel's height, sure, but he has none of Joel's strength, stamina, or pace – yet. When he gets everything sorted out – and he fills out a bit physically, a bit more beef on his backside – he could be quite formidable.'

Next morning, Gray dismissed Botham at once. He had steered him elegantly wide of second slip for four, then pulled the next ball violently for another fizzing boundary. He was given out, caught behind, off the over's last ball. 'I didn't hit it. It's as simple as that. My bat nicked my boot, it was nowhere near the ball – and I knew a few of the Surrey blokes realized I'd been "sawn off". But up went the finger and off went me. Of course I went straight away. In county matches I always walk if I nick it – ask anyone – and also if I don't nick it and the finger goes up!'

But the head-boy manner in which he had taken on Gray in the murk had mightily impressed two of Surrey's experienced greybeards. The former New Zealand captain, Geoff Howarth (whom Gray, on the overseas registration roundabout, was almost tragically keeping out of the county side) shakes his head in appreciation: 'Both is now a devastating mixture of hitter and batsman. He's changed from the days he hit less sixes, when he was much more across the line. As a person, he's grown in confidence and that has extended to his batting. He'll go for the sixes now. He has a magnificent eye, and a wonderful swing – he takes the bat behind him and brings it down in a perfect arc. He has very little foot movement, but the bat goes through straight, so it doesn't really matter. His hands are in control – the left controls the downward swing, keeping it straight, while the right hand gives that extra power when needed. It is a perfect balance of hands.

'In the New Zealand team we always thought a slower bowler like Jeremy Coney was the best bet against him – someone who could move it a little in the air and off the seam – just to tempt him. Then we would set a field to plug his strong points – straight, and cowshot corner. But now he's playing so straight and hitting it so far that fielding tactics are almost irrelevant. I really reckon Both will get even more controlled and cultured. He is a unique cricketer.'

The veteran off-spinner, Pat Pocock, not long back from the England tour of India, had first played county cricket 21 years before. He has bowled at – and bowled out – the legendary batsmen of the past couple of generations. The estimable, much admired Pocock is not given to thoughtless, unconsidered comparisons. He gazes across the wide and famous old paddock on which he and his wits and his nerve and his length have taken up many a champion's gauntlet. 'I maintain that Sir Gary Sobers, Barry Richards, Graeme Pollock and Viv Richards are the very élite I have bowled against. Botham is honestly now on his way up to that absolute top bracket. He has become a very accomplished batsman with a very sound defence. Top batsmanship is about scoring runs in a manner that will win you the match: on that basis, Both does it all the time. In county cricket, he is amazing – he can go from blocking, to hitting a six – with nothing in between. His confidence is so great that he never thinks the ball can possibly go anywhere but over the ropes when he gets after you. He is a frightening man to bowl at . . . and yet – we all know he's the best striker of the ball in the game, so if he whacks you, you just think, "Oh, it's Both – so that can happen to anyone." It puts less pressure on you.'

Pocock, nevertheless, thinks Ian lucky that his batting can complement the bowling. There are not many matches in which he fails to feature in both 'disciplines'. If there were, you usually look it up and find he has taken a couple of blinding catches just to get an oar in. 'I think he plays in this cavalier style because he has his bowling as a second string. Knotty (a stumper) was the same. A batter pure and simple has too much depending on him to think of playing like Botham. You never quite know what is happening when Ian's in – he must be a nightmare for a captain who's timing a declaration. Just 20 minutes of mayhem from Botham changes a day's well planned scenario. As a spinner, mind you, you don't need to bother about baiting him, as you do with other, more defensive players. You just know he'll go for it and attack. I try to vary my deliveries against him, so that he's not quite sure about my speed or my loop. If he's hitting me hard and often, I will open up my field and fire it in at his blockhole. If I'm lucky, he'll get frustrated and get himself out – or possibly he'll just stab it away for a single and the other batsman will get up to the striking end, which is where, of course, you want him.'

But for injuries, Surrey's fiery left-arm bowler, David Thomas, could have been playing with Botham for England now. He relishes the relishable: 'Both's whacked better bowlers than me. You must take your chance. He loves to attack the quicker bowlers, with the ball coming onto the bat. I love my jousts with him, although sometimes I think the only way to dismiss him is bounce him – and have two fielders standing in the Ladbroke's tent at The Oval, waiting for the catch! If that fails, bowl on, or just outside, the off stump – and pray it's your day.'

The match, alas, petered out. The weather had given it no chance. In reply to Somerset's soggy first innings total of 188, Surrey declared at once to see if Botham would like to set them a contrived last innings target. He happily obliged against the 'net' bowling of Richards, Clinton, and Stewart. He hit the thing to all points of the massive old ground, making 72 off 50 balls (8 fours and 5 more sixes) before declaring just before the deluge. 'They bowled rubbish – and I treated it like rubbish', explained the smiling boy at the end, and he quaffed his beers with the Surrey team as they watched the same rains come down that had quite drowned the opening of the Wimbledon tennis championships, say, some ten minutes earlier and ten miles to the west-sou'-west.

Apart from Botham's blaze, there were cheerful drinks, too, for Roebuck who had corpsed the whole field, let alone his own team-mates' dressing-room by plonking his first ball, from the most unlikely opening bowler, Richards the wicket-keeper, straight down a fieldsman's throat. Roebuck himself joined in. 'It was just a joke', said his captain. 'Funny, reactions vary when guys get out. Mind you, I can always tell when Roebey's walking off, after getting out, as to what his reaction is going to be. He might come in briskly and just nod and mutter "good ball, that". Sometimes he'll say nothing, seethe, and go very sulky – especially if he hasn't been getting many of late. Then he'll just take his pads off, stare into space, and then disappear, saying nothing; that always amuses me. If he's got a few runs, he's as chirpy as . . . well, as a cricket. Cluck, cluck, cluck, chat, chat, chat. On the other hand, say, Nigel Felton is always upset whenever he's out – and genuinely upset. "What was I doing wrong there? I must have done something terrible." He asks that, even if he's got a hundred. Viv? Well, it depends how he's got out. If it was a good delivery he always gives generous credit. Bloody good ball, that. Ruddy good bowler, him. If he's got himself out he can be annoyed. Sometimes, magnificently annoyed. Especially if it's put the team in trouble. But mostly he comes in, unpads – and just goes to sleep. Me? I take it as it comes. I think everyone knows that. Unless I've been "sawn off", mind. I suppose I was passingly annoyed in the first innings this time – simply because everyone knows I "walk". For one thing I was enjoying the battle with Tony [Gray]. Once it was only "no walking" against Australia: then it was in all Test matches abroad, because there have been so many bad decisions and there had to be a way of evening things out. But in English cricket, if I nick it I go.' He might not have nicked it on this occasion – and he went. But he had already scored 749 runs in next to no time in England's waterlogged 1985 early summer.

Over the river to Lord's. The Australian Test match at 'headquarters' – invariably the second of the series – in midsummer's sun evokes a timeless fixture of grandeur and magic. Old men in the Empire's outposts have, for a century, logged the five-day dates and cursed themselves they were not there. And there is a stately, breath-catching aura about the old pile when a full house, physically relaxed and knowing itself priviledged, is rapt in concentration at the every nuance of the play. Lord's is its singular self, and in a different 'class' than any other sporting stadium I have been lucky enough to visit all around the world – though I admit I have not yet seen Brazil play soccer in the Maracana, nor witnessed a world heavyweight title fight in the Garden at Madison Square. Lord's, it must be said, is also tops at having the rudest and most officious gang of fellows who man the entrances and exits.

MCC members in the exclusive vastness of the pavilion and Long Room are no longer gruff old Edwardian patricians in aspic. In recent years, they have let in some even more blindingly obnoxious and patronising nouveaux from trade and commerce and 'public relations'. But enough of the old buffers abound to set back the time-warp a few generations. Ian Botham has usually done well at Lord's – bar the Test, four years ago, in which he got the only 'pair' of his career and resigned the England captaincy – and though he cannot, in honesty, admit that the place he served his apprenticeship actually fires him up, there may well be a subconscious niggle here that drives him on. For Lord's was the place where, only a dozen years ago, the chief coach, Len Muncer, told the 17-year-old he should have stuck to soccer. Ian has always been at his most poutingly sullen when he walks, as players must four or five times a day, through the Long Room. The one-time apprentice still despises the masters' attitudes: 'I reckon some of the guys who populate that Long Room have a dust-cover put over them each autumn, a pink gin stuck in their hand – and are then stored up in the loft for six months before being brought down in April, dusted off, and another pink gin poured out so they can sit out the summer on their high chairs. One time, on the morning of a one-day final, us Somerset lads were coming through the Long Room on our way back from the nets, when I heard the shouted order, "Botham!" I ignored it and carried on through. "Botham come *here!*" I turned and told him simply and sharply, "It's either *Ian* or *Mr* Botham to you. Which one are you asking to jump around and beg?" And they think they're the educated ones: I'm only the lad from a secondary modern, but I'd never speak to anyone like they do to us sometimes.'

This time, four years on, it was Botham's captain, David Gower, who was being pilloried at the start of a Lord's Test, just as Ian had been in 1981. In spite of his century in the one-day international at Lord's three weeks before, Gower's form continued wretched. He had scored 17 and 9 in the Headlinglcy Test. Now Border won the toss. It had rained for a week, so he put England in to bat on a spongy field. Robinson was out at once. Gower went in and the gentlemen of the Press, in their glasshouse rim high above the Warner Stand, leaned forward, each vying to cast the first stone should he fail again. He made 86 courageous runs, easily England's highest score in their all-out total of 290. (Botham caught at deep point for 5, miscueing Lawson.) By the end Gower was even uncorking some of his vintage strokes. Next day, to a man, the Press said they knew he had it in him all along, and rejoiced in italics, exclamation marks and their boldest headlines. There was a warm feeling in the England dressing-room when their captain returned. 'None of us likes it when mud's being thrown at a fellow professional', says Ian. 'If only the Press were not so damn hypocritical. This whole thing with David has been another classic case of their obsessive hypocrisy. No wonder none of us take them in the least bit seriously. A year ago David Gower was the greatest thing since electricity or sliced bread. A bad trot and they are calling for his head – as if he has *never* known even how to hold a bat. Then one good innings and, hey presto! they're all swarming around him again. We just laugh at them, to be honest. If they used their brains and thought about why we have such animosity towards them, then they themselves would not expect us to treat them in any other way. Their insensitivity is pitiable: they are totally oblivious to the fact that we are just cricket players with families and friends and feelings just like anyone else, themselves included. I'm so embittered about it now that I've come out the other side and couldn't care less what they write about me any more, and I daresay David's exactly the same. He knows he has a Test average of over 50. That'll do him: because you can count the guys since the war who have a Test average of over 50 on one hand. He's already one of the "greats".'

From purely cricketing points of view, Ian of course allows the fact that journalist-critics have always been part and parcel of the first-class game. There are, nevertheless, some cricket writers he admires hugely; his list always starts with John Arlott. But the short-fuse starts crackling sparkily whenever he hears suggestions that his bowling is becoming a liability to the England team: for years something has always been wrong with Botham's bowling: it's either too slow, too short, too wayward, too 'off-hand', too experimental. Generally, critics have rated him a trundler who bowls himself into the ground for a lot of runs because successive captains over the years have been unable, once he had hold of the ball, to get it off him. So they let him bowl on for the sake of harmony, peace and quiet, and to stop him belly-aching at second slip. After his Headingley figures – 46-12-153-3 – the critics were growling again. So here at Lord's Botham bounds in with all the vim and zest of a colt playing in his first Test, not his 75th. The prancing young McDermott had taken six wickets for the Australians, but suddenly Botham was bowling with even more fire and nip – indeed was palpably the fastest thing in the match. Border's massively dominating 196 of Australia's 425 made the match totally safe for the visitors – England had not beaten the old enemy at Lord's since 'Verity's Match' all of fifty-one years ago – but Botham walked off with his 25th five-wicket haul in a Test match, beating the long-held world record of the legendary Sydney Barnes. It was the eighth time he had dismissed half the opposition against Australia in 25 Tests: he has done it six times against India (14 Tests) and New Zealand (13), twice each against West Indies (14) and Pakistan (7), and once against Sri Lanka (2).

In these matters, being the most innumerate of cricket lovers, I always hurry to Derek Lodge, stats wizard who has the knack of bringing decimal points to life. Ian's 8 bags-of-five in Ashes matches alone has yet to match Barnes (12), Tom Richardson, C.T.B. Turner, Clarrie Grimmett and Dennis Lillee (11 each). Curiously, each of these took five wickets in an innings in his *first* Test, as did Botham, of course, all those heady years ago in the heatwave summer of '76. The more remarkable achievers on this historical list are Barnes, who took five wickets 12 times in 20 Tests against Australia (and 12 times in 7 Tests against South Africa), and Richardson, who chalked up his 11 'fives' in just 14 Tests, all against Australia.

Now Ian needed only two more wickets in Australia's second innings at Lord's to pass Bob Willis's all-time England wicket haul of 235 (he was to get them in next to no time when Australia went in to win the match). Now only Dennis Lillee's historical haul of 355 was keeping Ian from being the most prolific wicket-taker in the game. But still the doubters in the press-box and Long Room, and the old bowlers in the commentary boxes, were chuntering on about how he couldn't bowl. 'I just don't know what's going on out there, Brian . . .'

Surely, by the end of this series, Ian would also gallop past Bob Willis's record of 128 wickets against Australia. At the end of Australia's first innings at Lord's, Botham was only 15 wickets behind with four and a

Now only Lillee's record to beat. Lamb catches, Wood wanders away, Edmonds applauds and England's leading all-time wicket-taker starts his war dance

half Tests to go. The only other Englishmen to take over a hundred are Rhodes (109), Barnes (106), Underwood (105), Bedser (104) and Peel (102). But the Australians, Lillee (167) and Hugh Trumble (141) stand above all. By the way, in the 1985 Headingley Test, Botham took his three wickets in four balls; the only other Englishman to do this against Australia was Voce, in 1936-37. Bates, Briggs and J.T. Hearne have taken hat-tricks. Ian would enjoy one of those one day. Meanwhile, he rests his case at his old apprentice shop, having taken more wickets at Lord's than any other bowler has taken in Tests on any other English ground – 68 at an average of 24.16, including a best performance at Lord's of 8 for 34 against Pakistan in 1978.

When Ian finally got rid of Border as the craggy Australian dasher went for the shot that would have posted his double century, the bowler was the first down the wicket to congratulate his friend and foe on such a sumptuous innings. The smiles of admiration were mutually heartfelt. 'It's always a battle out there with Both', says Allan. 'If you forget about who he is and just watch him from the dressing-room balcony, you always fancy your chances against him. He gives you a lot to hit and your attitude is that there are runs to be had. With front-line bowlers from some other countries, you tend to be a lot more wary. That's why they

117

probably don't have the strike-rate of Both. The adrenalin pumps when you face Ian. You know that no matter what the state of the game or what the wicket is like he's going to bounce you or do something similarly outlandish.' He laughs and sprays open another Castlemaine tinnie. 'The good old blighter can always get you into that frame of mind which makes it so easy to play a false stroke. He's got you pumped up. He's rushing in at you and doing all sorts of things. His aggression brings out the aggression in the batsman. That's when he can snare you, when you've got to go careful. He's a good bowler with it. I'm always hearing you people say he's not much of a bowler, but he's no mug. They say he takes a lot of wickets with bad balls – but he also bowls a lot of good balls that get you in two minds. You've got to believe it. Well, just look at all his world all-time records. In his earlier days he would swing the ball around a lot, but he's basically lost that now. He moves it around a bit, but his biggest attribute remains his aggression and his preparedness to be aggressive in any situation and to any batsman.'

G'day . . . and well batted, friend. Border departs, dismissed by Botham just four short of a double hundred. 'It's always a battle out there with Both'

Allan's wife Jane and his pride and joy, 16-month-old Dene, were arriving next day. Ian took out his Australian buddy for a last few 'bachelors' beers. Botham was well content with his own efforts, but knew England were up against it, especially having sent in two night-watchmen on the Saturday evening so, to all intents, they were probably four wickets down for just 40-odd, and Australia still 100 or so ahead. It meant Ian would be going in at No. 8 which could turn into a crucial waste. Some of us would love to see him bat permanently at No. 4 – Hammond's inviolate position, and Compton's. Says Ian: 'I've heard some of you "experts" say I shouldn't be either a strike bowler or even a stock bowler – that I should go in at No. 4 as a pure batsman. To be honest, I don't think that would suit my temperament. I think I've got it about right now – anyway, I know I enjoy it best – being a strike bowler, and batting No. 6. I think that's how I can be the best asset to the side. It keeps me fitter and stronger – I've looked after myself much better in the last couple of years. At 29, you know, fitness comes much harder to you than when you're 22. It came pretty easy to me to start off with. As a kid, fitness seems natural. Bob Taylor always used to joke about me and my excesses. No worry, Bobby, I'd say. He would warn me – "Fitness doesn't get easier, it gets harder", he'd say. I know that now.'

On Monday, England's middle was gone in no time – as had been so predictable when the nightwatchmen, Emburey and Allott, had been left holding the fort with their miners' helmets. Lady Bracknell's dictum held – to have to send in one was *unfortunate*, to send in a second was *carelessness*. So 57 for 4 became 98 for 6. Botham, now batting at eight, joined Gatting. An innings defeat was still on the cards. It was Watson and Bailey all over again (the staunch and historic partnership which had saved England in the corresponding match 32 years before: I was 15, and when they did it, my little school was given a half-day's holiday!). In other words, the day called for a Dunkirk spirit. But, as Matthew Engel chortled in *The Guardian*, 'Put Botham in charge of the retreat from Dunkirk, and he'll insist on marching on Berlin that evening.' And so it came to pass.

After the hearsay of India and his thunderous exploits in which all England – after so long waiting – had revelled in following on the crackly wireless every chilblained dawn, Gatting was suddenly being enjoyed as the most integral and chunky core of this Test team. Unselfish as ever, he now reined in his own flamboyance and organized Botham the strike. Not that Ian, by the blazing standards he was setting himself this summer, went potty. Let's say, he was not patting back half-volleys, nor clipping long-hops with a nervous jab to mid-wicket for a single, like some folk would. Simply, Ian batted with both the responsibility and the élan of a

119

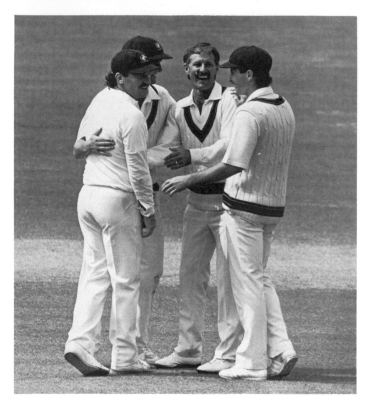

They planned for him to hit against the spin. It worked – and Holland is one very chuffed leg-spinner

man in supreme form. They knew it, we knew it, he knew it. 'I suppose it illustrated the way I've decided to play. Obviously there are times to shut up shop, to fight it out and never score a run. But there are really a lot more cases when you have to go out there and just *play*. If you're getting on with it, it takes a lot of pressure off the others. I've been trying to do if for the last three or four years – it's just that I sense it's all coming together now.'

Soon after lunch they had cleared the arrears and then Ian set about improving the account – announcing the decision with a gigantic six into the heart of the Mound Stand off Holland. He went to 50 out of 73 off 61 balls and, between them, they put on 131 when Botham attacked a fraction too exuberantly at Holland and holed out. He had scored 85 of them and the effortless and meaty six off McDermott over square leg will live in the recollection of every one of the 25,000 there. Ian was annoyed with himself. Another half-hour's mayhem only, and all initiatives would have been England's. But having showered, even he found himself warmly pleased that his wicket had set up the scenario for the veteran leg-spinner, Holland, to run in the classic return of 32-12-68-5. Especially as Bob claimed to have 'thought-out' Botham. Says Holland: 'First, our own former leggie, Richie Benaud, had taken me aside and said when bowling to Botham I should imagine that there is no batsman at the other end –

"pick out your spot and bowl line and length!" It's hard sometimes when you see Ian at the other end but I found it worked. Then, Allan and I worked out a plan to bowl on or outside leg stump to him. He hits fairly straight so we thought we could cramp him up on leg stump and tempt him to hit against the spin through mid-wicket. It worked!'

Bob Holland has been turning an arm over and revelling in his art and mystical craft for two decades now in all levels of cricket. 'Ian is the hardest hitting batsman I've ever bowled to. Viv [Richards] doesn't hit as hard. Botham is all brute strength whereas Viv uses more timing and placement. Ball after ball Ian tries to hit you right out of the ground. It can get a bit depressing for some bowlers but I always find it an enjoyable challenge bowling at him. He may smash you over the grandstand a few times but you always have the feeling you are in with a chance to pick him up. That's what keeps you going, most definitely. If he didn't allow you that optimism, well, you'd give up.

'I think, in a way, our pace bowlers have made the mistake so far of trying to bounce him out or beat him with the yorker. I think now we have all agreed to be patient and bowl line and length to him – like you would any other batsman in the world.

'You know, the challenge of bowling to someone like Ian Botham makes cricket such a fabulous game for me. I would hate to see where cricket would be these days without people like Botham. Well, you tell me? Nowhere. But just the other day I was thinking what sort of player Ian would have been if he wasn't an all-rounder. He certainly wouldn't bat the way he does in a Test match if he wasn't a bowler as well. He surely wouldn't be game and confident enough to take the risks, knowing he couldn't make amends with the ball . . . Or would he?

Border, Phillips, and young O'Donnell, improving at every entrance, knocked off Australia's runs. One-all. Anyone's series.

7 I thought I'd done everything right

GOOD to be back in pastoral Taunton. London's mid-summer sporty hurley-burley had transferred its fierce gaze from cricket's NW8 at Lord's, and across the Putney and Wandsworth Bridges to SW13 and the Wimbledon finals. Out in the sticks, it was still 'the cricket' for Englishmen. David Gower's Leicestershire had come to play Somerset, and Andy Withers, Ian's trusty helpmate, secretary and 'minder' had left his mother's home in Taunton earlier than usual to wake Ian with his morning tea. For after the day's cricket the England captain was coming to supper in the cottage. Ian, blearily, and Andy, energetically, set about tidying the shop. Ian is inclined to undress 'on the move', as pin-tidy Kathy, at home in Yorkshire, and Andy in Taunton, would verify as they follow with the laundry basket. Ian would far rather be at home with the family, of course, but he is lucky with his Somerset 'digs'.

'The cottage is out in the wilds, out of the way, nobody bothering me, nobody peering over the hedge or chinking through the curtains. Andy comes down from Taunton and wakes me up with a cup of tea after his own Mum has given him enough to keep that 28-ton bulk of his in good nick. [Andy's a bit more than half that!] I met Andy, oh, years ago; he used to play village rugby with Keith Jennings, the Somerset cricketer who was on the Lord's staff with me. Teaming up with Andy was probably one of the best moves I ever made – though don't tell him that, otherwise he'll go all lethargic and poncy on me. No, he's a great lad; a real mate, reliable, and very, very loyal. So once he's round and made the tea, another great day can start. No breakfast, just pots of tea.'

Botham won the toss against his longtime England friend. Leicestershire fielded three England bowlers – Agnew, Willey and Cook; one who was on the selectors' shortest of short-lists, Taylor; and Clift, the highly experienced, popular and canny stamp collector from Zimbabwe. Somerset, as ever – and for all their continuing problems with injured men, and inconsistent batting (let alone bowling that blew endearingly hot and cold) – purred into overdrive. Botham came in at 193 for 4. Nick Cook, England's former left-arm spinner, had just come on for the 59th over. Botham hit him at once for three whinnying, snorting boundaries. Richards had just departed after a bijou 47 off 51 balls (8 fours and a six). Ian was stumped by a mile after a glittering cameo – 48 in 42 balls (4 fours and 3 sixes). Later, and ruefully smiling, Nick reckoned his biggest mistake was taking a wicket as soon as he came on.

'That brought in Both. One six he hit off me went over long-on as soon as I had gone over the wicket. He then hit me "inside out" over cover for four – a beautifully controlled shot. If he just knocks it high and straight at Taunton, we'll never get him out – the straight boundaries are impossible to defend. He calls us spinners "step-and-fetch-it" fellows, yet we do have a chance against him – if only because he hits the ball in the air so often. It's just a question of sustaining your patience. If you can. I got him stumped at last. I had gone over the wicket; the field was scattered, because he was trying to hit every ball out of the county, let alone the ground. It was the last over before tea and he played three defensive shots in a row – all of a sudden, and every one exaggerated in its dead-bat care. I thought he was taking the mickey and taunted him down the wicket – "Both, you're not playing for tea, are you?" Next ball he rushed down the wicket – and was stumped by yards. He said nothing to me. But he smiled that big smile . . .'

Jonathan Agnew was fielding at long-off to Cook, in front of the old pavilion. 'Ian Butcher was at long-on. Both hit a four that went straight between us – just five yards either side, but it was going so thunderingly fast that neither of us had a chance of getting near it. The boundary can't have been less than 50 yards from the bat.' Botham was treating Taunton like his own private sands, hired for beach cricket. The fact remained, however, that this summer, soggy as it was, no spectator remained safe either as they picnicked in the top tiers of groundstands or on the great, wide arenas like Lord's, The Oval or Edgbaston.

Nigel Felton, the chunky left-hander, genuinely keen and comradely, had delighted everyone with his four-and-a-half hour century – not least his beaming captain – but for all that, next day, Leicester took up the play with just as much carefree calm, if not quite the same panache as when Richards and his blond warrior captain had been at the wicket. Whitaker batted well and Ian, at one stage, had marched over to the sponsors' tents and told them to stifle their private guffaws and allow a young batsman to concentrate. 'Sorry', said Malcolm Pearce, one of the county's leading sponsors, 'the wine had gone down too well.' But it had been a generous gesture from Ian – who, anyway, was himself on and off the field having treatment for the nagging tweak on the ligaments of his left ankle, leaving

the ever-willing enthusiast, Marks, to bowl his index-finger and his boots off for the richest and most rewarding of spinners' returns – 49-11-143-7. Vic was as 'over-tired' as the sponsors' clients.

Typically, neither Whitaker nor Marks made the headlines next day. If Ian was involved, that was enough for Fleet Street. As he said: 'No big deal. We were bowling, a keen young man was batting and doing his level best very well indeed. I just went across and told them to shut up. They had had a few too many. A nice day out, a bit boisterous, fair enough. I just reminded them that a professional game of cricket was going on outside their tent. Nothing wrong with it, really. Who am I to criticize anyone "over zealous" after a long lunch? Later, they sent over an apology: end of story.'

The high moment of Victor's lovely, long, lobbing, curling and curving twiddly tweaker's spell had been c-&-b'ing the England captain. Gower was still straining to break thoroughly free of his bad trot despite his runs at Lord's. He had scored four when he hit the thing back with the blazing fury of a Woolley trying to break Tich Freeman's ankle in the nets at

Canterbury. Vic hung on. Ian joined in the Somerset soccer-type adulation of their off-spinner, but he looked back to Gower departing, with a shrug. When the tide don't flow... it don't. To be honest, it *was* a most unlikely c-&-b. 'Well, Vic doesn't catch much off his own bowling. David smashed it savagely, Vic hung on – and I don't know whether the bat or the bowler was the more shocked and surprised! Marksey got over our back-slapping and his giggling and then announced how unlucky David had been. He had, too, I'm telling you!'

But the present England captain was, nevertheless, round with friends for supper with the former England captain in the cottage that Andy tidies. They don't talk much of cricket. Like the sage said, 'Who knows of Life who only Cricket knows?' But they laugh on life, and the circuit, and more than once or twice, great cricketing names from round the world might spice the un-cricketing conversation. The cabbage cooks briefly – and the music goes round and round. Outside all is silent Somerset, and Fleet Street is a million happy miles away. The host talks recipes.

'Self-catering? Of course. One of those lovely Marks & Spencer packets from the freezer; bung it in, 45 minutes later – Duck à l'orange! Chicken Kiev! Cumberland Pie! David fancies himself as more than a budding connoisseur of wine. Tonight, I agree, we invented champagne. I'd got in some Bolinger '75. Why not? We are old pals. Lately, I've been enjoying wines much more for their quality – as opposed to their quantity. I get my wine now through the *Wine Society*. I've been known even to ring up John Arlott and pick his brains about best buys, or what to drink or to put down. Reds? Something like a Fleurie, a good drinking wine. Medocs, too. If I was really going to buy a celebration bottle for Kath and myself, well Lafitte, of course, though they sting you through the nose for it these days, don't they?'

They were up early enough with Andy's cup of tea. Only Viv had 'food poisoning'. He did not bat. Ian strode in, windmilling his bat and looking surly, at 175 for 3. He immediately set about the morning. Well, someone at least did seem intent on warming up poor England's summer. Certainly Leicestershire's. His first six soared over the old pavilion and fell, with a crunch, on the clinkers under the old Main Gate. The next exploded out of Jonathan Agnew's palms at long-on, just like Harold Gimblett's did when a school-marm amateur was in the deep, smarmily re-adjusting the peak of his coloured cap. Then the missile soared like a diminishing dot into the sky, off Clift and over Cook's head at deepest mid-wicket, like a bombardment of Wellard, pre-war. This one – high, higher, almost highest – hit the steward, George Bouckley, on the right shoulder. It bowled him over. Six inches left and he would have been dead. Said the tottery George: 'I've always been aware in this job that even on the farthest

125

perimeter path of the ground, you make sure you're sheltered when Ian's batting. You hear the roar and you cower. This time, I heard the soaring roar alright – and at the instant I looked up, the ball crashed, crack! against my right shoulder.' George was bowled over. The crowd's crescendo whoop was stilled in concern. He was helped to medical attention in the home dressing-room. The collar bone was not broken. Ian signalled affection and – with a cupping-shudder of the right-hand batting glove in friendship – signalled that he would be standing George a very large pint at close-of-play.

Ian's 5 sixes and solitary four had posted his half-century in just 30 balls. Yet again he was poised for overtaking, with ease, his own fastest hundred of the season. Yet again he generously declared to help make a game of it. Once more the contrivance petered out. A draw, seven dull points apiece for a daring effort by both bristling captains. Somerset were still with just one win, for all their Viv, and natural verve – and bold, brash leadership. Ian had, of course, been peppering the pickets, first bounce, in one-day Player, NatWest and Benson farragos, but only 'first-class' cricket counted for the register of record sixes. Ian now averaged 62.5 runs per first-class innings. His aggregate was 937 runs – 576 of them in sixes. With 48 he was now in striking distance of Wellard's 50-year-old record. And it was just the beginning of July. Like the Taunton ice-cream seller told BBC reporter, Patrick Murphy, as she shut up shop for the duration this Saturday: 'Don't worry, me dear – when he's bashin' the ball about out there, I can see the queue vanish. When 'e's in there's no point sellin' ices out 'ere, is there?'

As he said cheerio at Taunton that evening, David Gower was still marvelling over just one shot. Ian's six over *extra-cover*: 'Nick bowled it a little wider to get him stretching. He just leaned over and stroked it away effortlessly. Clean over the extra-cover grandstand. I remember him doing the same to Iqbal Qasim a couple of years ago in a one-day international. Timing. Confidence. What else is there? Both has got them both to coin a phrase.'

Before they left the wild and woozy West, his England friends, the slim – too slim? – Agnew and the thoughtful – too thoughtful? – Cook, were still prepared to talk of the big, blond, barneying boyo who was hogging the rest of the bar. Cook's code is cunning: 'One of his straight sixes off me today was so high and far that I might well have got sunburn on the tonsils looking up at the disappearing ball. So I didn't even bother to turn round as it went back over my head. Truly, no one in my experience hits it so far, so hard and so often. I bet he'll emulate Sobers and get 6 sixes in an over before he's finished. "Appetite" is the key word – once he got that back this year, he was irresistible. Both's reflexes are unbelievable – both as a

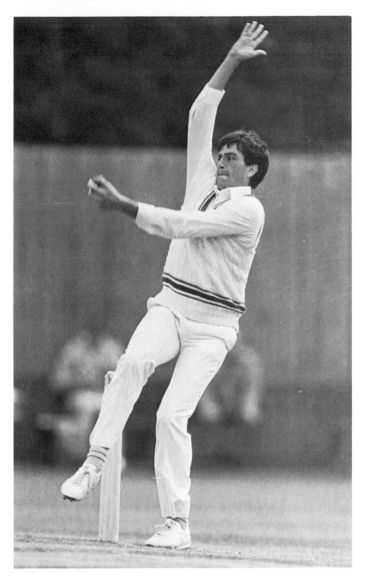

**Nick Cook . . . getting
sunburnt tonsils watching
the sixers fly**

fielder and batsman. He has a completely uninhibited swing of the bat, a
wonderful follow-through. I think that more and more people are appreciating his genius now. We are. He's larger than life, with no grey areas in
his attitude to life. I'd always want him in my side. He is a great team man,
and terrific in the dressing-room. I cannot tell you how he always wants
the team to do well. He is not a selfish cricketer. He's never happier than
when Somerset or England are doing well. His own performances don't
matter half as much to him.'

The delightful, considerate Agnew ('Spiro', wouldn't you know?),
chips in: 'There is no stopping him. In the second innings, I dropped him
at long-on off Peter Willey, who was bowling from the New Pavilion end.
Both was having a real dart at that stage, and the ball was no more than 7ft

in the air all the way. I was right on the fence and I didn't see it at first against the dark background. I was about 70 yards away, it was really motoring and it came at ear height to my right. It went straight through my hands for six – Willey's face was a picture. For the rest of the innings, the ball kept disappearing over the Old Pavilion, or straight over the press-box. As soon as he hits it, you think "he hasn't really got hold of that" and you look up and see it's miles away. Ian has that aura of confidence; a self-awareness. Like Border and Viv, he is totally aware of himself at the crease. It seems to us he has no nerves, no fear of failure. I remember one game last season when I bowled him two good-length balls on the off stump that he played defensively. The third ball was exactly the same: it disappeared over cover for four. I just thought, "What can I do about that?" Nothing.'

Agnew, like most cricketers, is touchingly generous about honouring a foe. Well, in this tight-knit game, friends are foes, and foes are friends. There's the yardstick. Botham, briefly, hit Leicester and Agnew into kingdom-come today. Agnew can twig the glory of that, cursing as he explains it: 'Ian is a magnificent batsman. He is so good that he can tick over at forty runs an hour without seeming to exert himself. He can hit the ball anywhere, at any time, and every bowler who has ever run into him knows that. He cashes in on that, I suppose, because county bowlers feel out-classed by him very early on. He just knocks the confidence out of you. That's where he's so great – that massive self-confidence. He loves to hit the ball on the up: that is very damaging to a fast bowler's *ego*. You want to bowl out-swingers, to get him edging – but a slip fielder needs very strong hands to pick up one of his nicks! They go like fizzing rockets. You bowl to begin with, and it is all in place and tidy. Just like any day, any summer. If Ian is in, a couple of early blows from him and the field is scattered at once. So as you're running in, you can't see anyone from your side except the 'keeper and a solitary slip who's dreading trying to hang onto a shell! I'd rather bowl at Viv than Botham. Because Ian is so unpredictable, he hits it so hard and so high. Anywhere, too.'

When Agnew, the breezily bright former Uppingham pupil, has played for England, he admits to bagging a balcony seat when Ian is batting. 'Honestly, we are all really disappointed when he's out. If you're on his side, you love to see him bat. He's great in the England dressing-room – not too brash, in fact rather quiet on occasions; he tells a good joke. And he really does encourage his team-mates; he's generous with praise and support for others, and us others have a fraction of his talent. Do you know, I feel sorry for any fielders when he's batting? The ball comes at them so hard and fast. And if you drop Both, well, you're in real trouble.'

Two or three years ago, I sat happily on the top table at one of Chris

Balderstone's benefit suppers in Leicester. Peter Wheeler, the England rugby captain was there, and so – ever generous in support of friends – was Botham. Chris looked across at Ian and said the boy could be as great a bat as, almost, Hammond, if he wanted to be. '*If* he had the cold-blooded hunger', he said. Now, as the Leicestershire team prepared to leave for home, Chris agreed that Ian has what it takes for a permanent residence among the all-time greats: 'I like his bravado, the touch of arrogance. I've been disappointed in him in the past, I didn't think he did himself justice as much as he might have. Not this season. I love the way he lifts the ball for six – especially on the leg side. He just manipulates the thing miles into the air. Today, I was standing on the boundary, watching the ball disappear into the crowd. You couldn't help admiring such dash. Years ago, when I started, no one used heavy bats. There were not so many hit sixes, I suppose. Still, no one can possibly rival Both for consistency with sixes.'

Botham hit no sixes in the Nottingham Test, however – the first week in the previous dozen that no sixer had sailed back, whirring past the earhole of an admiring, cursing bowler with his feet on the ground and a neck cricked. He hit 7 fours, mind you, in his 38 off 35 balls, till he misjudged a 'steer' off McDermott and miscued horribly to extra-cover. But he had come in with England already a whoppingly unbeatable 365 for 4 (Gooch and Gatting sharing successive stands with Gower of 117 and 187). The G-force had come among us. The captain's elegantly greedy rehabilitation of 166 was the highest by an England captain at Trent Bridge, passing Wyatt's 149 against South Africa exactly fifty summers ago. Ian was out at 416, after which England's tail curled up shyly – and Australia painstakingly overtook and continued to 539 all out and the draw that had looked certain from the Saturday morning. Wood fashioned a very well made, almost valiant 172 and the bracing young Ritchie hit a maiden Ashes century full of revelation and promise.

The pitch was a bland, lifeless featherbed. No bowler could flog any life from it. Botham took 3 for 107 in 34 overs, pegging manfully away at Wood's impassive technique and conjuring up a series of intriguing duels with the pleasantly precocious, puppy-plump and pugnacious-looking Ritchie, who had announced himself with that splendid 94 in the Lord's Test. After that innings, the former Australian captain and one of Botham's *bêtes noires*, Ian Chappell, had warned Ritchie about responding, out there in the middle, to Botham's general aggressiveness, to take no notice of the bowler's highly-charged mixed-bag of deliveries which were all loaded with taunt and tease and challenge. 'So I really tried to play Botham differently here at Nottingham', says Ritchie. 'For instance, Chappell told me to be satisfied with hitting him for one four an over.

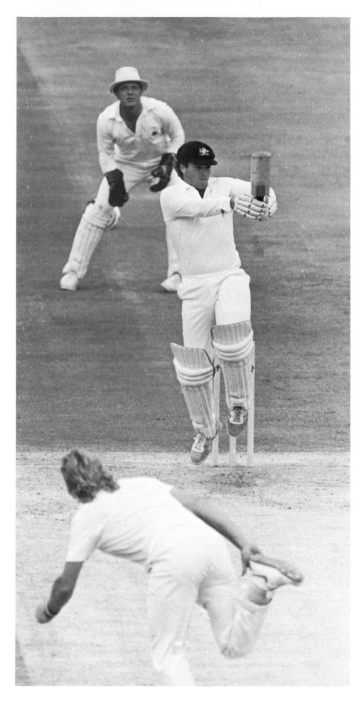

Ritchie gets his century . . . 'He left me a gap to allow me to play a pull shot forward of square, but warned, "you keep hitting but I'll get you in the end"'

Even if he bowled another bad ball, I went gentle on it. And it worked for the most part, didn't it? Except for the odd occasion, I also ducked all his bouncers . . . But, you know, just because you do it once you never have the bloke beaten . . . He is an incredible bowler. I faced overs out there when he bowled six totally different deliveries – an off-break, a bouncer, an in-swinger, an out-swinger, a half-volley and a long-hop. And he always tries to bowl to my strengths, making sure he sets up his field accordingly. To me he bowled a little short and left me a gap in the field to allow me to play a pull shot forward of square leg. But he would also put two fieldsmen down behind square leg. When he bounced me, he bounced me high, so I'd have to hit the thing behind square.

'Ian seems happy to concede four or six runs an over. He pretends to get the hump, but deep down it never really worries him. As long as he is taking wickets, he's happy to have 5 for 100 off 20 overs. He can move the ball both ways, and he's never, not in all the balls I've faced from him, bowled anything less than flat out.

'To be honest, I think he bowled best of all to me at Lord's. That was an amazing performance. He did everything in his power to upset me. Again he mixed it all up with a bit of poop – and I hit him a few times. As you went for a run, you'd pass him and he'd say "good shot – now get ready for the next one". Always there is the attitude, "you keep hitting them and I'll keep serving them up to you . . . until I get you out. Cos I'm going to, kid. No problem. Sooner rather than later . . ."'

Ritchie talks of the 'electricity' engendered at the batsman's crease when Botham paces out his run to begin a new spell. 'He's got the ball, and suddenly the whole level of competition is cranked up. Even the fielders are a bit more on edge. Certainly the crowd are. Everything's tensed. And up he comes to bowl and you just know *something* is going to happen. You always get a few balls to hit and you move up a cog to cater for this. Even when it's all at a very tight stage, he seems to deliberately bowl you a few easy ones to get you in the mood to play shots, to lull you into relaxing and thinking it's all too easy. When you feel that, bloody hell! suddenly he's got you! It's his supreme confidence, I suppose. It's just part of him – and not only on the cricket field. I've been on the golf course with him, and in a few bars. Both is a born competitor. He likes to think he can bowl the best, drive the farthest, and drink the most. Usually he can, too. You find that out pretty quickly.'

Ritchie and the estimable, patient Wood ensured the draw with their stand of 161. Gatting's stand with Gower was simply cancelled out. There were other diversions to warm the packed house, however. For one thing, the sun was so much in evidence as to have the cold drinks trolley wheeled on for the first time in the continuingly woeful summer. Suddenly it looked like a Saturday Test match should – and no better place for it than Trent Bridge which is a lovely ground, enjoyed alike by players and watchers. John Arlott called Trent Bridge 'the most convivial of Test grounds' and his days spent there 'some of the most companionable, hospitable and illuminating days – and nights – I have spent at cricket in my entire life.'

But if this somnolent Saturday seemed to be drowsing off into pleasant, sunny reverie, it was suddenly wakened by a jangling alarm call. Botham was responsible. In the day's final session, Wood and Ritchie bedded down. England's last throw was with the new ball. Ian paced out his run. First ball, Wood nicked – and Gatting dropped him at slip. At once, Ian's friend and new ball debutant for England, Arnie Sidebottom, hobbled off with a freak injury to his toe and carrying a bloodstained boot. England's other seamer, Paul Allott, was already sick with a tummy bug. It was all up to Ian: it trebled the fire in his belly. Immediately, he contrived to bowl a beauty, nipping back at Ritchie and hitting the pad. It was, as they say, very well worth a shout. The umpire, Alan Whitehead, impassively said 'not out'. Next ball, Ritchie backed away and slashed wildly over the slip cordon – to be thrillingly caught by Edmonds, plunging in from third-man. The whoop of applause from England and Englishmen died in every throat as they realized that Mr Whitehead had, late-ish and quietly, called a front-foot no-ball. In came Botham again, blood really up. Another edge cleared the slips. Then a predictable bouncer. The umpire stepped forward to warn the bowler that he had overdone his bumper quota. A minute or two later, Botham was being warned for running down the 'business' part of the pitch in his follow-through. Ian, livid, called across to his captain, Gower, nearby at mid-on, to come and mediate. The aspect ratio of the ground-level television camera made it seem the bowler was shouting at the umpire. Gower calmed everyone down and the game went on. Next day, Peter May, the chairman of the selectors, announced an enquiry. When questioned further, he had to admit he had only heard the sequence of events described on the radio. So, trial by hearsay; and another long-running Lord's bungle was instituted.

Ian's eyes still narrow momentarily when he recalls the occasion. Then he shrugs and smiles: 'For all the pandemonium in Fleet Street, you'd have thought I'd have strangled an umpire. It was blown out of all proportion. I reckon I did everything right and I will till the day I die. I'd seen my fellow opening bowler and great mate, Arnie, rip his toe half off in his first Test match – it was a really nasty injury, too. He had been so keen to do well. The new ball was there and England seemed to be in all kinds of trouble – Wood and Ritchie going well. We just had to get a wicket with the new ball and it was all down to me. England expects, and all that: so, okay, first thing is that I get Greg [Ritchie] going a treat and at once have him "in front of the lot". Alan [Whitehead] says "not out". I asked him, "Was it close? What was wrong with it?" like I do with every umpire when it's a close call. Always have: you ask them. Alan says, "He hit it", which completely baffled me because he'd missed the ball by a

'Look, David, you handle this, I'm not getting involved in any argument.'
Whitehead waits, Gower placates

foot. I was stunned. But I walked back to my mark and bowled again. He then no-balled me, late, and it was caught off the edge. Now you know I bowl very few no-balls, everyone knows that. Anyway, whenever I have done, I always ask the umpire how far over the line my foot was, so I can adjust it. But Alan couldn't – or wouldn't – tell me. That, for a start, put more doubt in my mind. So was it a question of me restraining myself or him getting officious? I called over to David and said, "Look Dave, you handle this, I'm not getting involved in any argument", and I went back to my mark. I thought I'd done everything right. Obviously I hadn't. Anyway, all water under the bridge now, I hope.'

The relationship between umpires and players has always been an intriguing one in cricket at any level. This momentary spat – or however you choose to describe it – seemed worth it if only to highlight the fact that tensions can get to umpires as well as cricketers when they are on the Test match stage. It so happens that on the eve of a previous Lord's Test, I had taken the two umpires, David Evans and Barry Meyer, to supper at the Westmoreland Hotel, where the players were also staying. As we went up the staircase to the dining-room, we passed Ian who had just checked in. The all-rounder had greeted the two men with his biggest smile and a warm handshake. They, too, were obviously pleased to see him. 'Yachi da!' (or however it is spelt) he had greeted the charming Celtic philosopher, Evans, and as we moved on, I asked whether it was difficult to be an umpire when Botham was performing. They both

133

Opposite: Just a gentle enquiry, umpire. At least Dickie Bird gets the joke (*left*), but the strain shows on David Evans (was it five 'not outs' today?) as he completes his most difficult Test match with two other law enforcers (*below*)

agreed, 'Oh no, good as gold, the big boy: never have any trouble with him: plays hard, but with a smile on his face.' Added one of them, *sotto voce*: 'More than we can say of some, mind.'

In the Lord's Test just finished, David Evans had, by the luck of the draw, been subjected to an awfully tough match. Every difficult decision had seemed to be at his 'end'. There was also, in the gloom, an unending traipse in and out with light-meters, always a cue for a groan from the crowd. Since the Test, the probably over-conscientious Evans had been on the sick-list and everyone on the circuit was enquiring concernedly about his recovery. Says Ian: 'I think that umpires have one of the worst of all jobs – especially these days. The ruddy critics, the so-called experts, sit up there with a back-up of numerous slow-motion machines, replay buttons, cameras in different positions, and what-have-you. They can loll back and make their rulings and bring in the verdicts at leisure – whereas the umpire stood out there has a fraction of a split-second to make his decision. And how many times are they wrong? Not often. Mind you, I do sometimes think umpires themselves should realize with more aware-ness – and less officiousness in just one or two cases – the situation and tensions of the players out there with them, and what's at stake for us, too. Nearly every player I know would rather help an umpire than be against him. Well, I know I certainly would. I can think of hardly any player who would deliberately go out of his way to con, or stuff, an umpire.

'But does it help – or embarrass – an umpire if you go when you know you're out – but he has given you, the batsman, the benefit? Alright, a batsman might decide beforehand he's not going to "walk" against Australia – "walking" is an individual thing, nobody seems to know whether "walking" is right or wrong, not even the umpires themselves. Only to say that, in general, every player is fully aware that umpires have a terribly difficult job. I certainly wouldn't like to be in their shoes at the ferocious level of Test match concentration these days. And don't get me wrong, all us cricketers know, too, that umpires, just like players, can have a bad match. Even dear old scorers can have a bad day, can't they? I know David [Evans] would not mind my saying that it might be less tough for him if he could relax a bit more when he's out there. He is probably *too* conscientious, if anything. Even Barry [Meyer] would admit he's had a bad Test – but he bounced back, didn't he? They are only human beings, umpires, and I think all us players realize that. But, in turn, one or two of them must realize we're human beings too. The "officious" umpire is the one that gets our goat. We all know them – and I reckon *they* know who they are, too.'

This time the House of Commons – a place of course not known at all for such a thing as 'Yaboo!' boorishness – got in on the act when the Tory

MP and apartheid apologist, John Carlisle, ranted about Botham's 'petulance and histrionic behaviour'. In return, Anthony Beaumont-Dark, MP, said, 'People only criticise Botham who have a fraction of his talent.' 'Yaboo' to you, too. Meanwhile, Alan Whitehead's report had Lord's announcing that Botham would be carpeted. As the Press that evening were composing their magisterial summations, Ian Botham and Greg Ritchie were enjoying a comradely night out. Michael Carey in the *Daily Telegraph* said, 'Whitehead, standing in only his second Test, emerged from the affair with rather more distinction than Botham, in his 76th'; John Woodcock in *The Times* said the bowler had 'behaved grotesquely'; Matthew Engel in *The Guardian* likened Whitehead 'to a new maths master who had been warned in the staff room that he must not let the Lower Fifth rag him', and the next edition of *Wisden Cricket Monthly* sanely printed a letter from Trevor Lee, of Lincoln, relating pertinently to the frustration quotient deemed allowable by Test cricketers: 'With reference to the Botham/Whitehead affair, here are some interesting facts gathered by myself in a 1983 survey for the final part of my BA (Hons) in Sport Studies. A questionnaire was compiled featuring 25 statements based on various situations which arise within the context of the game. Players were asked if they found the statements acceptable. Replies were received from 94 county professionals and 101 amateurs (county league players). The following two statements are appropriate to the incident in question:

Q11: A player criticizes the umpire's decision because he believes it to be incorrect.

ACCEPTANCE %

	Pros			Amateurs	
Yes	No	Don't Know	Yes	No	Don't Know
12.8	80.8	6.4	11.9	85.1	3

Q24: A player loses his temper through frustration

54.6	34	9.6	30.7	61.4	7.9

The difference between the pro and amateur attitudes to Q24 was the largest throughout the whole survey, except for a statement regarding the bowling of bouncers in fading light.'

That frustration quotient is borne out if you eavesdrop on any professionals' tales from the Long Room at close of play. Generally, the survey gives evidence of the essential good nature of first-class cricket, and I am regularly charmed by the close affinity in spirit and chivalry that the super-duper stars of cricket retain for their roots in pre-history on the village green.

8 Catching up on the paperwork

THE Fleet Street headlines which followed the barney at Trent Bridge could have been left in type. Immediately, the back pages were again screaming BOTHAM STORM. In Somerset's qualifying Benson & Hedges cup tie at Headingley – which they won by four wickets, chasing 209 – the game was clinched by a fifth wicket century partnership between Richards and Botham which ran the Yorkshiremen ragged. Early in his innings Richards survived an appeal for a catch behind the wicket. One of Viv's mannerisms on such narrow-squeak occasions over the years, has been to start to 'walk' momentarily, a cheerful and well-known enough gesture round the world, to tease the crowd, late to realize the umpire has turned down the appeal. Not in Yorkshire – and not for the first time up there the jeers that followed Viv's amiable mickey-taking contained some murky undercurrents of racialist abuse. Perhaps it was just a couple of the more notorious of Leeds United soccer supporters enjoying a summer holiday. Certainly it inspired Richards and his friend and captain to thrash the home bowling to all quarters, at over five an over, after which Botham, still seething, gave an interview to a local radio reporter, airing his disgust and suggesting the Yorkshire county committee put their house in order. At this, the Yorkshire chairman, Reg Kirk, did protest too much at the 'slur' on cricket's finest ever county – and, as the serial staggered on through the month, he in his turn was reprimanded by his club president, Viscount Mountgarret.

Says Botham: 'Reg Kirk is awfully naive if he thinks there isn't a racialist problem with a tiny minority of Yorkshire's supporters. I've had numerous apologetic letters from people who were at the game. When they played Gloucester the same thing happened to David Lawrence. David Bairstow [the Yorkshire captain] had to apologise to all the Gloucester lads. It's only a very small minority. Why at Yorkshire, I don't know. But they haven't done anything about it. I was fuming. I was very embarrassed, especially for Viv. He tends to shrug it off, but that's not the point – it was just sick to hear these 'brave' people shouting obscenities from 200 yards away and then running away to hide. Mind you, it goes without saying I also got letters from members of the National Front calling me "nigger lover" and all that. They are just a joke. They don't worry me. I don't give a stuff about them. It's not even worth telling them to be ashamed of themselves.'

In Yorkshire, the worms in the can that Botham had opened wriggled on. The apologies demanded by either side were not given and the whole episode seemed over when summed up by a 'neutral' letter that appeared in *Wisden Cricket Monthly* from Mrs Joan Underwood, of Pilsley, Derbyhire: 'I have attended matches, both Test and county, on various Yorkshire grounds and have been disgusted by the attitude of the spectators. But much worse at our home grounds. At both Derby and Chesterfield I have sat in our members' stands and had the misfortune to find myself in the proximity of Yorkshire supporters whose sole form of entertainment seems to be a mindless chanting of "We don't want no blackies"... Knowing of the friendship between Viv Richards and Ian Botham, I am not surprised that he finds the Yorkshire crowds offensive. As to Mr Kirk, if he insists that this does not happen, I can only assume that he watches his cricket from behind sound-proofed windows and suggest that if he went out among the spectators he would soon find that the racism most certainly, and very vocally, exists. Yours, etc....'

I interrupt the cricket at this time only to illustrate Botham's unflinching, competitive and dismissive gusto when confronted – whether it is a fast, good length ball on the off stump that needs to clear the mid-wicket fence, or intolerant bigots attacking an admired friend. The better if he can also scatter expletives into the dictionary of diplomatic language adhered to by the game's establishment and officers for over a century. Not many profesional county cricketers have taken on the chairman of a rival club – let alone Yorkshire – and got away with making him look, in public, to be a chuntering old windbag. Ask Len Hutton, or Johnny Wardle, or Brian Close or Ray Illingworth.

There was a more refreshing atmosphere in Somerset's following Championship match against Warwickshire at handsome, wide and white-painted Edgbaston. Nevertheless, Botham contrived another, this time minor, skirmish with the establishment on the second day. He attempted a bouncer at Anton Ferreira, dug it in but only succeeded in 'putting a hole in the wicket'. Members had jeered him. He then bowled Ferreira, turned and offered the members' enclosure what the *Daily Telegraph* described as 'an angry two-handed gesture'. Later, laughing, the two friends Anton and Ian went out for a meal together. The drinks were to summon up the most momentous spirits for the next day's cricket...

Somerset had batted first and made a measly 207 — only Roebuck, stoically, and Richards, savagely, giving the others anything to build on. Botham hit his third ball, from Lethbridge, over extra-cover for four, hit his foot with his bat as he aimed the next over fine leg, and swished airily at the fifth to be caught behind. In reply, Warwickshire's bespectacled political graduate from Durham, Robin Dyer, eked out a patient century before Botham, bowling fast, polished off the innings for 338, a substantial enough lead which Roebuck and Popplewell, in their contrasting styles, just about knocked off for Somerset's first wicket.

The match was intriguingly poised on the third day with Somerset needing some haste for a winnable declaration. Roebuck's anchor was finally prised up by the wily Warwickshire captain, Norman Gifford, and Richards cleared the stage for his captain's entrance with typically gleaming panache — 53 in 39 balls. Botham came in, No. 7, at 12.28pm. Somerset were 249 for 5, a lead of only 118. Gifford and Warwickshire could scent victory, especially as the ball was turning for the spin bowlers, and a heavy gloom of cloud cover had settled over even this most open and leafy part of the old city.

Within 26 scoring strokes, Botham was acknowledging rapturous applause for his century! The previous day's growls had turned to ungrudging wonder by the members. He had reached 100 — 94 of them in boundaries, 10 fours and 9 sixes — in exactly 50 balls, an astonishing 26 fewer than he had needed in the season's two previous, grievous, assaults on Glamorgan and Hampshire. For once, the stark figures themselves hold up as winking asterisks; they suffice as well for any adjectives. He strode in, took guard, and knew — as Gifford certainly did — that the home side had sniffed 'the kill'. With dead bat he examined minutely his first three balls from the highly promising young off-spinner, Adrian Pierson, whom he had not faced before. He hit the fourth ball for a withering four. Next ball, now facing Gifford, left-arm and longtime capped by England, ended up in a clattering, clinking ricochet around the members' seats. It was a spectacular six. He was off and away.

Lunch was only half an hour off — by which time he had made 74. In all he hit Gifford for 8 sixes, Pierson for 3; and Hoffman for 2, to round up the 13. One of the sixes off Gifford careered into the top tier of the East Wing stand, howitzered through an open door, bounced, binged and bonged down every flight of stairs to re-emerge at ground level, looking innocent, if exhaustedly battered.

Most of the sixes were hit on the charge; all but two of them (over mid-wicket off Hoffman and Gifford) were hit straight, in the arc between long-on and long-off. He faced four fewer deliveries than O'Shaughnessy of Lancashire who equalled Percy Fender's 35-minute hundred in 1983

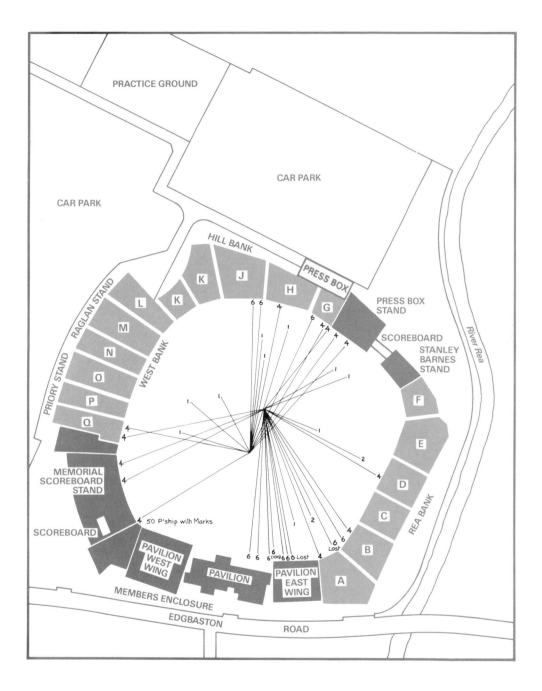

Norman Gifford: 'What awesome power. What pleasure he gives. You need a ground like Melbourne to keep him quiet.' July 26, 1985. Peppering Edgbaston, both inside and outside, on the way to the season's fastest hundred

141

– but the lobbists, Gower and Whitaker, had been bowling rubbish for Leicestershire that day. This time the Warwickshire bowlers never stopped trying. For all that, this was not history's fastest hundred for Somerset – Popplewell's versus Gloucestershire at Bath in 1983 took only 41 minutes. David Hookes, the Australian, hit the fastest century in all cricket at Adelaide off just 34 balls. When he declared – at 418 for 6 – (Marks having scored 8 of the final stand's 73) – Ian was undefeated on 138. The members greeted him deliriously. It had taken him seven minutes over the hour and, in all, he faced only 65 balls. He did not score off 28 of those – the remainder went, successcsively, for:

    1 4 6 1 4 4 1 4 1 6 6 4 4 1 4 6 4 6 6 1 6 4 1 6 6 4 6 2 6 6 4 6 4 1 1 1 2 4

There was one other Somerset man at work just as furiously. Up in his scorebox eyrie, David Oldham, the Somerset scorer, just sat there at the end, as he put it, 'totally stunned'. Then the press calls jangled at his telephone. 'It stirred me', he said, 'so I could catch up on all my paper-work. I cannot remember having had to concentrate so hard. If only I could have sat up there and just marvelled at it.'

By teatime, the wretchedly bad light had worsened and the game was called off (Warwickshire 74 for 1). The most experienced county cricketer in the game put his feet up and set the innings in context. Norman Gifford played his first Championship match exactly a quarter of a century ago – for Worcestershire in 1960. He is, by far and away, the only surviving cricketer who took part in the very last game – a now almost comically anachronistic fixture – between the Gentlemen and the Players at Lord's. That was in 1962 and the amateur Gents, represented by such as the Rev. D.S. Sheppard, E.R. Dexter, R.W. Barber and T.E. Bailey, lined up against such horny-handed sons of 'trade' and toil as Graveney, T., Trueman, F., and Shackleton, D. Gifford would have played many more times for England than his 15 Tests had his arch rival, the estimable Derek Underwood, not been so acutely good. He had recently, as manager of England tours, taken over from the late, still much loved Ken Barrington as the eminence of the élite professionals in the game. Now Gifford mopped his countryman's hale and purply brow – and shook it in appreciation. 'Ian was magnificent. He is a truly great player. What awesome power. What pleasure he gives to crowds. No one can contain him when he is in full flow like that. You need a ground like Melbourne to keep him quiet – and he's scored Test centuries there, too. It was unquestionably the most consistent display of long hitting I've ever seen. The ball was turning and young Adrian [Pierson] and I bowled pretty well, you know. But what can you do when you beat him twice on the outside in an over – and he hits the next two for six? With Ian, not every six goes off the meat of the bat, you know. He is just so strong. All the sixes off me went straight,

142

except for the one that he dragged round to mid-wicket. That's when he looked up the pitch and just grinned at me . . . All those he hit off me from the Pavilion end would be a carry of at least 100 yards – if the pavilion hadn't got in the way.'

In his turn, the hero concurred in that galumphing matter-of-fact modesty of his – sometimes it's almost shyness. You genuinely feel he would prefer to be remembering the fun of it than the fame of it. Ian puffed his little Café Crème cheroot: 'It was a funny wicket. It was turning quite a bit. Of every six balls from Giff, two would turn and go, and I'd play and miss; one I'd block; and three would go out the ground. When I went in, the match was extremely keenly poised, so it was both a challenge and fun. Well, Giff I admire hugely as a bowler. I've always loved him as a guy, too. A great man. Even in the nets when he's been on tour [as England's assistant manager] we've always enjoyed a real challenge together. And don't forget, he knows it all; he's bowled at all the greats in the last three decades, and probably got all of them out a few times as well – May, Cowdrey, Graveney, Dexter, Sobers, Worrell, O'Neill and Harvey . . . I remember the very first time I played against him, at Worcester, when I was a real kid: 1975, I suppose. I came in – and straight away hit him for four. Next ball I tried to do it again – and missed it. I wasn't out, but he came down the wicket, schoolmasterly, and said, "You know you can't hit every ball for four, laddie". I grinned back at him and said, "I know. But I can bloody well try, can't I?" He looked at me, baffled, and scratched his head as if to say, "Who the hell's this sprog, talking to me, an England player, like that?"' (That scorecard read: 'August 12, 1975: I.T. Botham c Yardley b Gifford 12.) 'Another thing with Giff over the years is that he will always try and get quickly into his run-up before you're quite ready, so he's on top of you and into his delivery stride as the batsman is still settling. I learned early to get him going on that one – to keep my eyes down at the blockhole and then hold up my left hand imperiously to stop him in his tracks – "'Ang on, Giff, 'old yer 'orses!" I still do it now to him. We were at it out there today. He'd finally bowl. I'd play and miss – or hit him for six. Either way, from him, it was always a shake of the head down the pitch and, "Stone me, I dunno, you spawny young bugger!"'

When Roebuck had been batting early in the day he had found himself in the regular third-day dilemma in as much as he knew that while nifty declaration runs were needed, survival was still imperative. Gifford was bowling very sharply and was also cussing the slow scoring under his breath. Later, Marks was of course in no such quandary: 'Peter [Roebuck] had played well in tricky circumstances. He had to think about getting runs as well as defend skilfully. Gifford wouldn't have been too unhappy about the treatment he got from Both – they were all straight hits and his

''Ang on Gif, 'old your
'orses. He's on top of you
before you're quite ready'

figures weren't all that bad eventually. He wasn't cut or pulled, and he
bowled the usual nagging Gifford length. I know this to my cost: when I
came in, I didn't know where I could possibly get a run on a turning pitch
against Giffie, with the field crowding me. So it proved. But it was no
trouble at all to Both. He sees it so early – and then just trusts his attacking
inclinations.'

Alongside the wicket-keeper, Humpage, the man with the closest view
of the mayhem was, by nice fluke, another legendary, long-standing
figure of the modern game, Dennis Amiss, prolific batsman on the world
stage through the 1970s who had played the first of his 50 Tests fully
nineteen years ago: 'I stood at slip throughout, though God knows why –
it was never going to come to me at a catchable speed. Every time Ian went
down the pitch I thought it would turn and get an edge or go up in the air –
but he always met the ball with a straight bat. You won't see an innings
like that again, I'm telling you. It was powerhouse stuff from a great
player. Ian played one slog against Giff – and half-apologised. Every now
and again, Giff would beat him on the outside, but it made no difference.
He kept his head down and still hit through the line with that wonderful

follow-through – when those arms of his just seemed to be thrown at the sky. Vivian [Richards] is more wristy – equally devastating, I agree – but Both is all arms and strength, and even more spectacular. There can't be anything worse for a bowler to bowl a good ball and see it sail right out of the ground. I truly revel to see an Englishman play like he does – and I only hope his example will inspire youngsters to bat like him. And, don't forget, all his runs so far have come in this terrible wet summer we are having.'

Amiss, generously, thought the other hero of the hour had been Warwickshire's young spinner, Pierson, who had finished with figures he is unlikely to find repeated in such double-quick time, even if he plays the first-class game as long as either Amiss or his captain – 34-8-164-1. (Gifford's were 42-20-128-4.) Amiss explained: 'It was, actually, a fine effort by Adrian. At lunchtime, David Brown [Warwickshire's manager] asked for volunteers for the post-lunch session in the dressing-room. Adrian said, "I'll have a go." Terrific. He had been hammered, by Viv too as well as Both before lunch, but he still thought he could get him out.'

Of his Test match batting, Amiss says he thinks it terrific the way Both has ignored all the press criticism when he gets out cheaply by playing his shots – 'others would go into their shell and play cautiously next time, but he is his own man and knows just what suits him best.'

Next morning, one of the newspapers carried a pocket cartoon showing a glazier at Taunton Glassworks apprehensively reading the headline BOTHAM NEARS WELLARD RECORD. And to be sure, this latest effort had carried his season's sixes total to 60 – only six behind Wellard's figure that had stood alone in *Wisden* for exactly half a century. Earlier in the summer, some claimed that Wellard had cleared the ropes 72 times in 1935 – indeed, so logged *Wisden* – but the 'official' figure had been determined after some scrupulous re-checking of the files by Somerset's chairman and archivist, Michael Hill, and the meticulous schoolmaster-author, Gerald Brodribb, who has made a rewarding and always fascinaing study of the game's big hitters over the years. Like many leading sportsmen, Ian genuinely thinks he is oblivious to the game's legend and lore of yore, especially in the matter of ancient and dusty records. But, time and again, I have found that players are not as careless of them as they make out. They know, y'know. This time, Somerset's scorer was to give the game away. At lunchtime during Ian's epic innings at Edgbaston, David Oldham was asked by Botham in the players' dining room: 'How many more do I need?' 'I knew he meant the Wellard record. We were still working on 72 – to make sure – at that stage, so by now he had got to 54. "Another 18, Ian", I said. "But don't get them all after lunch." He looked thoughtful and said, "Perhaps another six". He did just that. I

145

Dennis Amiss: 'I stood at slip throughout, though God knows why. I truly revel to see an Englishman play like Ian – and only hope his example will inspire youngsters to bat like him'

Opposite: The confidence of a man in prime form

could sense he was budgeting for twelve more against Essex in the next two innings.'

Such daredevil budgeting was slightly out. Enough to say that, having hit the fastest century of the summer at Edgbaston, Ian came home to Taunton – and sublimely hit the *second* fastest of the summer against Essex. He ended up with 152 (out of 195 from 121 balls). He posted his century off 68 balls, and his half-century off 32. The comparative pottering at the end of his knock came when the Essex and former England captain, Ian's old friend Keith Fletcher, put seven men round the boundary perimeter to stem the flood. Botham responded by turning down singles to keep the strike. It was stalemate – not the way Botham enjoys his cricket and, as the chucklingly wise old bird, Fletcher, suspected, it needled his young friend. Said Ian, who cannot hide his admiration for more than a few minutes when an old captain of his rings the ropes with fieldsmen to cramp the style and the sixes: 'I just blocked him. "Two can play at that game, Fletch", I sneered. But I know, like Giff, that the old boy represents simply one of the very greats in all the history of county cricket. As England captain, you know, he was treated appallingly. He turned down a lot of money from South Africa – a real golden nest-egg for him at his age – to stay loyal to England after the tour of India. He had done a fine, fine job as captain of England on that trip, and

Keith Fletcher . . . 'one of the best thinking captains of all, and looked up to by everyone'

he did only one thing wrong, which scarcely anybody even noticed at the time – he flicked off a bail when he was "sawn off" at Bangalore. In a tour of Pakistan once, didn't Donald Carr actually throw a bucket of water over an umpire? What happened to him? Secretary of the TCCB, now. Quite. Anyway, I'll always have a lot of time for Fletch. So will every man he ever led. He has been one of the very best thinking captains, to be looked up to by everyone in my era.'

The innings first. It had been a quite beautiful exhibition, less crackly, 'impossible' and dramatic than the day before in lucky Birmingham: this was more a proof-of-pudding for those purists who would like to see Botham give up bowling and take his place as a natural successor at No. 4 to Hammond and Compton. He hit 16 fours and 'only' 4 sixes. The niggly war of attrition came after he had reached his century with an enchantingly late cut off Topley. Thereafter he hit only 3 fours in his next 52 runs – an extremely limp quota by him. For the rest, Felton and Wyatt made a heartening few for Somerset and Botham declared at 363 for 9 – the better to be able to buy a succession of large drinks for the popular Essex

148

wicket-keeper, David East, who took eight catches in the innings to equal the 26-year-old record set by the Australian gloveman, Wally Grout.

Most day's play, when anybody plays Fletcher's Essex, ends with an evening of good fellowship. For one thing they have had a settled and (suddenly) successful team for over half a dozen years now – the same, exactly, as Somerset till this wretched, unlucky summer in which they had just gone to the bottom of the Championship – and it was a side that had struggled together as kids, and matured gently into their triumphs. As well as the venerable and loved Fletcher, Ian had a specially long established relationship with his often-times England touring room-mate, John Lever. Then there was his sometime current England colleagues, that honest-to-goodness dasher Graham Gooch, and the relentlessly improving Derek Pringle (ridiculously force-fed when he was still, comparatively, in his county bib and high-chair by the *Oxbridge-über-alles* new selector, Peter May). Then Essex, too, field such friendly, knowing stalwarts with no axe to grind as Ken McEwan, in his last season as one of the world's most graciously accomplished bats, and David Acfield, the off-spinner and British Olympian at fencing, who had first played his beloved county cricket all of twenty years before.

The first drinks were for David East. And the second. The new round, and the conspiratorial huddle was for Botham, and what splendours they had tried to stem.

Said Keith Fletcher: 'It was a superb knock, a pleasure to watch even if I was the fielding captain. It suited us that he got narked because we ringed the boundary, only offering singles. That's the only way to contain him – even then he's so strong that the ball usually carries the fielders. He's not just a long hitter, he's magnificent off the back foot. Also a superb timer. Great self-confidence. I thought I'd seen everything . . . I know how to bowl at him – with fast bowlers pitching it short. He thinks he's a good hooker, but he's not. He puts it in the air, he's a compulsive hooker. He should learn to duck under them, because he has so many other shots he doesn't need to hook.'

Derek Pringle, who could yet, one day, succeed Botham as England's all-rounder: 'He got bored because we didn't make it easy for him. What a player! But I bet he wouldn't bat like that if he couldn't bowl. Never mind, he puts bums on seats.'

Ken McEwan: 'I was fielding on the boundary, just watching the ball sail over my head, feeling so very envious of a man who can bat that way. As a batsman pure and simple, I am jealous of his supreme confidence, his way of playing in the same manner in or out of form. A batsman can be out of touch and his day is over after five munutes; but Both always has his bowling. He is always in the game, whatever its state, and that suits

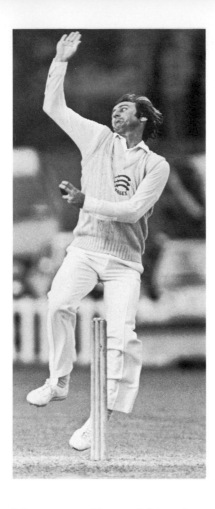

J.K. Lever ... 'Actually, I reckon Ian does get nervous. He needed Brearley to tell him how great he was'

his personality and his talent. I only wish I had the physical strength to play like he does. For the longest hitter of my time in the game, he is also amazingly consistent. I love particularly the way he picks the bat up from the gully area with such a flourish – that helps him to play inside-out, and so hit sixes over extra-cover. He is truly an amazing player, and a pleasure to know and watch.'

David Acfield: 'Normally he smashes me first thing for six, then says, "Morning, Ackers, how are you, ol' boy?" Not this time, funnily enough. I was pleased I didn't go for many. I just fired it in at him and he complained that he was only getting ones. The boundaries at Taunton are so short that there seemed no point in tempting him. His bat is far too heavy – there should be a poundage limitation! He refused those singles when we put men around the boundary – but why should we co-operate with his talent? His trouble is that he has no fear of failure, no nerves. I'm not sure he has any. He's a wonderful entertainer; I love the banter out there in the middle with him. For us, Graham [Gooch] can hit the spinners as far but, honestly, not the quicks in the way that Botham does.

150

Graham is more responsible, actually, and far more run-hungry. But, you know, Botham is the only one I would rush like mad down to the ground to watch if I heard he was 20 not out.'

John Lever: 'He is, simply, the longest hitter I've ever seen. The small Taunton ground helps him chase the sixes, but don't forget he's hit many on bigger grounds, not only this season but all round the world. But I genuinely think Ian could become an even better batsman, once he learns more judgment. He's playing *so* straight now. He always gets his bat to the ball, rather than the pad when he plays defensively. That's the test – not only does he avoid an lbw decision, but he picks up the singles from defensive shots. That pick-up of his off his legs is working so well that you just can't fire it in at the blockhole like you can with others. The margin for error is very, very small with him. When he is going for the big hit, he doesn't move his left foot too near the pitch of the ball as they say you should – because he wants to swing his arms and he needs room for that. If you want to hit it a real long way, you mustn't get too close to the ball. Actually, you know, I reckon he *does* get nervous. He needed Brearley to tell him how great he was. And also – he needs to feel the adrenalin from the crowd, he loves to be roared on.'

Next day, Sunday, in the picnicking Player League knock-about, Ian hit 58 in 57 balls and, in the course of the innings became the first English-man to hit 100 sixes in the Sabbath slogs – after the West Indians, Greenidge, Lloyd and Richards.

But old Arthur Wellard's was a much more intriguing record. He forfeited the chance of even attempting it in the second innings of the Championship game against Essex, for after a wash-out on the Monday, Botham declined even to start the Somerset innings and simply set Essex 296 to win in 90 overs. With the rampagingly decisive Gooch in the visiting side, it turned out to be a gift-wrapped target. His England friend set about Botham's variable and wondrous experiments with the new ball to such effect (2×6, 6×4) that he had 41 off the Somerset captain's first four overs. Ah, well, you can't win them all! Gooch ended with an undefeated and thunderous 173 in 90 overs to win the game for Essex by seven wickets with an almost ludicrous 21 overs to spare. Wisely, Garner (knee) and Richards (tummy) stayed away from Somerset's humiliation. The county now woodenly propped up the bottom of the Championship table – though, somehow unaccountably, Richards led the country's batting averages, with his captain second – 1,270 runs at an average of 70.55. And history – after the Test match – was just around the corner at Weston-super-Mare.

9 Arthur's 66 and all that

WHEN he rejoined the England team at Old Trafford, the dust had still not settled over the incident with Umpire Whitehead at Trent Bridge. Fleet Street, of course, was happy to turn on the wind-machine each morning. Ian's own ghosted column in the *Sun* had been headlined GET LOST! YOU'RE TALKING A LOAD OF TWADDLE, in answer to the equally banal spoutings from the two former England legends, Fred Trueman and Denis Compton in their own respective pop paper columns (over the years, Botham has particularly lost any respect for the former's opinions). In the *Sunday People*, Trueman sneered, 'Botham's been bowling rubbish for fully ten years... I don't think he can even bowl a hoop downhill.' In 1984, ten years after his first-class debut, Botham overtook Trueman's hitherto world record haul of 307 Test wickets.

Meanwhile, in the *Sunday Express*, the old maestro, Compton, had written that Botham 'was disgracefully thinking himself bigger than the game' and likened him to John McEnroe, the unruly tennis player. Ted Dexter, another former England player, also chipped in with a school-masterly 'open letter'. (Ian, by the way, was now just a hundred runs off Dexter's own Test match aggregate of 4,502 runs in 102 innings, with 9 centuries: before Old Trafford Ian had reached 4,400 runs in 120 innings, with 13 centuries. He had also taken a couple more wickets than Dexter.)

All this criticism of Botham stung the Australian captain, Border, to call the most unlikely press conference. 'I just cannot believe these three guys', he said. 'They, of all people, spending so much time knocking Ian yet the man is a national hero. The comments make me fume. It's almost as if Trueman never bowled a bad ball, or Compton and Dexter didn't play a bad shot in their whole careers. All I can say is that there is no player we want to see the back of more that Ian Botham – I can pay no higher compliment than that. You get guys who win a match with their bowling and some who do it batting – Ian can transform a game with either. He has done it so many times that I wonder where English cricket would be

Story of the soggy summer. Rain again and off they go. Border has the cap; rain might frizz up Gower's waves nicely, but it might dull Botham's highlights

without him. It owes him a great debt of gratitude.'

Border said if Britain wanted to deport Botham, 'then we'll take him off your hands with pleasure. If Botham was wearing the green cap, there would be not a shadow of doubt about which side would win the Ashes,' he said. 'Look at his sportsmanship', he went on. 'England were really down when we won so well at Lord's – but who was the first man into our dressing-room to congratulate us and pour the beers? Botham, of course. I agree, sometimes it's tough when you've had a hard day in the field to go into the opposition dressing-room and put on a happy face. But Botham never fails to turn up. Whichever team it is. He's respected throughout cricket for that and we love playing against him. I simply regard it still as a treat and a privilege just to be in the same match as him – and nearly every other opposition bloke does too.'

On another low, slow pitch the England spinners, Edmonds and Emburey, made the first inroads into Australia's chilled, damp batting order. Boon, Phillips, and young O'Donnell (with one or two clinking drives which Botham was seen to applaud) put the only gloss on an all-out score of 257. Mind you, we were lucky to get any cricket and, for once, dear Old Trafford belied its reputation by keeping comparatively dry when all the rest of England had its dripping umbrellas hoisted. Looking out from the pavilion, from the first Thursday morning, unfriendly grey-black little scudders skidded down the spine of the Pennines yonder, over what is cricket's most famous railway line – unless you count the

Vindication! He had moved Lamb's fielding position the ball before. The catch came. Boon went

Bakerloo that rumbles under the Nursery end at Lord's. For four days we watched the clouds and the rain – and their rainbows – tauntingly circle the ground from the high moors right round to Crewe and the Glossop line and the nicely-adjoining stations of Hattersley and Broadbottom. But on the fifth day, wouldn't you know, the rains came down and Border, with a clangingly competent century, batted out the match with resolute help from Phillips.

Botham had braked any threat of a substantial Australian score in their first innings with a bounding second spell which accounted for Boon, Phillips, Matthews and Lawson. He had to wait till Saturday afternoon to get to the wicket again as England pressed on and on, this time led by the tubby and truculent revivalist, Gatting. (What with "Fat Gatt" for England, and "Fat Cat" Ritchie for Oz, even the nicknames of these two friendly sides were alliding.) After Gooch and Gower had put on 121 together, Gatting shared a partnership of quite scintillating strokeplay with Lamb. England had thus cruised into a formidable lead and it was akin to following the Lord Mayor's Show when Botham came in, greeted with an expectant roar from the crowd who had been fuelled by every newspaper's banner headline prediction that morning of STAGE SET FOR BOTHAM BLAST.

'In those circumstances I never get many. I'm not much good at "exhibition" knocks. I tried to hammer a few, of course. But perhaps my subconscious was saying, "Let them wait till it really matters". I don't know, but I never get runs in that situation and I don't think I ever will. What was the score when I went in? Over 300? England well ahead. That's no challenge. Well, why waste energy batting when I've got to bowl for a long spell? No, I honestly don't mind being in the dressing-room while the others are piling up the runs. It means the team's doing okay, doesn't it? It is specially necessary to get a rest if you've had a long bowl. If I was down at No. 5, it means that I've got to start getting ready as soon as one wicket goes down. At No. 6, two wickets can go before I even have to think of preparing myself and padding up. It just gives me that bit more breathing space.'

In the event he hit 3 fours – two claps of thunder to the sightscreen off McDermott and O'Donnell – and another inside-edge mow through mid-wicket off the latter. In between there were some flailing drives and whirring hooks which made no contact – till he steepled a massive thing high to fine-leg which O'Donnell held well. A case of the biter bit. 'I'm not saying it wasn't "planned", like', said the bowler, McDermott, in the evening, 'but if he'd caught it right it would have cleared that railway station.'

That, by the way, was the galloping, strong, precocious and broad-bottomed Queensland colt's fifth wicket on the trot. Botham was most impressed: '"Billy Craig" has learned something with every ball he's bowled this tour.' In the end he finished with eight – to become, at 20, the third youngest Test bowler to have such a haul, after Alf Valentine (on the same ground in 1950), and the Indian mystic, Venkat (at Delhi twenty years ago). McDermott had heard of neither of them.

On the Monday evening, before the rains came, England seemed to have one chance in the last over of the day when the whole field went up for a bat-pad 'catch' by Botham off Ritchie. It would have left Australia 33 behind with only five wickets standing. Umpire Shepherd said 'not out'. An hour later, at the bar, some of the England players were still cursing their luck. Botham put them wise. He had, of course, been in for a drink with the Australians. And he had asked the batsman: 'Greg Ritchie swears he didn't hit it. That'll do for me. If "Fat Cat" says he didn't hit it, then he simply didn't hit it. By the same token, he has "walked" before in very tight situations, like a bat-pad on the off side – and if he's hit it, he's gone before the umpire's even thought of putting up his finger.'

One-all, and now only two to play. But suddenly it seemed to be all coming together for England. So, of course, was the deplorable English weather. It would surely relent, for history's sake, at Weston.

Someone should make a film of county cricket's festivals before they vanish. Posterity needs to know what civilized Augusts were once enjoyed. I fancy they will be lucky to see out the century. Still, and hooray, here they were again – 1985 vintage but still unchanged and unchanging, ordered as if by statute of pastoral high summer England. The tent pegs were sharp, the guy ropes taut, the bunting untangled and now, once more, decorating the trim marquees which encircle the grand green fields of Canterbury and Cheltenham, of elegant Eastbourne, and the seagull-squealing flats of Scarborough and, of course, Weston-super-Mare. Flower baskets bloom. The Band of the Buffs no longer stirs old men's memories in Kent, but otherwise things will remain the same at the most serene and snooty of all the 'weeks'. Is the Old Stagers tent still next to the tree and are there eclairs for tea in the Band of Brothers corner? For sure, the glasses will tinkle most in the Rotary tent, from whence the guffawing laughter will interrupt occasionally the serene calm of the evening's play. And Mr Swanton will stride the scene with his now benign, but still overwhelming episcopal presence.

At Cheltenham, the College Chapel will oversee the week, basking as always in the honeyed, Cotswold warmth. Just as at Canterbury, a major feature of the day will be the million schoolboy matches that flash the field at lunch and tea with higgledy-piggledy 22-yard certainties. The same at Weston. I've always fancied the West in August. Weston has more of the feel of a countryman's charabanc choir outing. Bill Andrews is the patron there. He first played on that field as a tea interval urchin when he was 12 in 1921. When he was 13 he was selling scorecards at 4d a dozen commission. At 14 he was operating the scoreboard. Ten years later he was chosen for the county at last and, in dazed awe, he asked the senior pro, Tom Young, 'Am I the worst cricketer that has ever played first-class cricket, Mr Young?' The answer was brief: 'No, son. There is one worse than you. Arnott of Glamorgan.'

Weston will hum as ever with the reminders of Andrews, and of Wellard and the whoop of joy his sixers brought; of Walford's holiday batting; and Gimblett's; of Hazell's waddle and Buse's untangling action; and, in later years, of Greg Chappell's fleeting English springtime.

Last summer was Weston's cricket jubilee. Somerset first played there in 1914. It ought to have been a one-off gala, for as the contemporary report says, 'Consideration of the amenities failed to include the quality of the pitch'. The Yorkshire bowlers, Drake and Booth, bowled

Wellard must have thought his 50-year-old record pretty well inviolate...

unchanged through the match and in Somerset's second innings Drake took all 10 wickets in 9 overs. That pitch probably resembled the famous beach just across the way that I remember as a child – the first time I'd seen the sea. 'That last blue sky and an infinity of mud stretching away to the shadows of Wales', as Laurie Lee also remembers.

Robertson-Glasgow enjoyed his bowling here, and he wrote some sixty summers ago, of 'the ring of marquees where the right stuff could always be found, and deck-chairs and wooden chairs under which the spade and bucket could be parked for an hour or two...' Something odd

157

always happens at Weston week. Once, in the Royal Hotel, the captain of Surrey, P.G.H. Fender, complained to the manager that there wasn't enough room in his bedroom to swing a cat. The manager looked The Oval's city gent up and down, curled his lip and said, 'I 'adn't realised, *sir*, that you'd come down to Weston merely for the cat-swingin' festival.'

Fender died, at 92, just before this current season began. Wellard, too, has gone: Somerset's smiling, summery smiter died on New Year's Eve, 1980. Ian Botham cannot be certain, but he thinks he met Wellard once when he was a kid – introduced at Weston by his old new ball buddy, Andrews, of the bustling bonhomie. Was Wellard a long, gaunt man with a twinkle in his rheumy, soft-boiled eye? That would be him. Little did either of them know that the single handshake that day in the 1970s would have to suffice, when the time came, as acknowledgement and congratulations for the handing over of a famously long-standing record. With bowling as it had become tight and taut, and fielding so athletic and ruthlessly sharp – and the decline in the number of matches deemed 'first-class' – old Arthur must have thought his record pretty well inviolate.

Botham, mind you, is not of an age yet to succumb to romance. Perhaps, with his often uncomfortable realist's nature, he never will. (Though I wouldn't bet on it.) Northamptonshire had come to play cricket at Weston and he needed two sixers to level Wellard's figure; the tide was in, and the WI flower baskets were plumply overflowing with colour. Yet Weston, to Botham, means Andy has to wake him up an hour earlier in the cottage for the curvy drive to the channel coast. 'Well, with our newly superb facilities at Taunton, why don't we stay there for every match? I suppose, with reason, the folk at Weston and Bath think me selfish – and it is laziness on my part, I admit. But it always seems odd to me to have to travel for over an hour to a home game!

'Surprisingly, to me, I've got quite a few runs at Weston over the years. And a few wickets. But the facilities are pretty ropey – crummy dressing-room, one shower between the teams. Actually, I feel far less sorry for us players than poor old Gordon Prosser, the groundsman: there's a guy who has to produce a first-class cricket pitch for one week in the year – while the other 51 weeks he has hockey matches all over it, or dogs crapping wherever they feel like it.'

Ian was also despairing of Somerset's woeful results. The wooden spoon looked likely. They might be unbeaten, but they were very much bottom of the Championship. The sick list was as long as ever – indeed for this match they had to pick for his first-ever county match the slim, long-limbed man-child, Jonathan Atkinson, 17-year-old son of Somerset's former captain and chairman, Colin. At once the troubles continued. By noon, Wyatt and Felton were out of their pads with 40 on the board. Roebuck and Richards – who faced, for him, an astonishing 25 balls before getting off the mark – batted grittily and wisely through and past the lunchtime pudding. It was a yeoman's plod. Mallender and Griffiths were bowling with considerable tartness and edge. Botham came in at all the fours – 144 for 4 – and not, for some superstition going back to the mists of time, an auspicious set of numbers for cricketers. For most, that is: Botham hit his third ball, from Griffiths, for a clumping boundary four. In his next over, Griffiths went for a steepling six; and, in his next, another – high, wide and handsome. It equalled Wellard's 66 of 50 years ago. Not all the crowd were aware of it. There is no PA loudspeaker at Weston. They should have had a man with a megaphone on top of the pav.

Marks came and went for a duck. The West Indian Test player, Harper, had come on. Young Atkinson, slim but of confident tread, arrived to join his captain at 193 for 6. Botham spoke to him – then hit the experienced, nippy Mallender for two great sixes. One for the record, which sailed into the faraway clump of parkland trees – and one for luck and Jonathan. They went into tea – Botham with 50 in 53 balls.

Says Jonathan: 'He had been to my father's house for dinner. I was allowed to stay up, but just sat there taking it all in. He was an absolute hero to me, you see. I was only eight when he first played for England. This match, I was meant to be playing for the Under-19s when I was told to get to Weston, pronto. They only said I was in the thirteen. That was staggering enough, but then I was told I was playing – and within a few hours I would be batting with Ian Botham ... well, I just couldn't let it sink in. Mind you, I didn't really get the chance to feel nervous because it all happened so quickly. Vic Marks was out second ball, and I had been putting a solution on my injured foot and also some medicinal stuff on a mouth ulcer. *How's that!* And I was in! In the confusion I mixed the solutions up – foot stuff in my mouth and vice versa. So I was in a fair amount of pain as I walked out to bat.

'I got off the mark immediately, with a lucky push off Harper. Botham shouted down "good shot". He never stopped encouraging me. All the time between overs he was saying, "Don't be afraid to play your shots, loft the ball if it's there for it." I was amazed at how helpful he was, a great encourager. I was overwhelmed at it all, and it really only started to sink in the next day. It's a day I will never forget.'

Says Botham: 'I really mean this: if Jonathan sticks to cricket I can see him going a long way. I know this sounds a bit romantic, but as we were batting out there I had a lovely sort of soppy feeling that I could see myself a dozen years ago in him. It was almost eerie – thinking I was seeing the young Both at the other end. He wasn't overawed; he was enjoying it,

159

Geoff Cook: 'Ian could bat anywhere in the world for any team at No. 4'

relishing the challenge; not scared. Okay, up comes Mallender, a good bowler and an England prospect – Jonathan hits him straight back over his head for six. I really had a lump in the throat at that. He's a big lad, bigger than me. I just hope he sticks with cricket.'

It was, simply, very touching. The joyous record-breaker of all swash-buckling, big-time cricket was giving not a fig for his own figures, just nursing the tyro – in whom he could see himself. Ian was 39 when Jonathan came in. Together, they battled for just 31 overs, adding an astonishing 177 off a good attack with its tail up. Nor did the captain dominate: Ian made 95 of the partnership, Jonathan 79 (off 91 balls). They were out, somehow appropriately, off successive balls from Mallender. Botham ended with 134 – in 147 balls, with 8 fours and 10 sixes – and Somerset were contentedly all out just before the close, at 409.

The captain offered his blushing sprog a drink – then bought a large one for his long-time friend – and rival captain – Geoff Cook. The Northamp-tonshire skipper gives best, as ever: 'Well, Ian always knows what he's about, doesn't he? He exploited that one smallish boundary, of about 65 yards. He played very sensibly, well within himself, but he is always bristling and looking to play shots. Griffiths and Mallender bowled jolly well in favourable conditions. For me, his duel with Harper was engrossing. No reverse sweeps, no swash or buckle, just a lot of mutual respect – unless he was just sizing him up for the winter in the West Indies.

'From a cricketing point of view you just have to admire the innings – from a rival captain's angle, you just had to hope he'd get himself out. He didn't go for the straight hits as much as usual, he was more selective – that short bourndary was simply milked. He's not daft – in fact he has a very good cricket brain. He just works it all out for himself. His only mistake was when Harper almost ran him out with an astonishing piece of fielding.

'It was really touching to see him with the kid. He was very good at encouraging young Atkinson – and the lad responded with some handsome, powerful batting. I could see who he modelled himself on. Sure, Ian could bat anywhere in the world for any team at No. 4. He has a marvellous technique now and all you can do is keep him away from the strike or hope he gets himself out.'

The match petered away down the drain. Weston was washed out for the next two days – which Ian spent mostly in bed with a stomach bug. The thrilling partnership with young Atkinson prompted me to ask colleagues from both country and county whether Botham, so original, sometimes so intemperate, is good to bat with. To a man, he was almost the favourite batting partner. Nigel Popplewell, who has, of course, also shared many stands with Richards, was by far the most articulate: 'Well, things can certainly never be dull when Ian is batting. He is marvellous to bat with. He takes so much pressure off his partner in several ways. Firstly, he is so powerful that he can score runs quickly and allow his partner to become established. He will also take pressure off in another way, and it is instructive to compare him with Viv. If both are batting in a tight run chase, their moods are ostensibly very different and while both want to win passionately, they are poles apart in the impression they give. Viv is intense and taut. His passion flows out from every pore and he stares and scowls at all around him. This can put pressure on his partner although it is usually best for the team – for Viv in that sort of mood is indestructible. But play a maiden out in a tight situation with Viv at the other end, and you can feel the pressure physically increase as he glowers down the wicket at you.

'Ian, on the other hand, is almost the opposite', says Nigel. 'Botham wants to win just as much, but will go to the other extreme, appearing as outwardly casual as he can to make things easier for his partner. I

Shot of the Year – One. Batsmen at the Belfry . . . 'I said I was going for the green. Allan said I was barmy. "Bollocks, A.B., let's have a go." Perfect'

remember vividly batting with him in just such a close situation in the 1983 NatWest semi-final against Middlesex at Lords. Chasing 220-odd we were 50 for 5. Ian played a defensive innings, picking up singles; and even when I played out a maiden he was nothing but encouragement. Indeed, he sometimes told me to calm down – talk about pots and kettles! His only moment of chancy belligerence came to knock John Emburey out of the attack – a calculated risk that succeeded for the team. On the last ball of that game he padded up and denied himself the chance of a 100 – but had ensured that we won the game. It was a generous and whole-hearted innings and just typical of the man.'

Ian, however, was not getting to bat for long with any English colleague – so sumptuously had the early order started to play. Suddenly, England were just one new ball partner away from being a very good team indeed. Allott and Sidebottam had not been fit, while Cowans and Foster were out of favour. Ellison, of Kent, had begun to bowl swingingly for Kent after his early season injury and the England side were delighted to welcome him back for the fifth Test at Edgbaston, as well as the knowing Leicestershire bowler, Les Taylor, the old 'coal-seamer' much admired by the circuit's pros for some seasons, but another who had doused his chances by the South African adventure.

Australia batted, and after Botham got rid of Wood, the perky Ellison

162

bustled the bat into all sorts of nibbling edginess; he ended with 6 for 77, in 31 overs, as Australia logged only a reasonable 335. When the drizzle was not actually rain, the light was so gloomy that nobody was betting on a result. England lost Gooch at 38. The next wicket went down 331 runs later – Robinson for 148. Gower went on to make 215. Gatting made exactly 100. Having spent all Saturday in his pads, waiting to take guard, Ian next day joined the Australian team in a golf competition at the nearby Belfry, the course that was to host, in a week or two, the Ryder Cup.

The Belfry is a newish course, with a devilish 'turn' at a famous 10th hole, a 301-yard par 4, with a small, stringy, kidney-shaped, faraway green with a canal and, on the front apron, a lake, to serve in the office of a moat. The professionals don't often dare drive it. Greg Norman, the blond, aggressive Australian, did once. There is a plaque there, celebrating the fact that the already legendary Spanish hitter and genius, Seve Ballesteros, had plopped an accurate screamer over the water and into the heart of the green. No one else. It was a soft, serene day when Seve did it. When Botham did it, it was raining. His partner in the better-ball pair's stableford was Allan Border. First, just for kicks, these amateurs and cricketers were allowed a free hit at the famous green, not counted in the tournament. Says Ian: 'We all had one go at it for fun: I hit a screamer – but straight, no fade. I missed the green, of course, and it went well past the green, about 25 yards left. No problems with length, I thought. So we resumed our match and teed up. The knack now was to lay up in front of the lake. I thought "Why not?" and said I was going for the green. A.B. said I was barmy – I'd just missed with a "free" practice shot, so why "blow" the match? I said, "Bollocks, A.B., let's have a go." He buried his face in his hands, cursing me. So I just hit it; I let go and faded it. It landed plop on the green. Perfect.'

The golf correspondent of the *Sunday Times*, John Hopkins, is one of those few sportswriters who can relate a hero's game to a hacker's. Now Hopkins had seen an amateur hit a ball further and more accurately than any golf pro in Europe, bar the nonpareil, Ballesteros. Next day, Hopkins developed a fascinating piece: 'Technically, the best golfing cricketer is Ted Dexter, who was once considered good enough to have made a living as a pro golfer. In his hey-day, Dexter dispatched the ball vast distances and now, at age 50, he is still sufficiently powerful to have holed in one on the ninth at Sunningdale recently, a distance of 260 yards. But whereas Dexter was a classical stylist, as elegant with a golf club as he was with his bat, Botham is a slogger. Brian Rose, Somerset's previous captain, says of Botham's style: "Ian's got a short backswing, and a long follow-through. When he's hitting sixes, he lets the bat go straight through. You have to if you want the power, and most cricketers do that when they play golf. They tend to swing straight through the ball, and that's why so many of them tend to push their shots. But Ian's follow-through in golf is more like that of a golfer's. He gets his hands up and around, and that's one reason why he hits the ball so far."

'If Botham could hit the ball so far in the rain, how far could he hit it on a still, sunny day? The longest recorded drive in a contest is 392 yards, by the Irishman Tommy Campbell, a tiny figure at 5ft 8½in and 10½ stone, when compared with Botham at more than 6ft and 14 stone plus. "My ball carried 325 yards", Campbell recalled, fully 21 years after he had set the record. "So you could add at least 50 yards to Ian's shot to take into account the roll of the ball. Believe me, if Ian used an ordinary ball [he did, a Wilson Staff, 100 compression] and it was raining, then that's a helluva dig. He must have superb timing."'

Next day at Edgbaston, Ian had to wait almost till tea-time for another hit. England were 572 for 4 when he went in. 'As quick as you want, mate', said the showering Gower as his friend picked up his heavyweight bat. McDermott had just dismissed Lamb and, in spite of the long day's drubbing, might have raised some optimism, as Australians can, that his luck was changing. Botham took guard, looked around and, as ever, waited calmly . . . took a half-stride from the crease and hit the fast bowler a rapturously thrilling blow, followed by that golfer's follow-through to the heavens: nasally know-all Birmingham businessmen boozing in the executive boxes that quiff the pavilion scattered for dear life like a cowering swarm of Jack Woolleys. Can Jessop ever have been so dramatic? Or Grace, even? Or Bradman, or Hobbs, or Hammond? Or Trumper? Wellard played on county grounds. This was a wide and handsome Test match field where a full house and full responsibility perforce must go together.

It represented, too, (though the batsman didn't know it) a celebration not only of an impending Ashes victory, so rampant were England now, but of Botham's very 100th sixer of the summer, if you included the no-less serious, but deemed by Lord's as 'second-class', one-day competitive (and often defensive) matches for the NatWest Trophy, the Benson & Hedges Cup, or the John Player League. A ball later, he hit McDermott for another straight and blazing six into the pavilion – then went, caught by his old pal, Thomson, crouching on the boundary. Thomson 'V-signed' the disappointed, jeering crowd, then gave a return thumbs-up to his departing, smiling friend – and, briefly, foe. Australia went in again. England's batting had made them punch-drunk. Immediately Hilditch

Shot of the Year – Two. First ball, Edgbaston members scatter

Australia go down with the sun – Edmonds catches McDermott off Botham to win the fifth Test and the Ashes get nearer

again fell for Botham's sucker ball and holed out to fine-leg. Ellison ran through the rest with verve, swerve and crummy batting. The tourists' one grouse remained a disputed catch when Gower pocketed the lob off Lamb's instep after Phillips's square-cut. Did it come up on the half-volley? Ian, at slip, had a better view than the umpires. 'It was out. No doubt at all. It hit Lambie plonk on the top of the foot. The full round bruise was there as perfect proof within hours. No way it could have been a bump-ball. It was a brave decision by the umpires, mind you – but also a very good one. Of course I bought a few drinks that evening to commiserate with "Flipper" Phillips. He'd long accepted it by then, though.'

Border, meanwhile, allowed himself an uncharacteristic spat about the decision at his press conference, but in truth his prostests held as much conviction as a 'we wuz robbed' claimed by the manager and mentor of a boxer who had been cruelly out-jabbed over the full 15 rounds. Which is how the Australians must have felt.

In Australia's capitulation, the suicidal played-and-planned-for hook by Hilditch had given Botham much pleasure – but he knew the critics would readily blame Hilditch and not credit Botham for the wicket. He

166

Golf under a warmer
sun at La Manga. Such a
full follow-through . . .
he might as well have used
a 3½lb bat!

and Andrew grinned ruefully at that certainty. Botham also ordered up, and put his arm round the shoulders of Simon O'Donnell. Alongside Ellison's exuberant splurge of 9-3-27-4, Ian had chipped in with figures of 14-2-52-3. He had too, and yet again, clean bowled O'Donnell, the young all-rounder who had started the tour with the awesome Press-induced, job of trying to square up to Botham. During this farewell evening to Edgbaston, Ian – still full of his golf – asked Simon to join him in September, when cricket was over, for a golfing holiday at La Manga in Spain. O'Donnell was thrilled to accept. Could this be the opponent he had been warned to loathe? 'No, it wasn't very odd that I never really got on with him at the start of the tour. I could tell that as the Australian all-rounder, he saw me as a direct opponent. If I dared have the temerity to think I could challenge him in that area, he was going to teach me a lesson. He did – but hopefully I'll be good enough to take him on when he gets back to Australia for the next Ashes battle . . . I suppose I regard myself as pretty competitive so I was determined not to be overawed by Both's reputation. When I first bowled to him in England I tried to treat him as just another batsman. But there are times when he overpowers you, mentally and physically. It is an awesome power he has – and the worst thing for me was the realization that at times I could do nothing about it. He can leave you feeling pretty devastated. For one thing, how do you cope when he gets at you so quickly? It can take him only four or five balls to dominate you, not an hour like any normal human being. Suddenly, after ten minutes, he's taken a grip on you and the whole game, and he's strangling you . . . It's thrilling, and dangerous, and extremely competitive, an almost frightening thing to have to cope with, isn't it?'

Yet, suddenly the two of them – the attractive, but as yet untested tyro and the triumphant Test match hero of a decade – were in the warm and chummy conclave of old, firm friends. Spurning a round of the hard stuff, O'Donnell breaks away for a moment to order himself another Coca Cola. 'Two months ago I was meant to be his enemy. I was determined not to like him. Now, I think we are pretty good friends. Already we have talked a fair bit about bowling and he's given me a lot of good tips. He has a definite plan for every batsman. Once he believes he has a guy worked out he keeps chipping away at any weakness he has spotted. Whenever he talks about bowling, I enjoy listening. It probably sounds odd for an Englishman to be helping out an Aussie, but that's the sort of guy Both is.'

What did the old Aussie leg-breaker, Arthur Mailey, say when he was chastised for giving advice to England's young spinner, Peebles? 'Art and science', he said, 'is international', or words to that effect. Mailey also said, 'The size of the crowd, or the stumps or the ball or the leg-side squad, is not nearly so important as the "size" of the man or the sportsman.'

10 Showdown with a champagne shampoo

BETWEEN Test matches there was one last epic innings for Somerset. In the event, it was to be Ian's last entrance of the season for the county, and his last as captain. Increasingly, as the summer squelched on, Ian had been niggled and uneasy about his enforced absences from the injury-wracked team, still firmly plonked on the bottom of the Championship table. A decision would have to be made in September, he knew... Meanwhile, back at Old Trafford, it was Manchester with a vengeance as rain washed out Saturday's play against Lancashire. A start was made after lunch on Monday – and the grey, drabness of the previous weeks and months was once again rainbowed in primary colours as, first, Richards and then, inevitably, Botham matched each other, vivid stroke for vivid stroke. By the time Ian declared Somerset's innings after only 81 overs, Somerset had reached 329 for 4 – Viv 120; Ian, in later, 76 not out. Paul Fitzpatrick, of *The Guardian*, was one of those cowering up there in the press-box chicken coop: 'Richards went on to complete his sixth hundred of the summer and there were echoes of the one-day innings he played for West Indies on this ground last year. One of his 5 sixes, off Allott, went over the longest boundary from nothing more than a flick. Another, off Fairbrother, almost looked as if it came from a backward defensive stroke. There was no way that Botham could watch this innings and not try to produce something at least as good. And, of course, he did. By the time he declared he had completed another remarkable batting feat, 76 off only 47 deliveries and including another 4 mighty sixes – all off Simmons – bringing his total for the season to 80.'

They were to be his last sixes of the summer. Somehow, too, it tied up the unities with perfect neatness, for had not this chronicle of one man's season started far away in Spain – at La Manga in April when old Jack Simmons, along with Norman Gifford the county circuit's seen-it-all grey-beard, put his foot on the bar-rail, cupped his sulphurous cigarette butt to his lips, supped his ale, and talked of young Botham's place in his litany of saints? Now, at Old Trafford at the end of August, Jack was almost eager, as ever, to give credit where it was due: 'You know, the blighter came down the wicket to my first ball and tried to smash it back over my head. It was just a little too short and he played it back to me. But he had signalled his intentions! I bowled from the City end. Three of the sixes were over long-on; for the fourth I beat him in the flight and he dragged it round to mid-wicket. One of the straight sixes was no more than seven feet off the ground all the way, a real skimmer. It crashed against an advertising hoarding. At the very start I said to the skipper, John [Abrahams], "four men out – long-on, long-off, mid-wicket and deep square leg" – and pretty soon it was a "John Player" field. Then he hit me for 3 fours in an over – two of them absolute screamers. I thought of getting down to them for a caught-and-bowled – but quickly thought "bugger it". Eventually I bowled him a low full toss and he smashed it past me to long-on. It was going so fast he could only get a single. It was a deliberate ball from me, good enough for most batters, designed to avoid being hit for yet another six. I was happy just to give him a single, to get him away from the business end.

'It was quite something, especially coming after Viv's innings. One can only keep raising your glass to the lad. During the knock, Ian had laughed and told me that he had got a bit bored and wanted some fun. What superb nerve! It was a serious match! Of course, Viv's marvellous hitting geed him up. Viv's sixes soar away with perfect timing, whereas Both's are more powerful, bludgeoning things. I think only Clive Lloyd can rival him as a long hitter in all my time. But that's when Clive's well set. With Both, the ball can disappear as soon as he comes in.'

In the event, and in spite of the two friends' pyrotechnics that had whizzed and fizzed and exploded all around the grey, oystery-damp Old Trafford skies, Somerset contrived next day to lose the match. Lancashire had agreed to forfeit an innings, so they just had to beat Somerset's score. It was a generous decision by Botham (shades of Sammy Woods's old dictum – 'Draws is only good for swimmin' in!'), though it should have paid off if Lancashire's batting had lived up to its brittle reputation. It didn't. The two uncapped kids, Chadwick and Hayes, each scored centuries – though the defeat by six wickets, when it came, was not seen by Somerset's captain who had limped off in mid-afternoon to seek out urgent treatment on the old knee injury that had begun to play up again. The Australians were assembling at The Oval for the Ashes' decider in two days' time – and, on the way, England's all-rounder had been summoned to Lord's, where officialdom's prevarication had finally ended and a 'court' was assembled to hear the Whitehead case. Chief witness for the defence was England's captain, Gower.

Meanwhile, Somerset's caravan moved on down the road to Derby. The captaincy issues would be resolved when the cricket was all over. If Ian stood down, the two heirs apparent were Marks, the present vice-captain, and Roebuck, who had stood in as leader on many occasions. For the present, they were both happy, as ever, to sit down and reflect on their friend and, still, captain. The three of them have been close since school-days – coming together for county colts' games – Vic and Peter from, respectively, the celebrated public schools of Blundell's and Millfield, Ian from Buckler's Mead Secondary Modern. Vic is even more in awe this summer: 'Well, he has simply made really good professionals like Tremlett, Cooper, Mallender and Griffiths look like amateurs. Look what he did to Jack Simmons today. It gets to them and they don't do themselves justice. He bends bowlers to his will. Spinners haven't a hope against him at grounds like Taunton. He's also hit sixes at big grounds like Edgbaston, The Oval, and here at Old Trafford. But at Taunton, a spinner hasn't a chance against someone with such a great eye, superb timing and heavy bat. I suppose our early batting this season has been so brittle that Both has had many chances to shine. But he's pulled us round at speed without appearing to take any risks. He has looked simply masterful; his striking of the ball has been so clean, so certain.'

Peter nods: 'His batting has become almost irrelevant to what's going on around him. We ordinary mortals have to play good county bowlers carefully, but he just smashes them off their length. Then the bowlers feel they have to get him out in a hurry – so they fall apart under the pressure. His back foot play is now simply awesome. He is a little wilder off the front foot but it's all based on sound orthodoxy. Notice that he is rarely clean-bowled . . .'

Inevitably, comparisons with Somerset's other coruscating champion dot such conversation. Vic remembers when Ian used to play across the line, trying to work it through mid-wicket like Richards. 'Now he plays much straighter. He and Viv don't have too many big stands because Ian tries to be too spectacular. Viv bides his time – and is still there after Ian has tried one exotic shot too many. But, however short, you can rest assured it's been a glorious partnership.'

Yes, but don't forget, says Peter, that Richards rarely swings the bat like Botham. 'Viv is like a boxer (jabbing) whereas Both is like a golfer (swishing). Ian is also a better player of "delicate" shots than Viv – you need a light feathery touch to play the reverse sweep, for instance, and that lovely late cut off the fast bowlers. I adore watching him when he's playing well, when he can score so *easily* off a ball that's coming at him so *quickly*.'

Next day Ian was carpeted at Lord's. The hearing wasted over fours hours. He was flanked by David Gower, who spoke in his defence, and Pat

Pocock, representing the Cricketers' Association, his 'trade union'. A written statement was submitted by Peter May, chairman of the selectors, who had of course 'seen' the incident in question by way of his car radio. Ian himself was at his most sullen throughout; fumingly narked, for with the Test starting the next day he was desperate to be on the treatment table for work on his damaged knee. The TCCB spokesman then came out to issue a statement: 'From the evidence of the umpires, and repeated examination of a video recording of the third Cornhill Test at Trent Bridge on Saturday, July 13, the disciplinary committee of the TCCB found that Ian Botham showed considerable frustration and an element of dissent amounting to misconduct on the field, which the committee felt would bring the game into disrepute. Botham has been reprimanded and warned that any repetition of this conduct would be likely to have serious repercussions for him.'

It was not good enough for *The Times*, who wheeled out their big guns, frothing and spluttering. Their chief columnist, David Miller, dreamed up some obtuse reference to the train robber, Ronnie Biggs, for heaven's sakes; and he then pootled on: 'It is important that the TCCB should not let the matter pass – however maladroit their handling of it has been so far – because there is an increased tendency for Botham to consider that he is free to behave as he pleases . . . His introduction of friends and children into the team environment and his flamboyant commercially motivated dress are not separately so bad but collectively can be divisive. What the TCCB need to remind him is that without umpires, opponents and colleagues, his extravagant play has no platform. Most of his colleagues would agree, even if his captain opts to give evidence on his behalf.'

Nor did the warning satisfy the august journal's cricket correspondent, John Woodcock: 'I find it hard to think that had Lawrence, for example, making his England debut, or Dilley, making an England come-back, done exactly the same as Botham that they would not have paid more dearly for it. But Botham is held in greater awe than the ordinary mortal.'

The Guardian simply commissioned a piece from a man who at least understood the matter from first-hand experience, not from a pulpit. The former England pace bowler, Mike Selvey wrote: 'Botham's lid rattled and the steam poured out of his ears. Then, sin of sins, he swore – a man bowling his socks off for his country and so pumped up that he swore. It has been done before, but Botham's mistake was to do it in TV close-ups, offending a blinkered minority and apparently umpire Alan Whitehead. Make no mistake, Whitehead is a good umpire and deserved to be on the Test panel, but he is a hard-liner. He has already been involved in one similar situation this summer, with Imran Khan, and was believed to have over-reacted. At Trent Bridge, the occasion screamed out for tact and it wasn't there. We cannot condone anyone swearing at an umpire, if indeed that is what he did, but I saw him let rip at his captain, and what are they for? All this was exacerbated by TV. If we are going to use the visual evidence to condemn Botham, then in fairness we should use it to mitigate as well. The disputed lbw decision looked palpably plumb, the short-pitching probably excessive, the running on the wicket debatable and the no-ball was signalled tardily.'

To complete the rout, the editor of *The Guardian*, in next morning's editorial, cheerfully shot down its rival's apopletic righteousness with just one well-aimed fusilade: 'The jury was out for some considerable time before delivering a verdict as pusillanimous as we have come to expect of those who presume to rule the greatest of games. Mr Botham was reprimanded, and warned of the serious repercussions if he erred again. His reaction can be easily imagined, and was thankfully not delivered on the square. The TCCB, inevitably, felt constrained to put out one of their pompous statements. The final Test of the Ashes series begins at The Oval today, and if Mr Botham is fit he will give his usual eleven tenths and be the one cricketer a sizeable proportion of the crowd have come to watch. The connection the TCCB fails to make is that seen by Mr Botham's many fans, the character is the cricketer. He is not demure or gentlemanly or retiring. He is larger-than-life, swashbuckling, out-going. And he is that kind of cricketer. He hits sixes rather than plays forward. Those excesses of character make him the heroic figure he is, and lead to his overstepping, on occasion, the bounds of Long Room decorum. But who would be the poorer without him? The story is told, probably apocryphally, of W.G. Grace being bowled first ball and refusing to leave the wicket. When the umpire tried to insist, W.G. is supposed to have said: "The crowd have come to see me bat, not you, umpire." The same could be said of I.T. Botham.'

Suffice to say that I.T. Botham himself – unlike men found guilty of far more heinous crimes – knew better than to comment himself on a TCCB conviction. He muttered darkly about considering an appeal through the Cricketers' Association, then settled back for his urgent physiotherapy, and psyched himself up for the morrow. The sun came out at last and once again England batted with a staggering certainty and rollicking tempo. This time Gooch led thunderously from the front, scoring a massive 196. At Gower's 157, the Australians metaphorically stretched themselves meekly on the grass and limply fluttered the white hand-kerchief. They were totally spent, and only Ritchie and Border resisted as the ancient enemy was meekly laid to rest. England won by an innings and 94 runs.

Botham took six exuberant wickets for 105 runs in 37 overs, including

England's
G-force . . . Gooch,
the uncomplicated
man who stands up
and gives it one;
Gower, goldilocks
with the languid
charms; and Gatting,
barbed and bristling
at the wicket like a
young Henry VIII
looking to get at a
new wife

Wood in both innings, and Hilditch, hooking again. When he had finally got in to bat – at 405 – he was caught behind for 12, driving. It mattered not. After his two clinking knocks in the opening two Tests, when the series seemed even, Ian had not batted again in the next four till England – thanks to Robinson and the G-force trio – had scored, successively, 365, 304, 572 and now 405.

Before going out on the last morning to administer the *coup de grâce*, Ian looked around the cluttered dressing-room at his friends. 'I can honestly say this lot make up the best England team I've ever played with. David and the others started it in India in the winter and the impetus just kept going. I'm convinced it's the start of something very big for all of us. Our team spirit has never been higher – and a lot of that, of course, has to do with Gower. He set a marvellous example by leading from the front and I speak for everyone who was part of the England set-up this season by putting our admiration for David on record. And the warmth that went out to him when he came back to us in the dressing-room after that first "comeback" Test hundred at Trent Bridge was something really moving.'

The partnership between Gooch and Gower had been so murderously clinical that it now put them both 'simply up there near the all-time greats'. He surveyed the others near him on the bench, each concentrating on their clobber and last minute, private, readiness to take the field: 'And what a player Gatt's become. He's both very good fun and a very good team man. All of us have known he was a great county player, but once he got into the big arena he thought he had to play a bit more like a "Test" player instead of just being natural. Not any more. He's a tremendous man to have on tour, particularly – a competitor, a motivator, a fighter. But basically he's just a real good lad. I've nothing but admiration for him. I love his company. And look at Lambie there. He's a particularly close friend; he's great to bat with: gutsy, and always a sense of humour. He can play and miss, play and miss – but doesn't give a stuff. "C'mon, I've survived, let's get on with it, next ball, please." He just switches off in between deliveries; that's probably why he can bat for a long time.

'Funnily enough, I always tremendously enjoyed batting with Chris Tavaré. That may have seemed an unlikely combination, but Tav was so good at nursing you into the strike when you were going well. He ended up generously getting the single to give you all the opportunities to score – and then, of course, he'd be criticized in the Press, or slow handclapped for a boring two-hour innings or whatever. He just put up with it, made sure you'd got going – and go on just nibbling a single to get you the bowling. A marvellous bloke.'

On one bench those two inseparable buddies, Gooch and Emburey, conspire in warm comradeship. Alone, the loyal, constructive, charming team man, Downton, prepares his gauntlets for the fray. Robinson is making sure he's the neatest turned out of all. Taylor meditates, Ellison is quite at home.

In one corner, Phil Edmonds was holding his usual smiling, all-knowing court, laying down the law of the day, having just finished his *Financial Times*. 'Dear old Phillippe. I've always got on pretty well with him, mind – though he'd agree, there are times he infuriates me and, I know, I infuriate him. And I don't ever deny I've been known to go out of my way to infuriate him! We have had some fantastic arguments over the years. But out there, I wish he'd sometimes just get on with his bowling instead of wanting to change his field 15 times an over. He's got so much ability, but is sometimes obsessed with a brand new theory for every other ball he bowls. And he tries to draw attention to himself too much at times – even like that silly hat with the brim turned up, or standing far too close at bat-pad. But, you bet, I enjoy his company. I love trying to take the mickey out of him, too. He likes taking it out of me, mind – so it's probably good for both of us.

'That's the lovely thing about team games. A dressing-room is made up of *totally* different guys. That makes everything so refreshing and stimulating. We spend a lot of time cooped up in here over the year. There are a million different ways to have a laugh – you get quiet ones, sulky ones, moody ones, boisterous ones, mad ones . . . every type part and parcel of the team. No, there are very, very few shitty ones.

'Some read, some write, some brood, some play silly-buggers all the time. Some get very nervous, others ludicrously pretend not to . . . Most dressing-rooms now have a television. In the Tests some of the fellows like to have the cricket on. I prefer the golf. There's always quite a move by some to switch over to the horse-racing. I used to have the odd wager when Big Bob Willis was around – just friendly bets – but not much these days. To be honest, more often than not, I like to take a nap. A siesta on the physio's couch can be wonderful; earphones on; music; doze off: lovely. No, it doesn't depend on whether I've had an extra few jars the night before – like I told you, I never get hangovers. I'm lucky there so far.

'No, I never, ever, watch the cricket out in the middle when I'm waiting to bat. Or very, very seldom. I will probably be playing cards, or reading a magazine – say *Golf World*, *Golf Monthly*, *Penthouse*, you name it, whatever's hanging around. No, never a cricket magazine. Perhaps the air magazine, *Flight*, or *Fishing, Trout & Salmon*, or *Shooting*. Possibly my favourite mag of all is the *National Geographic*. It's a superb read, fascinating. There's always the day's newspapers floating around, of course – and I'll always get the *Sun* to see my article in it. It's my one chance to put the Press right. And it's got a pretty good all-round sports-page range, too, hasn't it? I never seem to read any novels in the summers – but knock off a hell of a lot on tours. You really need to be stuck into a good book then. I'll read anything going then, but Robert Ludlum, I suppose, is my favourite novel writer.'

Botham's own legendary rumbustiousness in the dressing-room is not all it's cracked up to be. His captain, Gower, says: 'Sometimes Ian's surprisingly quiet and keyed-up. He is not totally without nerves, you know.' David also summed up his all-rounder's Test summer: 'He's a million times better bat at 60 for 4 than 300 for 4, so he didn't have much batting pressures, did he? Thus his bowling become more important to us – so we could use him as a shock, rather than stock bowler. But how he loves to prove people wrong – he really enjoyed taking so many wickets after being totally dismissed by the Press as an expensive stock bowler.'

And not only with his bowling. Here at The Oval he had caught two quite stupendous catches; the first high to his right like a flying, back-somersaulting goalkeeper from Lawson; the second, from McDermott, a breathtaking blinder, low to his left. He had dropped one catch at Edgbaston and the critics had at last found a valid excuse to launch an attack on his method of (a) so defiantly daring to stand at least a foot closer than the other slips, and (b) preparing himself for the ball with his hands on his knees, instead of the orthodox crouch with expectant, extended fingertips. Again, like the reverse sweep, they were attitudes which horrified the compilers of Mr May's *MCC Coaching Book*. These two catches had thrilled the nation as they were replayed through the week on television (the first, actually, was almost too fast for one cameraman!). Says Ian: 'They can say what they like. I'm just more comfortable with my hands on my knees. And I've seldon failed to get my hands to the ball from that position, have I? It suits me, that's all. Why so much closer than the others? No, it's nothing at all to do with bravado. Over the years, when I've been bowling, there's been nothing so frustrating as to get a nick from the bat and then having the ball drop short of the slip fielder. So I'd far sooner be in the position of having a go at it, giving myself much more of a chance to get a hand to it and, okay, sometimes drop it; it's a tragic waste for a slip fielder to have to take a ball on second bounce.

'It's tiring, concentrated work. You wait and wait, often all day. It's all reflex stuff, slip catching, and in a way the less time you have to think about it the better – that's why I always enjoy second slip more than first.

First catch it, then do the backward somersault: this one (*above*), off Lawson, was too fast for the TV cameras. In the diving catch off McDermott (*below*), Botham is far advanced on the line of the other three slipfielders – 'the less time you have to think about it, the better'

At first slip you can see the ball all the way, you're virtually a second wicket-keeper; at second slip it comes at you after a change of direction. Much more exciting. Over the years at second slip, I've had a lot more success standing up, closer, because (a) I've held catches that wouldn't normally carry, which is a real satisfaction, and (b) I think bowlers like to see you there being really "aggressive" for a catch. It gives them a real extra buzz and zippiness. I must say, though, Joel sometimes say he thinks I should stand back a bit – but I say, "don't worry, Bird, I won't drop them off you." It's more than my life's worth! It's cock to say that first or third slip mind me standing up there ahead of them: they've got to like it over the years, in fact – for one thing it allows them to stand just that little bit wider.

'Some say the rule is that second slip focuses his concentration on the edge of the bat. I don't. I watch the ball from the bowler's hand. I see the edge of the bat like a slip-cradle, or practising catching off the edge of a bat, I like to see the ball come. Graham Roope and Tony Greig have been great second slips in my time; I can't rememeber which, but one of them would only watch the edge of the bat, the other would watch the ball all the way, like me. But does it matter if it's effective? Just horses for courses. Do what suits you best. Most satisfying catches? Every one. [Long think.] Funnily enough, in Tests, three in Roope's old sentry-box here at The Oval: okay, this one from Lawson; one from Larry Gomes; then that one from Shastri off Bob Willis, when I was really close because the wicket was so slow – pure reflex that one. There was a caught-and-bowled off Kallicharran in a one-dayer at Adelaide . . . oh, lots have given some real warm pleasure.'

The diving, electrically quick catch off McDermott put Ian once again top of the series in the catching list, level with England's other first-division fieldsman, Edmonds. It was Ian's 92nd catch in 79 Tests which puts him very high in the all-time list of prolific catchers, in which it must be remembered, he was a regular bowler so limiting his chances for catching (in his tally of 92, 8 were c-&-b's). In other words, non-bowler Cowdrey's 120 catches for England in 114 matches came throughout his career at either 'end'. In Botham's Tests, he has now bowled 18,391 balls. The other two legendary 'catching bowlers' are Sobers (21,599 balls) and Lock (13,147) – and to a lesser degree, Hammond (7,967). The table for those who have taken over 50 catches now reads:

	CATCHES	TESTS	CATCHES PER TEST
E.D. Solkar	53	27	1.96
R.B. Simpson	110	62	1.77
G.S. Chappell	122	87	1.40
I.M. Chappell	105	75	1.40
B. Mitchell	56	42	1.33
W.R. Hammond	110	85	1.29
I.R. Redpath	83	66	1.26
G.A.R. Lock	59	49	1.20
G.S. Sobers	109	93	1.17
I.T. Botham	**92**	**79**	**1.16**

For those who revel in such maths, an interesting little addendum to the list is:

W.G. Grace	39	22	1.77

Indeed, as Gower, Botham and their delighted colleagues wantonly shook and shampooed themselves in champagne, the musty men with the slide-rules and calculators were already figuring out their decimal points for posterity. Perhaps one of the reasons the dear old gasometered

The Captain, the King and the Castlemaine

Oval is such a fondly-loved place in cricket (suddenly, says Ian, the players' food was much, much better this time) is because it always contrives to stage the final, famous curtain calls. Now the happy scenes and balcony merrymaking evoked memories right down the century. In recent post-war years, the ground has staged sterling deeds like, off-hand, Pakistan's famous first victory, Dolly's serenely mischievous hundred that set the pigeon among the snarling cats of apartheid, and those two glittering innings by Asif and Gavaskar... but all would agree that The Oval is most cherished for being the place where the Ashes come home to. It was now 83 years since Gilbert Jessop, at 29 exactly the same age as Ian Botham, sat in the Grand Central Hotel, had his first glass of Pommery to induce, on his own genteel admission, that feeling of more-ish, and took bets, at odds of 20-1, that he would get a century on the morrow. He did, of course, in 80 balls – three of which whizz-banged into the pavilion – and then, the legend goes, Hirst and Rhodes retrieved the Ashes 'in singles'. That was August 13, 1902. Twenty-four years and a grievous world war later, on August 16, 1926, Arnold Bennett's *Journal* read: 'Suddenly went off to The Oval... crowd very quick to take up every point. Every maiden over cheered for instance. Women fainting here and there. Attendants to look after them. Cricket cautious and very slow. Great roar when Woodfull's wicket fell. Heat of the crowd. Great difficulty of seeing anything at all, even by tiptoeing and craning.' The man who bowled Woodfull was Larwood – and home came the Ashes again. And then there was the day twenty-seven years later, August 19, 1953, when they returned once more as Compton punched a long-hop from Morris down to the gasometer scoreboard to release a tide of jubilation. In that match, Australia had been Lakered and Locked after Trueman had venomously blasted the defences. It struck me as sad, watching Botham being garlanded in the common man's affection and admiration this September afternoon thirty-two years on, that Trueman was in the vanguard of the British critics' circle of Botham-bashers. More like degrading, when you think about it. Ah me, old men will never learn...

Trueman's public announcement that Botham 'can't even bowl a hoop downhill' had not stopped the young man's relentless pursuit of Dennis Lillee's all-time Test record of 355 wickets. His astonishing haul of 31 wickets in this series – only the steady, beautifully controlled and cunning Emburey was remotely near him with 19 wickets – puts Botham now only 12 behind the Australian demon. Trueman's 307 languishes far, far behind now. In just about every facet, Trueman's fine record as a strike bowler looks limp beside that of Botham. Trueman took five wickets or more in an innings 17 times, to Botham's amazing 25; Trueman took ten wickets in a match on three occasions, to Botham's four. Blunt-speaking

Fred, of course, doesn't even get a mention in the catch-match ratios, or the batting averages. Ye anciente fierie one, does, however, pip the young man (who gives him the pip) in the matter of runs conceded per wicket taken – just. Botham's image as a Test bowler is that of a typical strike bowler, taking wickets frequently, but not particularly economically. This is borne out by the figures, although the rates of 'balls per wicket' and 'runs per 100 balls' do not in fact vary very much as between good-class bowlers of the same type. To illustrate: Botham's striking-rate, that is, the number of balls he has bowled for each of his Test wickets, is 53.62. Of the bowlers who have taken 200 or more Test wickets, only six have bettered this, and not by very much:

Trueman	49.44
Holding	50.82
Lillee	52.02
Thomson	52.67
Willis	53.41
Garner	53.50
Botham	**53.62**

Slow bowlers tend to need more time to get their wickets; for example, Underwood's rate is 73.61, Bedi's 80.32 and Gibbs's 87.75. Most fast and fast-medium bowlers concede runs at about the same rate, 45-48 per 100 balls. Botham has given away 49.19 per 100, and of the '200 club', only Kapil Dev at 50.99 is more expensive, but there's not much in it. This, of course, is where the slow men come into their own; Underwood, Bedi and Gibbs conceded at 35.10, 35.75 and 33.15 respectively.

For once, at The Oval, Lamb did not take a catch off his friend's bowling (Lamb's fielding through the series also warrants high praise). During the summer, Sir Frederick's Critics' Guild also passed a resolution snidely intimating that the great majority of Botham's wickets were those of tail-enders. This is palpably untrue. He has dismissed more 'top five' bats than Trueman himself did – and it was nicely illustrated in Australia's last innings at The Oval when he made Wood chop-on and so join his own 'double figure bunnies' club. Ian's Test dismissals have been obtained thus:

		%
Bowled	50	14.6
LBW	73	21.3
Caught	219	63.8
Hit wicket	1	0.3

His chief collaborators in the field have been Taylor (60 catches), Lamb (14), Gooch (14), Downton (12), Gower (12), and Brearley (10). The Taylor-Botham combination is the second most successful in all Tests, Marsh having caught 95 off Lillee. Fascinatingly, Lamb, brilliant 'all-round' fielder, caught 12 of Botham's last 76 victims. Ian's favourite victims? He has dismissed Kim Hughes 12 times, Border 11, and now Wood 10. After these come Marsh (8), the brothers-in-law Gavaskar and Viswanath (both 8), Burgess and Kapil Dev (7 times each).

Ian has always claimed to disregard records, but he will readily admit that Lillee's all-time 355 has been a target all summer. 'I suppose I set my stall out for that about 18 months ago. Well, between me and Dennis, it's the old rivalry rearing its head again: I admire Dennis hugely, he's simply the best bowler I've ever seen or faced. Even in his later days he could ping one in very, very quick – but overall his magnificence was in his variations, his control, his ability to do virtually anything with the ball, seam, swing, stop, swerve, he could almost make the ruddy thing sing. And what a good mate he's been: we always had a healthy respect on the field for each other, I think, and then inevitably repaired afterwards for an ice-cold tinnie together. Or two or three or four . . . Out there earlier that afternoon, mind you, it had always been a real, rotten, no-holds, narrow-eyed contest. How else can you play Test cricket?'

Lillee, by the way, dismissed Ian seven times in their series of epic duels – though the Test bowler who has dismissed him on most occasions, eight up to the end of 1985, is his even better buddy, the big smiling bird with the rickety knees, Joel Garner. Another mate, Jeff Thomson, has sent Ian on his way on six occasions. In all he has 16 times been both bowled and leg-before in Tests, twice stumped, thrice run out, and caught 85 times – 19 of which, like here at The Oval, snaffled up by the raucous men in gloves. Thus, he has been caught in 69.97 per cent of his innings, a higher proportion than that of the average Test player – currently 63 per cent. This will surprise nobody – indeed it helps bear out Ian's carefree assertion after the celebrated reverse sweep dismissal many runs, sixes and wickets ago at Old Trafford in May, that 'I've got myself out in many dottier ways – in fact I wouldn't be surprised that I've got myself out more often than I've been got out.'

And so a season ended with the Australians shamed and English jubilation and truce all round. The splendid Mr Woodcock in *The Times* even apologised with grace and charm to Ian – 'Quite simply, he is a law unto himself . . . and I promise never to say again that he deprives himself

D.K. Lillee – 'Simply the best bowler I've ever faced . . . and always time for a few "tinnies" afterwards'

at slip of a potentially crucial split-second by standing with his hands on his knees.' In the same's Sabbath sister, his old captain, Mike Brearley, wrote, 'Simply, he is the greatest match-winner the game has ever known.' And on the main leader page of the *Daily Telegraph*, by no means celebrated for its adjectival affection for Botham on other pages, Michael Kennedy most handsomely made amends: 'He is a hero in an age of anti-heroes, and it is a pity the over-exposure of publicity so often offers ammunition to his detractors. No one plays the game harder, no one is more wholehearted in delight at a colleague's success, and no one is more likely to turn a game round single-handed . . . time and again he takes the vital wicket and his miraculous catching is the equivalent of having an extra bowler in the side.'

11 Knackered!

S EASON'S end, but only for his cricketing. There was Somerset and the captaincy to sort out. Then some golf in Spain with Simon O'Donnell and friends. Some shootin', fishin' and deerstalkin'... oh yes, and also a little matter – rather long, in fact – to begin at John o' Groats.

In the event – and in spite of a great deal of speculative press hype, not least in Ian's 'own' *Sun* – the captaincy of Somerset changed hands in a chivalrous and gentlemanly manner. Peter Roebuck accepted the job, and nice Vic Marks, who had been vice-captain, accepted the decision with charm and a voicing of honest disappointment. Ian had played only ten first-class games of the county's 24 so it was a sensible decision, arrived at, also, with regret and disappointment. He loves being the official leader from the front and has never denied it. He enjoys the intrigue of tactics and the *oomph* of being first over the top and rallying the troops to the charge. 'I gave a hell of a lot of thought to giving it up. Was it fair to be away at the Tests so often? Was it fair to all my other outside commitments? Were those new 'business' interests with Tim [Hudson] themselves fair to the team? There is also all the backroom 'committee' work a captain is expected to do. Some of it was fascinating, but suddenly, you got a couple of days off because of some fixture quirk or whatever – anyway, a period that gives a player time to recharge the batteries or rest up a niggly injury – and then you realize you have to turn up for a committee meeting or stay to sort out some crisis or whatever. Also, the older I get – and the faster the kids grow up – then the more I find I'm missing being with the family. Liam and Sarah are at a wonderful age now. More and more, I want to take advantage of any days off from cricket or business to go and watch my own son play his sport at school. Or take him fishing. Or just crash out and enjoy us all watching a video together after going out and bringing back some fish-and-chips.

'But, actually, during match-play, I admit I love captaincy. Certainly, I'd dearly love to captain England again one day – even just for one game.

And David knows that too – but also that I'm going to give him 110 per cent while he's captain. Mike [Brearley] would know that too. Without question, as captain of Somerset, and playing well for England, I find I've enjoyed my cricket more over the last couple of years than I had done for the previous half dozen. I think it helps actually, having a number of business activities not totally related to cricket.

'Honestly. It was a real wrench giving up. I'm a Somerset cricketer. I love Somerset. You couldn't wish for a better county, better people. But, all in all, I suppose I regard myself a basic Northerner. My roots are Northern. I was born there. My home is in the North. But, do you know, I think that every day I get a bit more cosmopolitan. My accent gets a bit of a burr in it when I'm a long time in Somerset: the vowels are much more broad and 'Yorky' when I've been at home: in London, I've been told, I can get a bit nasal and Cockney – in Scotland I've even been known to say to a barman, "Och aye, Jimmy, set up a few large drams, d'y'ken!"' When he laughs sometimes it can be a great rumbling job that shudders the rafters.

Roebuck is also a good laugher. Less an Orson Welles rumbling-thunder about it, mind you. Everyone calls him 'studious', for some reason. He is a very witty man – though, certainly, a 'studious' bat – and a smashing writer who was putting the finishing touches to his much-awaited biography of his suddenly former captain as his call to the colours came in the autumn. Actually, the particular night he was named captain, Peter was at the cinema watching the studious Clint Eastwood in the studious *Pale Rider*. Next morning he recalled his long friendship – since they were both 14 – with the man he had succeeded: 'I remember putting on 90 with him in one of our very first matches. He got 82 of them in 25 minutes. So you see nothing much has changed. He was exactly the same then as he is now – noisy, likeable, roguish. Good fun. I've known him since 1970 when we were in the Under 15s. He's tremendous, a colossus of a cricketer. I've always liked the way he imparts life into everything he does. Perhaps we live different lives but we hold a lot of similar views and I don't see any problems just because the captaincy has changed. The only problems he's going to set will be to the opposing captain and the people who make cricket balls. I'd like to talk to him over a whisky or two... once I can get hold of him. I'm delighted that he's staying. Good not only for the county but for Ian too. We'll talk as we've done over the years. It's important that cricket remains centre stage. That's what he's a genius at. We'll talk, but how a person leads his life is up to him.

'He will give his heart and soul for Somerset. It's no use pretending he

The captain resigns, with regret: his successor tries the parking space for size

189

is going to turn up in a collar and tie every day and pat me on the head. He is a robust, buccaneering character, and I'm glad of it. I expect people to stand up and say what they think – and Ian has shown he has plenty of ideas. Both, Viv, Vic and I all joined the Somerset staff on the same chilly April day in 1974. We've travelled a long way together and I believe we have a long way to go yet.'

For some, however, it was the end of the road. Before he left Taunton for the summer, Ian had to say goodbye to friends who would not be rejoining the jokes of April. Tall, cheerful Richard Ollis, for one, had not been re-engaged. Ian was genuinely sorry. 'Somehow old "Aulage" [his family run a transport firm] never got full recognition for some real gutsy knocks. He's a good lad, an athlete, a good fielder, and he's brave enough to have got his runs usually when we've been in trouble. Perhaps, in the end, he just lost heart. In a lot of ways I can't blame him for that. It just all went wrong. But I'm really sorry he's going.'

Nigel Popplewell, at 28, was also going. He was going to take up law studies. Perhaps, in 30 years or so, he might follow his father to the red robe, permed wig and gavel. He had played with particular vigour this season, volunteering to open for the injury-stricken side – and, of course, fielded with a demon's verve, as ever. Ian was devastated when 'Pops' put in his notice. Things wouldn't be the same. 'He's not only a ruddy fine player. We're going to miss him for hundreds of reasons. Such a refreshing attitude all round. A great man.'

Popplewell, in his turn, reflected on his once and former leader: 'Ian's friendship, persona, and presence was a reason I enjoyed my seven years with Somerset so much. He has a huge desire to cultivate team spirit, but if people are down or the team is tired, he does not quite know how to pick them up. I remember being sent to Hampshire when I was only slightly injured to be told by the acting captain that there was never any chance of my playing – I was there to improve team spirit! Because he is such a good player people perhaps feel that he has not gone through a confidence "crisis" that others often have and are therefore reluctant to confide in him. He appears to be so confident himself, but that too can be misleading: when I had some troubles at the start of the season, I found him sympathetic, reasonable and, rather surprisingly, full of sound common sense.

'Yet Ian does not suffer fools or incompetence gladly and in close games when the tension is high his temper can boil over and be directed at a friend. I have heard him shout across the field in a game at Birmingham when someone made a fielding error at a crucial time. But it is soon forgotten and win or lose the culprit will be the beneficiary of a pint of lager in the bar afterwards. That can, however, have a more damaging effect on younger players who are looking for consistency in their lives. Cricket dressing-rooms provide a harsh environment to develop in and this overbearing character who rants at you one minute and calls you his best mate the next may be difficult to come to terms with. He believes that people should behave the same way towards him – if he makes a mistake, confront him with it, give him a bollocking, but then forget it and harbour no grudge. Unfortunately, most people do not see behaviour in such black-and-white terms and will bear him ill-will for mistakes in the past.

'Ian is often movingly concerned with team spirit and the success of the team rather than of himself as an individual. One of his proudest boasts is that he'd rather the team did well and himself fail than vice versa. It is true, too. I remember in 1981 when he had just made the only "pair" of his career against the Australians at Lord's, the day he resigned from the captaincy of England. We were in a Benson & Hedges quarter-final the very next day against Kent at Taunton. In spite of his own troubles, he turned up at the ground at 8.45am, looking absolutely dreadful. Drawn, pale, a shadow of his real self. Yet he still managed to take a couple of wickets, bowl tidily and generally contribute, despite his desperate psychological condition. And yet when we had won, he was overjoyed and took huge delight in our victory – indeed, he threw me fully clothed into a bath and poured beer on my head as a "reward" for winning my first Man-of-the-Match award. It must have been a dreadful time for him, and yet he really delighted in someone else's success. And it was only about a month later that he smashed Lillee and Alderman all round Leeds.'

And then the rods and guns, wife, kids, parents, in-laws, and, it seemed, sisters, cousins, aunts, cats and dogs, were all piled into the boot and off to Scotland for a bit of rest and recuperation in the blissful hills and forests not a million miles from dramatic old Stirling.

To be sure, one of the most warming aspects of Ian's cricketing has been the continued family presence. To me, it underlines his villagey roots in the game. Go and watch him in an exhibition, evening game for a fellow county player (turning up to which he is famously generous on the circuit: ask anyone: and the more 'bread-and-butter' the beneficiary the more he will put himself out), and there in the deck-chair throng with the Thermos more often than not will be some member of the Botham-Waller family. They are as readily in evidence at a Test match in one of cricket's huge stadiums as they are popping in with a picnic at county games from Taunton to Cheltenham, Chesterfield or Chelmsford. Any man might take, say, his schoolboy sons to watch the great British baron of beefiness bat or bowl through a day's county cricket in the shires – and as likely as not, in the lunch or tea intervals, they will be playing in the children's games that criss-cross the field alongside the raucous, cheery 8-year-old

Liam Botham, amiably bullocking and barging about with his baseball glove. With Mum throwing the catches. There is something touching and wholesome and heartwarming whenever I see them so.

Liam is in many ways a chip off the old block. I wonder if he is like Ian was, around 1963? Liam is rumbustiously cheerful; slightly earnest; confident, courteous, enquiring, but sensitive with it. He is athletic and competitive, too: and a good team man. At eight, he is already No. 9 for his school's Under-11s. When it comes to wide-eyed charmer's charm, even Liam would agree 6-year-old Sarah takes the cream cracker. She likes the cricket, too, not for the buzz and bonhomie of the man's-man changing-room that Liam revels in, but for the possibility of starting totally trusting conversations with totally trusting strangers. As likely as not, Kathy's parents, Gerry and Jan Waller, might have popped in from Doncaster. No son-in-law could wish for more support there. And Les and Marie are often in evidence plus any other member from the family chapel at Yeovil.

While Ian was destructively moving cricket balls to all points through the year, Kathy was moving the family home, from the bureaucratized Humberside of 'old' Lincolnshire up the M1 to North Yorkshire. She was also pregnant again, which delighted Ian. 'If it was left to him, he would love six kids at least', she laughs. 'I suppose it's just because's he's really no more than one big kid himself!' The new home is a converted coach house on the edge of a village. It seems perfect for them – a large L-shaped country kitchen in scrubbed pine and a big cosy sitting room with crackling logs in the fireplace. You have to look very carefully indeed to find evidence at all that cricket plays any part in the owner's scheme of things. A dog lover, sure: there are two lifesize ceramic models of a boxer and a brown-spotted pointer. It might be Mrs Woodhouse's sitting room. 'Barbara' Botham, indeed. There is a set of soft and delicate watercolours by the Yorkshire artist, John Hurst – two ploughmen-pastoral jobs, one of York Minister, and one of a winter countryman homeward plodding at dusk, shotgun over one shoulder, brace of partridge over the other: on close examination it is Ian, looking like a young Prince Hal, with his cropped and gingery beard of '81 vintage. At the foot of the staircase is hung a copy of that Victorian oil of a young Downland shepherd's lad taking gawky guard at Hambledon. In the bookcase there are more cricket books than you might have expected, and in a corner cabinet there is a delicate ceramic figurine of W.G. Grace, and also a presentation plate which shows the scorecard of the 1981 Headingley Test. Kathy keeps the place spotless – 'somebody has to when Ian's around.' In the gravelly drive, stands a Jaguar and a Corvette. In the paddock a few pairs of waddling geese gobble.

Botham, beaters and bearers. Huntin', Himalayan style, 1982

One autumn morning I stepped on a dew-sodden hunk of wood. It had been there for weeks. Liam had left it out. It turned out to be a cricket bat. Ian picked it up. 'I got a century with that against Australia at Melbourne', he said, matter-of-fact, as he leant it against the fence. It's probably still there. I didn't dare ask if I could have it, but said, instead, 'Where's the bat that scored the 80 sixes?' He supposed Kathy had slung it in the loft with the rest of his summer clobber.

They met in the car park at Leicester cricket ground. She had come down with her Dad to see Brian Close, an old family friend. She could not find her car. A gawky Somerset colt had helped her look for it. They married in January 1976. They were both 21.

A few years later, they were on a walking holiday near Ullswater when Ian told Kath that one day he would have a crack at walking the length of Britain, end to end. To raise money for leukaemia research. The charity had been dear to Ian since he had visited the special children's unit at Taunton Hospital. 'They seemed as normal and happy as my own kids: OK, some had lost their hair, but they were all bubbling with health and laughter. But I was told many of them would soon be dead. It was shattering.' You would not have thought that the great trek was about to begin had you visited the October family holiday in Scotland. The only give-away – four bottles of surgical spirit on the table of the holiday cabin in which to soak daily the soles of his feet.

The sly weather of summer, wouldn't you know, had suddenly put on its brightest side for the holiday. Autumn was a blissful delight and Ian was indulging in one of his favourite pastimes. 'Fishing is a fantastic relaxation. Salmon is what I go for most. It's hard work, good fun, frustrating; it's tranquilty, peace of mind... I can spend a day, a week, a fortnight, and don't even have to see, speak to, or meet another person: just me stood there, on the river; heaven; a flask and a sandwich on the bank; I just stand there on my own. That's it, that's me for the day, I'm happy. Liam's just getting into it now, so the two of us just go off for the day. I don't think there can be any better way for making friends with your child. Salmon fishing only for the rich? Balls. I can buy a ticket for £12 for a whole season in Scotland. No, I'm not telling you where! You find out for yourself! Anyway, in Scotland every river has its town beat – even the Tay. I first got into salmon fishing about a dozen years ago; and trout fishing, too. I'd done some coarse fishing as a lad, as most people do. A kid's jamjar first: then a keep net; then a few roach, you know, chuck 'em all back...' Happy days.

This year's new sport was deer-stalking. One night after a cheery family supper the three of us, Ian, myself, and father-in-law Gerry, had sat up chewing the cud and measuring out (and measuring out) the malts. I was in no fit state to do anything for the next 24 hours at least! I sense Gerry felt *roughly* the same. Ian was up at dawn, clambering up mountains and down dales, sometimes on all fours, sometimes at the same lick he comes in to bowl. You could cover 30 miles a day, no problem. 'The exercise is fantastic. I'm sorry to say it, but the Anti-Bloodsports people have no idea. I respect their sincerity, of course I do. But I'm afraid, for the most part, they are talking through their backsides. Do you know that there are more deer in this country than there were in the days of Henry VIII? And if you don't cull deer and keep the herd controlled, then what are you going to do, just sit back and watch them die in the winters? There's nothing more horrific, I'm telling you.

'What happens is this, if you've ever watched a herd at a feed hole: the strongest beasts, the big stags, are the first onto the feed, obviously; then it goes in circles of brute seniority, not need. So the hinds and the calves are on the far outside ring of the pecking order. So the younger generation can starve. It's as simple as that. Starve to death. There's no more gruesome way for an animal to die. Last winter, on just one estate in Scotland – one I've stalked on – they lost 260 beasts. All because the outer circle, made up of the weak ones, could not get at the feed. Like all primitive life, it's the survival of the fittest. So you have to cull the herd, control its greediness if you like. And let's be quite frank about it, too – venison is very lovely, very edible meat. And unlike butchers' red meat – beef, lamb, etcetera – that goes, on the hoof, to the abattoir, there is no fear for the animal in stalking. Have you ever seen a bullock, or a lamb, in an abattoir? They can "smell" death: they are tense, neurotic, very scared. They know they are going to die.

'Culling is different. They have no remote hint, no possible premonition of death. With a gamekeeper, and his binoculars, you select the beast that has to be culled. Say it's 1,500 yards away from you: okay, you have to get to 500 yards of it without him realizing. Then, perhaps, if the wind is behind you, you have to manoeuvre around – out of sight, out of scent, out of earshot – and the whole great circle could be a few miles. And on these hills, that can mean a ruddy heck of a lot of work, I'm telling you. Then, one shot – and the beast has gone. It *had* to be culled. My only message for the townees – most Antis are townees – is to take a trip down to the abattoir or wholesale butchers' depots near their home to see how they are preparing next week's Sunday lunch.

'Or next time they think of having a chicken for supper, go along to their local battery farm to see how a chicken is killed – let alone how it has lived for all its pitiful life with 3,000 others in a shed as big as someone's garage. No daylight. Fear and tension in their eyes. That's cruelty. At least the animal I shoot has lived a full and wild and natural life. An expert gamekeeper tells you which one to shoot to cull. These people who attack me for stalking and shooting should look around them at what's going on as regards cruelty to animals, and do something about that. I've lived all my life in the real country, and I'm afraid I just laugh at these people.'

The swish family motorcade moved on towards John o' Groats. As mile upon mile, hour upon hour, was ticked away, a simple, basic truth hit us. It was a long way. An awful, awesome long way.

Ian set out from John o' Groats on a grey, pewtery dawn on October 25. A hundred or so saw him off, including the family. Kath was heavily pregnant and proud; Liam told the TV that if his Dad said he was going to do it, then do it he would. Ian's collecting target had been set at £100,000: typically, at the last minute he said he would be going for £500,000. He put a toe in the water, re-laced his trainer shoe, and started walking.

It was, as far as I could discover, the 105th year of this dear and dotty crackpot craze. In the visitors' book at the gaunt old pseudo-Gothic John o' Groats Hotel, you can still read the faint Quinked chronicle of the first two pioneers – H. Blackwell, of Camberley, and Chas Harman, of Southgate. In a breathless copperplate, they logged details of their 'hitherto unattempted journey from Land's End, through Shropshire and the Lakes'. The 890 miles took them 13 days – on bicycles. They arrived at

Day 1 ● JOHN O'GROATS *26 October* **30 miles**

Day 2 ● LYBSTER *27 October* **37 miles**

Day 3 ● BRORA *28 October* **28 miles**
Day 4 ● ARDGAY *29 October* **28 miles**
Day 5 ● EVANTON *30 October* **18 miles**
Day 6 ● INVERNESS *31 October* **23 miles**
Day 7 ● CARRBRIDGE *1 November* **30 miles**

Day 8 ● NEWTONMORE *2 November* **20 miles**

Day 9 ● PITAGOWAN *3 November* **25 miles**

Day 10 ● DUNKELD *4 November* **32 miles**

Day 11 ● KINROSS *5 November* **25 miles**

Day 12 ● FALKIRK *6 November* **23 miles**

Day 13 ● FORTH *7 November* **12 miles**
Day 14 ● BIGGAR *8 November* **26 miles**

Day 15 ● MOFFAT *9 November* **37 miles**

Day 16 ● GRETNA *10 November* **32 miles**

Day 17 ● PENRITH *11 November* **27 miles**

Day 18 ● KENDAL *12 November* **22 miles**

Day 19 ● LANCASTER *13 November* **31 miles**

Day 20 ● BLACKBURN *14 November* **33 miles**

Day 21 ● MANCHESTER *15 November* **22 miles**

Day 22 ● CONGLETON *16 November* **23 miles**

Day 23 ● STONE *17 November* **24 miles**

Day 24 ● WOLVERHAMPTON *18 November* **31 miles**

Day 25 ● OMBERSLEY *19 November* **23 miles**

Day 26 ● TEWKESBURY *20 November* **29 miles**

Day 27 ● NEWPORT *21 November* **28 miles**

Day 28 ● BRISTOL *22 November* **19 miles**

Day 29 ● HIGHBRIDGE *23 November* **26 miles**

Day 30 ● WELLINGTON *24 November* **23 miles**
Day 31 ● CADBURY *25 November* **24 miles**
Day 32 ● OKEHAMPTON *26 November* **24 miles**
Day 33 ● TWO BRIDGES *27 November* **24 miles**
Day 34 ● VICTORIA *28 November* **28 miles**
Day 35 ● CAMBORNE *29 November* **25 miles**
● LANDS END

**It was a long way.
An awful, awesome long way**

the topmost tip of Britain in time for supper on July 24, and reported – 'Both of us are in better health and spirits at the finish than at commencement of our tour, and our trusty machines ran as well as ever. We cannot conclude without extolling the charming ignorance displayed on the subject of distances by the Scotch peasants, having received in one place the perplexing intelligence that it was (either) 16, 15, 4, 10 or 3 miles to so-and-so. The Road Surveyor's office staff obviously hide the milestones up here.' Five years later, now exactly a century on, another immaculate entry, by Thomas Marriott, of Ratcliffe-on-Trent, claimed the new cycling record on September 28, 1885: 12 days 23 hours 12 minutes – 'and accomplished in a time of year highly unpropitious for a performance of this description and under a succession of adverse circumstances.'

Ian was going even later in an already 'unpropitious' year – and on foot as he retraced the steps of, it is reckoned, some hundred or so hikers who have done the deed on shanks's pony, right up to the doughty duo of Barbara Moore and Jimmy Saville. It was going to take him five weeks of his life.

The Gods could not do much for his feet, but they did turn on the most blissful of autumn weeks as he strode down the side of the milky-white sea. To the right the hills were speckled with sheep and the forests with the most blissful shades of old golds and faded greens, and browns and reds and russets, oranges and lemons . . . Tang Head and Wick, Thrumster and Lybster, Berriedale, Helmsdale and Brora, Spinningdale and Bonar Bridge . . . By now, blisters beating the bravado out of all the early, bettaking boastful hangers-on, there were only three men left with will and guts enough to consider going the whole hog with the hero – John Border (Allan's brother, no less), a courageous barrelly little koala bear of a fellow; Phil Rance, a Manchester hairdresser, whose father had died of leukaemia the year before – and such a mourning pledge was always going to overcome five weeks of pain; and Chris Lander, the 44-year-old rugby writer for the *Daily Mirror* who had done the first 30-mile leg to Lybster, for a story and a wheeze, and now found himself caught up irretrievably in the cause – though the effect remained mutilating to his feet, his achievement stirred the spirit of every hack in the Street. The grimacing trio followed their leader, across Dornoch and down the side of Cromarty; through Carrbridge and Kingussie; and on, on down to Kinross by way of Pitlochry and Perth. And still shone the lukewarm autumn sun: the Tay was silvery, the Spey soft, and the textures, tones and tints of Birnam Wood can seldom have been more moving.

And all the time, the crofters waited at crossroads, and the common folk came out from their cottages to chip in a groat and good cheer, to fold it either personally into Ian's hand or toss it into the back-up lorry that chugged behind the Pied Piper and his posse. Each night, at the hotels, there was a masseur ready, a hot bath, and a session with the local chiropodist. Each morning, at dawn, a new set came to join the stage, schoolboys or schoolgirls or sports teams, or super-duper stars to lend their weight: John Conteh, Bill Franklyn, Billy Connolly and, 'the most memorable superstar of them all', says Ian – 8-year-old Anthony Shuttlewood, who walked 20 miles, some on the cricketer's shoulders, having just come out of his two years of intensive treatment for leukaemia.

The weather broke at last, but on and on they walked . . . down through the plump hills of Buchan country – at about 3,900,000 steps, said somebody; Moffat and Mosspaul were enveloped in fog; Shap was very sharp and the Lakes looked frozen. Brian Close, Botham's bald and brave boyhood mentor, completed a wincing stage, then went at once to hospital for a knee operation; Arnie Sidebottom was the first summer sidekick to present himself; Blackburn was bitter, where Bill Beaumont did the honours.

On the night of November 14, with Ian sleeping deeply in a hotel on the other side of the Pennines, Kathy gave birth to their third child in Doncaster Infirmary. At dawn, Ian was driven to say his 'Hello and Welcome' to his 7lb 7 ouncer. A television camera crew was at the family bedside and Ian was asked if he had considered a name for the babe. 'Gertrude', he announced with his widest grin – at which Liam piped up, 'Well, I'm leaving home then'. They settled on Rebecca ('Beccy', for short), though later that day I half-expected to hear that Lord's had fined him £1,000 for bringing the name 'Gertrude' into disrepute, the same sum they relieved him of when he said he would not wish a fortnight's holiday in Pakistan even on his mother-in-law, or when he played soccer for Scunthorpe – in the same winter that other eminent England cricket tourists were left scot-free when playing regular soccer or even skiing.

Back to the plodding parade . . . Manchester's lunch hour did not quite know what hit them – but the Black Country was generously ready all right, and the kitty had by now passed its official target . . . but the limping leaders, their blisters long turned into hardened layers, were suffering now in shin and calf, and the sciatic nerve was complaining with piercing regularity. Congleton, Stone and Stafford; and a wander past Wolver-hampton to Worcester . . . Bill Tidy, Bob Taylor, Bernard Thomas . . . two former captains, too, Brearley and Willis . . . and Dennis Amiss, who had stood, solitary at slip, as Ian hit his 13 sixes in his summer's most rampant riot . . . and the bands played on through November and the collecting tins rattled . . . Gloucester and Bristol, plus a peek into Wales . . . Brian Barnes, Barry John, and a most triumphant tramp by Max Boyce, whose shoes

Doncaster stopover ... Sarah, Liam, Mum, Dad, and 'Gertrude', er, sorry, Beccy

were seeping blood when he unlaced them.

Graham Gooch brought his footballer friend, Paul Brush, whose wife had died of leukaemia ... and another good man, Gatting, also pledged a plodding stage. So, at the last, did David Gower. Down the length of Somerset it was a prodigal's progress ... at Taunton, the old market town turned out in droves and lined the streets, just as they had over fifty years before at Sammy Woods's funeral, but now there was no sadness in the day, just hoorahs for a hoofing hero ... Highbridge and Wellington, Tiverton ... ancient Cadbury, Crediton and on down to the tip of Dartmoor.

It was the final lap at last. Every step was wretchedly painful. The weather remained wintry cruel. Eight hundred miles done, and just two days to go. Tempers frayed. A traffic policeman chivvied Phil Rance for peeing in public on top of Bodmin Moor. There was a pushing match and Botham bonged the policeman on the helmet. No charges were preferred, but they could have been. There were two mentions for Ian next day in the House of Commons.

Peter Bruinvels, Conservative MP for Leicester East, said: 'According to the reports I read, Botham behaved disgracefully – and it is equally

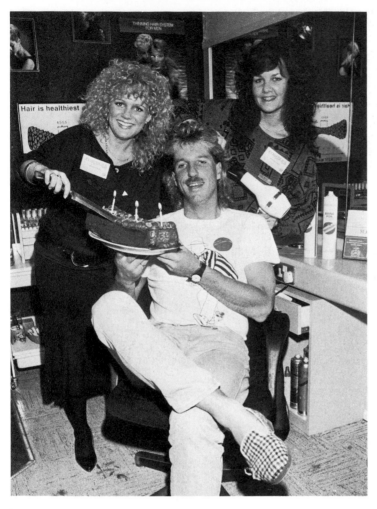

Birthday cake and hair-do highlights at Taunton. Three more days to go

disgraceful that the police are apparently not charging him.' But already David Harris (Conservative St Ives) and Mr Robert Maclennan (SDP, Caithness & Sutherland) had tabled a motion describing the walk as a 'magnificent achievement which had won admiration from one end of the country to the other.'

Next morning, the mazy Camborne road to Penzance was festooned with good will and cheers. The charity total had passed £500,000 and was still ticking on. Land's End's 'first-and-last' house loomed at last through the midday murk. The skein of stone-walled lanes tied in the cars. Five hundred folk or so got through to greet the four proud walkers, newly changed en route into toppers-and-tails. At the finish, the Penryn School brass band competed with the loudspeaker that was playing the country-and-western recording by Botham and his buddy, Bobby Buck, 'Just Take Time to Care – For the Helpless Kids Out There'. Ian then gave a smiling, one-only word press conference: 'Knackered!' At once a damp grey tarpaulin of mist closed in over the headland to muffle eerily the sound of

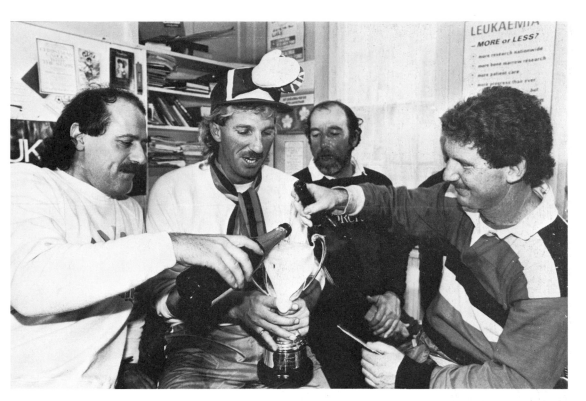

The prisoners released from the walk . . . Rance, Lander and Border spike the mineral water

the BBC's hired helicopter and the general squawk of the Desert Island Discs seagulls. 'It is', he said later, 'the best thing I have done in my life.' At 874 miles it was about £572 a mile. He averaged 4mph, walking for 220 hours or nine complete days. The distance was the equivalent of 70,000 cricketing singles. No wonder he prefers sixes.

The *Sun* said there was now no reason to quibble with Tim Hudson's view that Ian 'is Britains's biggest hero since Nelson – and that includes Churchill'; and a letter to *The Guardian* suggested a Cabinet re-shuffle – 'Bob Geldof for Chancellor, Princess Di for the Foreign Office, David Blunkett for Health . . . and Botham for Prime Minister.'

The swelling scene the Saturday before, at Taunton, had been witnessed with awe by Ian's fellow Somerset cricketer, Nigel Popplewell. It had stirred him to quote some lines from another legendary figure with Somerset connections, the poet, T.S. Eliot:

> No, I am not Prince Hamlet nor was meant to be
> Am an attendant Lord, one that will do
> To swell a progress, start a scene or two.

As Ian walked on, there was no doubt in anybody's mind just who was

Home is the hiker: 'It was honestly the most satisfying thing I've ever done'

Prince Hamlet. The role of the rest of us, and indeed that of the many who had joined him on his march from John o' Groats, was very much that of attendant Lords, swelling his progress.

Reflected Popplewell: Quite simply, Ian is less of the stuff of an attendant Lord than anyone else I've ever met.

12 West from Land's End

HE might almost have carried straight on, sou' sou' west, by walking (as any schoolboy will assure you he can) on the water all the way to Barbados. For in no time he would be sending Kathy up to rummage in the loft for his bat before setting forth for the England team's winter tour of the West Indies. Between times, there were a few blissful, blister-resting days in which to loll on the floor at home with Tigger and the kids, and cuddle Becky in the crook of his great arm in hours of chin-chucking, baby-talk reveries – only putting her down to her cot softly in order to go and bark with often terse rudeness to anyone who dared to telephone him. Some afternoons there was a chance, too, to stand on the fog-shroudy school touchlines to watch Liam play football or rugby. 'Get stuck in lad', he would murmur to the 8-year-old – and he would run to field the balls when they went out of play, and earnestly toss them back to the breathless, midget thrower-in like he was proud to have been chosen the school's official ballboy.

One evening, on the video, we watched the classic old 1950s film *The Vikings* – Tony Curtis's coracle versus Kirk Douglas's longship. All cudgels, claymores, and clamour. 'With a bit of coaching, you could do that', I told him. Indeed, next day, Botham was going to Hollywood – for a ten-day holiday with Hudson who, when all the cricketing was over, liked the idea of Ian being the next Errol Flynn. 'Sure, there's a thought about acting. Why not?' says Ian. 'If something like that came up, I think I could give it a real go. But I've no illusions. We'll just see what happens. This time I'm going over to have a holiday with Tim, a rest in the sun at his beach-house, and we might meet a few of his film friends. Have a few lunches, say "Hi!" If anything did come of acting in the future, well fine. It's no big deal as yet.'

He was back for a warm family Christmas just as a fresh blanket of snow wrapped itself around north Yorkshire. Mrs Thatcher's House of Commons tea-party touchingly brought together again all the walkers and workers from the great trek and after a group of Peers had taken them on a tour of the House of Lords, Ian laid on a Bacchanalian late night supper at a Battersea bistro to round off quite a year. Now, as he packed his bat and baggage for the West Indies, a brand new one beckoned.

In professional cricketing terms, I wondered how many more there might be for Botham. A career at the very top in professional sports can be cruelly short. Ian insists he has enjoyed the game more in the last two years than he has ever done. He has never deviated, either, from saying he will retire only when he stops enjoying his cricket. The England team's new assistant manager for the Caribbean tour was England's immediate past captain and longtime friend and champion of Botham, Bob Willis. The year before, Bob had said he would not put it past the younger man, one of these days and out of the blue, to stun the cricket world. 'Ian, to his credit, has never minded spending his money; but soon he will be losing count of all he is earning. Then perhaps thoughts of retirement might start nagging away at him... He is such a single-minded character that it would be just like him to go out at the top, rather than run the risk of getting kicked on the way down.'

In fact, only in professional cricket terms, is Ian's earning capacity a high one. In a rough earnings 'league table' of British sporting stars, Botham comes in far behind the likes of Steve Davis, the snooker player, Sandy Lyle, the golfer, Steve Cauthen, the jockey, or even the runners, Sebastian Coe and Steve Cram. The latter was said to earn at least £20,000 per four-minute mile – each evening's paypacket much more than Botham earned in his whole season for Somerset. Indeed, in the summer, the British racing driver, Derek Warwick, got nowhere near a chequered flag, yet was still paid a £350,000 salary by the manufacturers, Renault. In one televised race at the Crystal Palace in 1985, the newly naturalized, 'former' South African athlete, Zola Budd, earned for a ten-minute race in which she finished way down the field more than *twice* as much as Ian made in his whole year of playing for Somerset, England *and* his newspaper column in the *Sun*. Tim Hudson has a hectic as well as highly delicate job in guiding Botham's immediate future, and as Nigel Popplewell says: 'Ian's proudest boast is that he is an individual, affected by no man, who doesn't give a damn what people think. I hope that he retains this individuality and does not allow himself to be manipulated by lesser people than himself. He has mellowed to the good recently, becoming more aware that his indiscretions have repercussions beyond his immediate environment. I hope that he will not change for the worse. He is a great man with splendid qualities, the sort of person who makes you feel good to be with and a privilege to know, and his friendship is one of the reasons that I enjoyed my playing years so much.'

Oh, what a short life they lead, I thought as the England team's flight

The England touring party in the West Indies: left to right (standing) R.T. Robinson, D.M. Smith, L.B. Taylor, J.G. Thomas, P.H. Edmonds, N.A. Foster, P.R. Downton, B.N. French; (sitting) G.A. Gooch, I.T. Botham, M.W. Gatting, D.I. Gower (capt), A.J. Lamb, P. Willey, J.E. Emburey

BA 257 left the snow-flecked, freezing paddock at Heathrow for the tropical textures and terrors of the Caribbean early in the new year of 1986. As the aircraft levels out – the cardsharps, Gooch and Emburey, Downton and Ellison, settle four-square for the tour's first hand of bridge; Gower rattles through *The Times* crossword and then casts about to beat his record for the *Telegraph*'s; Gatting pores over chapter one of his latest whopping sci-fi novel; and the new boys, Smith of Worcester, and Thomas of Glamorgan (so challenging at Taunton a million months ago in May), uneasily and shyly integrate themselves amongst their new comrades. Botham and Willis share a glass of Ian's Côtes du Rhône, specially stowed away to toast the certain triumph of the trip. It has been nine years since they met – on another tour like this one. In the transient world of top line pro sport, nine years is an age. And in that time, Botham especially has crammed in so many hours of glorious life. What else can be left in his locker? What follows for this man who, as Spender had it, 'has travelled a short while toward the sun, and left the vivid air signed with his honour'? Willis recalls their first meeting nine years ago. It was the Centenary Test in Melbourne. 'Ian and Graham Stevenson of Yorkshire had been both playing club cricket in Victoria – having come

Right: Adjusting to the glare and the bounce in the Barbados nets . . . Ian has never been a studious 'netting' swot, prefering to resemble the urchin on the sands intent on a few last swipes before the tide comes in

Below: A long way from Land's End. Captain and chief lieutenant acclimatize above the coral reef before the guns of battle sound once more

Sir Garfield Sobers . . . the great all-rounder's one and only greatest all-rounder. Botham had the West Indian's picture pinned on the wall of his schoolboy's bedroom in Yeovil . . . along with those of the 1960s Chelsea FC stars. If Chelsea, not Crystal Palace, had asked the teenage Botham for trials, he might well have 'stuck to soccer'.

along to help out in the dressing-room. "Stevo", acting like the model junior pro, was very subdued, but Ian clearly considered himself to be one of the lads, behaving without the slightest sign of inhibitions. His main topic of conversation – more a monologue, actually – began: "When I'm playing for England next season . . ." I admit I did not take to him at all, wondering who on earth he thought he was, for even among the many legendary cricketing figures who were scattered around Melbourne during that frenzied week, Botham showed no shyness or humility. He would mingle with the likes of Percy Fender and Eddie Paynter, boasting about how he intended to take more wickets than Jeff Thomson and score more runs than Greg Chappell. I hate to imagine what the old-timers thought of him, but the wonder of the whole thing was, first, that he believed every word he was saying, and, second, that he was very soon proving that they had not been idle words. I knew nothing of his personality when I met him in Melbourne, nor of the eccentricities and the excesses which were to mark him out both as an unusual person and an unusual cricketer. He has not significantly changed from that day to this – he remains just as combative, just as indomitably self-confident and just as happily outrageous in company.'

The nation remained uncertain, but the subject highly approved when the painting by John Bellany was unveiled at the National Portrait Gallery. The distinguished artist said he had aimed to capture 'an essence of the chivalrous young knight of mediaeval times, the Arthurian paragon and champion'. The only other cricketer ever to be honoured by the NPG was W.G. Grace – 'who played with the whole man of him in full action, body, soul, heart and wits'

Already, as we landed in Barbados, Ian was at once smotheringly embraced by welcoming, laughing, noisy Caribbean friends. Our first taxi ride, appropriately, diverted us through Bayland and we passed the little house where Ian's first cricketing hero, Gary Sobers, was born. A poster of the greatest West Indian all-rounder was sellotaped to the wall of Ian's boyhood bedroom a long time ago in Yeovil. It also seemed a long time since John Arlott's farewell 'God speed' for a safe trip. In an ITV interview before they left, Brian Moore asked if it wasn't sad for sport that Botham continually attracted all the wrong sort of headlines – 'Oh dear, oh dear, oh dear', retorted the gravelly-voiced old sage of Alderney. 'With the present day Press as it is, the wrong sort of headlines would be attracted by the Archangel Gabriel if he came back to earth. It's incredible to me, we expect this chap Botham to work cricketing miracles every day and still behave like a sombre vegetable – well, you just can't expect that, the two things just don't go together.'

It was a far longer time ago that the Somerset captain bagged his place in front of the radiator at Oxford and sent out for whisky for his team: an age, it seemed now, since he got old Arthur Wellard's record in his sights, as well as the bowling of such stalwarts as, offhand, Cooper and

208

Graveney, Gifford and Holland, Lawson, McDermott, Mallender, and Marshall... Marshall, the demon (and Botham's 'skinny wimp') came down to watch England's first practice in Barbados. He and Ian laughed fraternally over the old times, then went off into the hills for a convivial evening – before narrowing their eyes for the new times...

In the ruthless nature of these youthful things, the new times will, very fast, simply all be old times. And then only those of us lucky enough to have lived for the decade that spanned the 1970s and '80s will *really* know of the old times. 'Cos, as the song says, we were there. Cardus saw W.G. Grace only once, but it was enough for him to tell how 'he played cricket with the whole man of him in full action, body, soul, heart, and wits.' And so say us who saw Botham in his pomp of 1985. On the cricket fields, we would not forget him if we could (and could not forget if we would), as morning after morning the summer's sun rose for him and he went forth and trod fresh grass – and the expectant, eager cry was sent about the land:

Botham's In!

I. T. Botham, 1985

SOMERSET v OXFORD UNIVERSITY

At Oxford, April 20, 22, 23. Match abandoned.

Somerset
Somerset 351-1 dec (J. G. Wyatt 145, P. M. Roebuck 123 not out, N. F. M. Popplewell 67 not out)

Oxford University
Oxford University 247-5 (J. D. Carr 115, G. J. Toogood 59)

SOMERSET v NOTTINGHAMSHIRE

At Taunton, April 27, 28, 29. Nottinghamshire won by nine wickets.

Umpires: B. Dudleston and A. G. T. Whitehead.

Somerset

J. G. Wyatt c Rice b Cooper	28	c French b Cooper	18
P. M. Roebuck c Johnson b Saxelby	12	c French b Cooper	36
N. F. M. Popplewell c French b Rice	2	run out	13
R. L. Ollis c French b Rice	44	c Broad b Such	0
B. C. Rose c Robinson b Pick	43	c French b Such	7
*I. T. Botham c French b Pick	90	(8) c Robinson b Such	50
V. J. Marks b Rice	10	(6) b Such	3
†T. Gard c French b Pick	1	(9) c Rice b Cooper	1
G. V. Palmer not out	45	(7) c Randall b Such	0
M. R. Davis not out	21	run out	1
A. P. Jones		not out	1
L-b 17, n-b 1	18	L-b 2, w 1	3
Total (101 overs — 8 wkts dec)	314		133

1-27 2-44 3-44 4-121 5-201 6-239 7-243 8-246

1-47 2-70 3-70 4-70 5-77 6-77 7-96 8-119 9-131

Bowling: *First innings*—Saxelby 23-7-49-1, Pick 25-5-79-3, Cooper 25-5-119-1, Rice 18-6-38-3, Such 10-5-12-0. *Second innings*—Saxelby 6-0-25-0, Pick 5-0-16-0, Such 18.2-5-73-5, Cooper 18-10-17-3.

Nottinghamshire

B. C. Broad c Gard b Jones	27	not out	56
R. T. Robinson c Gard b Davis	105	c Ollis b Jones	54
D. W. Randall c Gard b Davis	18	not out	32
*C. E. B. Rice c Wyatt b Marks	27		
P. Johnson b Davis	0		
J. D. Birch c Popplewell b Marks	38		
†B. N. French c Gard b Marks	18		
R. A. Pick c Roebuck b Marks	15		
K. Saxelby c Gard b Marks	0		
K. E. Cooper not out	17		
P. M. Such b sub b Davis	8		
B 1, l-b 8, w 2, n-b 4	15	B 7, 1-b 4, w 1, n-b 6	18
Total (78.5 overs)	288	(1 wkt)	160

1-86 2-119 3-185 4-187 5-188 6-235   1-98
7-244 8-244 9-275

Bowling: *First innings*—Davis 24.5-3-83-4, Palmer 10-0-46-0, Marks 23-5-66-5, Botham 7-1-22-0, Jones 14-2-62-1. *Second innings*—Davis 9-1-30-0, Palmer 7-1-28-0, Marks 18-4-52-0, Jones 12-2-39-1.

SOMERSET v GLAMORGAN

At Taunton, May 1, 2, 3. Glamorgan won by nine wickets.

Umpires: D. J. Constant and P. B. Wight.

Glamorgan

J. A. Hopkins b Davis	8	c Gard b Jones	12
A. L. Jones c Rose b Palmer	11	not out	18
G. C. Holmes st Gard b Marks	88	not out	9
Javed Miandad c Gard b Davis	86		
Younis Ahmed c Wyatt b Palmer	59		
*R. C. Ontong b Davis	64		
J. G. Thomas c Jones b Botham	37		
J. F. Steele not out	11		
B 5, l-b 4, w 8, n-b 6	23	L-b 1, w 2, n-b 1	4
Total (98.3 overs — 7 wkts dec)	387	(1 wkt)	43

Did not bat: J. Derrick, †T. Davies, S. R. Barwick

1-11 2-26 3-209 4-209 5-301 6-367 7-387   1-24

Bowling: *First innings*—Botham 18-4-45-1, Davis 20.3-2-61-3, Palmer 20-2-97-2, Marks 26-6-109-1, Jones 5-0-20-0, Popplewell 9-0-46-0. *Second innings*—Davis 5-0-14-0, Botham 2-1-4-0, Marks 4-2-7-0, Jones 2-0-9-1, Rose 1-0-8-0.

Somerset

J. G. Wyatt lbw b Derrick	45	c Jones b Barwick	19
P. M. Roebuck b Thomas	2	b Barwick	26
†T. Gard c Davies b Thomas	1	(6) lbw b Holmes	0
N. F. M. Popplewell c Thomas b Derrick	5	(3) b Holmes	81
R. L. Ollis lbw b Barwick	38	(4) c Barwick b Steele	14
B. C. Rose b Derrick	8	(5) c sub b Steele	0
*I. T. Botham c Derrick b Steele	112	lbw b Holmes	3
V. J. Marks not out	9	(9) c Davies b Ontong	18
G. V. Palmer c Jones b Steele	0	(10) c Miandad b Ontong	0
M. R. Davis run out	0	(8) lbw b Thomas	21
A. P. Jones c Holmes b Steele	0	not out	1
B 5, l-b 7, w 2, n-b 3	17	B 1, l-b 6, n-b 1	8
Total (71.1 overs)	237		191

1-6 2-12 3-47 4-79 5-89 6-222 7-228 1-30 2-53 3-111 4-119 5-120 6-134 7-153
8-228 9-233   8-190 9-190

Bowling: *First innings*—Thomas 22-7-43-2, Barwick 21-6-54-1, Ontong 14-1-69-0, Derrick 12-0-53-3, Steele 2.1-1-6-3. *Second innings*—Thomas 12-0-50-1, Barwick 12-3-33-2, Derrick 10-2-23-0, Ontong 11.5-2-36-2, Holmes 12-3-25-3, Steele 10-5-17-2.

SOMERSET v AUSTRALIA

At Taunton, May 8, 9, 10. Australia won by 233 runs.

Umpires: R. Julien and D. R. Shepherd.

Australia

A. M. J. Hilditch c Davis b Botham	20	c Harden b Booth	46
K. C. Wessels c Davis b Marks	41	c Botham b Booth	156
D. M. Wellham c Davis b Botham	64	not out	26
*A. R. Border c Botham b Marks	106		
D. C. Boon not out	62	not out	21
†W. B. Phillips not out	56		
G. R. J. Matthews		c Roebuck b Booth	22
C. J. McDermott		c sub b Marks	0
J. R. Thomson		lbw b Marks	7
R. G. Holland		c Popplewell b Booth	35
L-b 7	7	L-b 2, n-b 1	3
Total (4 wkts dec)	356	(6 wkts dec)	316

Did not bat: G. F. Lawson.

1-47 2-85 3-221 4-248   1-125 2-173 3-179 4-191 5-264 6-273

Bowling: *First Innings*—Davis 14-2-71-0, Turner 15-0-85-0, Botham 12-3-28-2, Marks 25-4-87-2, Popplewell 3-0-21-0, Booth 11-1-57-0. *Second Innings*—Davis 7-0-32-0, Turner 11-1-58-0, Botham 6-2-16-0, Marks 28-6-110-2, Booth 22-2-98-4.

Somerset

P. M. Roebuck c Phillips b Lawson	13	not out	33
R. J. Harden c Phillips b McDermott	0	c sub b Thomson	17
N. F. M. Popplewell c Boon b Thomson	25	lbw b McDermott	0
R. L. Ollis run out	11	lbw b Thompson	4
R. C. Rose retired hurt	81	absent injured	
*I. T. Botham st sub b Holland	65	c sub b Thomson	4
V. J. Marks c sub b Holland	50	c sub b Holland	48
†T. Gard c Wessels b Holland	30	c sub b Holland	0
S. C. Booth not out	4	c Boon b Holland	5
M. R. Davis st sub b Holland	11	c Holland b Thomson	4
M. S. Turner b Thomson	9	c sub b Thomson	0
B 4, l-b 4, n-b 7	15	B 4, l-b 1, n-b 5	10
Total (9 wkts)	314	(9 wkts)	125

1-34 2-54 3-65 4-65 5-170 6-273 7-290 8-308 9-314   1-10 2-15 3-43 4-49 5-111 6-113 7-114 8-118 9-125

Bowling: *First innings*—Thomson 17-3-75-2, Lawson 8-2-31-1, Holland 29.3-11-87-4, McDermott 11-1-71-1, Matthews 9-0-42-0. *Second innings*—Thomson 14-1-44-6, Holland 17.1-5-30-2, McDermott 12-2-46-1.

SOMERSET v HAMPSHIRE

At Taunton, May 22, 23, 24. Hampshire won by five wickets.

Umpires: C. Cook and R. Palmer.

Somerset

J. G. Wyatt c R. A. Smith b Marshall	7	b Connor	13
P. M. Roebuck b Tremlett	18		
N. F. M. Popplewell c James b Marshall	28	(2) c Greenidge b Tremlett	68
I. V. A. Richards c Greenidge b Tremlett	0	(3) c Greenidge b Tremlett	186
R. L. Ollis lbw b Tremlett	4	(4) c Terry b Marshall	34
*I. T. Botham b Marshall	149	(5) c Connor b C. L. Smith	19
V. J. Marks c Cowley b Connor	17	(6) not out	1
†T. Gard run out	9		
M. R. Davis not out	18		
J. Garner lbw b Cowley	17	(7) not out	19
M. S. Turner lbw b Cowley	17	L-b 9, w 1, n-b 8	18
B 4, l-b 6, w 2, n-b 5	17		
Total (73.4 overs)	298	(5 wkts dec)	358

1-12 2-51 3-51 4-58 5-70 6-108 7-166 8-251 9-272   1-34 2-146 3-298 4-328 5-338

Bowling: *First innings*—Marshall 22-4-81-3, Connor 18-5-68-1, James 13-1-64-0, Tremlett 15-5-36-3, Cowley 5.4-1-39-2. *Second innings*—Marshall 13-0-50-1, Connor 14-2-67-1, James 11-0-81-0, Cowley 15-2-80-0, Tremlett 14-4-43-2, C. L. Smith 4-1-28-1.

Hampshire

C. G. Greenidge lbw b Botham	12	c Botham b Garner	2
*V. P. Terry lbw b Garner	3	c Popplewell b Marks	83
C. L. Smith st Gard b Richards	16	b Botham	121
D. R. Turner c Marks b Richards	5	(5) c Davis b Botham	8
M. D. Marshall c sub b Garner	24	(4) c Popplewell b Garner	33
N. G. Cowley c Gard b Garner	0	not out	49
K. D. James c Davis b Marks	124		
T. M. Tremlett not out	102	(7) not out	7
B 1, l-b 7, w 2	10	B 12, 1-b 10	22
Total (110.3 overs – 8 wkts dec)	334	(5 wkts)	325

Did not bat: †R. J. Parks, C. A. Connor.

1/11 2/21 3/68 4/76 5/87 6/94 7/107 8/334   1/4 2/184 3/251 4/257 5/283

Bowling: *First innings*—Garner 22-7-39-3, Botham 15-2-69-1, Turner 21-4-46-1, Richards 20-8-55-2, Davis 15-3-53-0, Marks 17.3-3-64-1. *Second innings*—Garner 12.3-2-45-2, Botham 13-0-60-2, Davis 11-1-37-0, Turner 4-0-22-0, Marks 17-1-105-1, Richards 8-1-34-0.

GLOUCESTERSHIRE v SOMERSET

At Bristol, May 25, 27 (no play), 28 (no play). Match abandoned.

Umpires: D. G. L. Evans and K. J. Lyons.

Somerset

J. G. Wyatt c Russell b Curran	46
N. F. M. Popplewell c Russell b Curran	31
N. A. Felton c Russell b Lawrence	29
I. V. A. Richards c Lloyds b Bainbridge	26
R. L. Ollis c and b Graveney	8
*I. T. Botham c Stovold b Lawrence	5
V. J. Marks c Athey b Lawrence	0
†T. Gard c Stovold b Graveney	30
M. R. Davis c Lloyds b Graveney	7
J. Garner not out	8
M. S. Turner not out	13
L-b 5, w 1, n-b 2	8
Total (70 overs – 9 wkts)	211

1-66 2-91 3-126 4-136 5-141 6-141 7-166 8-183 9-194

Bowling: Lawrence 22-3-76-3, Walsh 15-3-38-0, Curran 10-1-36-2, Bainbridge 9-2-30-1, Graveney 11-3-22-3, Lloyds 3-1-4-0.

FIRST TEXACO ONE-DAY INTERNATIONAL – ENGLAND v AUSTRALIA

At Old Trafford, May 30. Australia won by three wickets.

Umpires: D. G. L. Evans and K. E. Palmer.   Man of the Match: I. T. Botham.

England

G. A. Gooch c O'Donnell b Holland	57
G. Fowler c Phillips b McDermott	10
*D. I. Gower b Lawson	3
A. J. Lamb c Phillips b Lawson	0
I. T. Botham b Matthews	72
M. W. Gatting not out	31
P. Willey b Holland	12
†P. R. Downton c Matthews b Lawson	11
P. H. Edmonds c Border b Lawson	0
P. J. W. Allott b McDermott	2
N. G. Cowans c and b McDermott	1
B 2, l-b 7, w 2, n-b 9	20
Total (54 overs)	**219**

1-21 2-27 3-27 4-143 5-160 6-181 7-203 8-203 9-213

Bowling: Lawson 10-1-26-4, McDermott 11-0-46-3, O'Donnell 11-0-44-0, Matthews 11-1-45-1, Holland 11-2-49-2,

Australia

G. M. Wood c Downton b Cowans	8
K. C. Wessels c Botham b Willey	39
D. M. Wellham c and b Edmonds	12
*A. R. Border c and b Allott	59
D. C. Boon c Botham b Gooch	12
†W. B. Phillips c Gatting b Cowans	28
S. P. O'Donnell b Botham	1
G. R. J. Matthews not out	29
G. F. Lawson not out	14
B2, l-b 12, w 4	18
Total (54.1 overs – 7 wkts)	**220**

Did not bat: C. J. McDermott, R. G. Holland.

1-19 2-52 3-74 4-118 5-156 6-157 7-186

Bowling: Cowans 10.1-1-44-2, Botham 11-2-41-1, Edmonds 11-2-33-1, Allott 11-0-47-1, Willey 9-1-31-1, Gooch 2-0-10-1.

SECOND TEXACO ONE-DAY INTERNATIONAL – ENGLAND v AUSTRALIA

At Edgbaston, June 1. Australia won by four wickets.

Umpires: D. J. Constant and D. R. Shepherd.   Man of the Match: A. R. Border.

England

G. A. Gooch b McDermott	115
R. T. Robinson c and b O'Donnell	26
*D. I. Gower c Phillips b O'Donnell	0
A. J. Lamb b Thomson	25
I. T. Botham c Wellham b Lawson	29
M. W. Gatting c Lawson b McDermott	6
P. Willey c Phillips b Lawson	0
†P. R. Downton not out	16
P. H. Edmonds not out	6
L-b 2, w 2, n-b 4	8
Total (55 overs – 7 wkts)	**231**

Did not bat: P. J. W. Allott, N. G. Cowans.

1-63 2-69 3-134 4-193 5-206 6-208 7-216

Bowling: Lawson 11-0-53-2, McDermott 11-0-56-2, O'Donnell 11-2-32-2, Thomson 11-0-47-1, Matthews 10-0-38-0, Border 1-0-3-0.

Australia

K. C. Wessels c and b Willey	57
G. M. Wood lbw b Cowans	5
D. M. Wellham lbw b Botham	7
*A. R. Border not out	85
D. C. Boon b Allott	13
†W. B. Phillips c Gatting b Cowans	14
S. P. O'Donnell b Botham	28
G. R. J. Matthews not out	8
L-b 13, w 2, n-b 1	16
Total (54 overs – 6 wkts)	**233**

Did not bat: G. F. Lawson, J.R. Thomson, C. J. McDermott.

1-10 2-19 3-116 4-137 5-157 6-222

Bowling: Botham 10-2-38-2, Cowans 11-2-42-2, Allott 10-1-40-1, Willey 11-1-38-1, Edmonds 10-0-48-0, Gooch 2-0-14-0.

THIRD TEXACO ONE-DAY INTERNATIONAL – ENGLAND v AUSTRALIA

At Lord's, June 3. England won by eight wickets.

Umpires: H. D. Bird and B. J. Meyer.   Man of the Match: D. I. Gower.

Australia

G. M. Wood not out	114
A. M. J. Hilditch lbw b Foster	4
G. M. Ritchie c Gooch b Botham	15
*A. R. Border b Gooch	44
D. C. Boon c Gower b Willey	45
†W. B. Phillips run out	10
S. P. O'Donnell not out	0
B 2, l-b 13, w 6, n-b 1	22
Total (55 overs – 5 wkts)	**254**

Did not bat: G. R. J. Matthews, G. F. Lawson, C. J. McDermott, J. R. Thomson.

1-6 2-47 3-143 4-228 5-252

Bowling: Cowans 8-2-22-0, Foster 11-0-55-1, Botham 8-1-27-1, Allott 7-1-45-0, Gooch 11-0-46-1, Willey 10-1-44-1.

England

G. A. Gooch not out	117
R. T. Robinson lbw b McDermott	7
*D. I. Gower c Border b McDermott	102
A. J. Lamb not out	9
B 2, l-b 9, w 2, n-b 9	22
Total (49 overs – 2 wkts)	**257**

Did not bat: I. T. Botham, M. W. Gatting, P. Willey, †P. R. Downton, N. A. Foster, P. J. W. Allott, N. G. Cowans.

1-25 2-227

Bowling: Lawson 9-0-37-0, McDermott 10-0-51-2, Thomson 8-1-50-0, O'Donnell 11-0-54-0, Matthews 10-0-49-0, Border 1-0-5-0.

SOMERSET v GLOUCESTERSHIRE

At Bath, June 8, 10, 11. Match drawn.

Umpires: D. J. Constant and J. H. Hampshire.

Gloucestershire

A. W. Stovold b Garner	0	c Botham b Garner	2
P. W. Romaines c Felton b Botham	2	not out	22
C. W. J. Athey lbw b Garner	52	(4) c sub b Davis	2
P. Bainbridge lbw b Garner	0	(3) c sub b Davis	17
B. F. Davison c Gard b Davis	43	b Marks	26
K. M. Curran c Botham b Marks	83		
J. W. Lloyds not out	95	(6) not out	6
*D. A. Graveney b Marks	0		
†R. C. Russell lbw b Marks	0		
D. V. Lawrence c Ollis b Marks	8		
C. A. Walsh not out	33		
B 11, l-b 5	16	B 9	9

Total (103 overs – 9 wkts dec)	332	(4 wkts)	84

1-0 2-8 3-15 4-80 5-139 6-262 7-262   1-2 2-27 3-31 4-68
8-264 9-294

Bowling: *First innings*—Garner 28-7-68-3, Botham 16-2-54-1, Richards 27-7-62-0, Davis 11-1-57-1, Marks 17-5-65-4, Booth 4-0-10-0. *Second innings*—Garner 7-2-21-1, Davis 8-3-17-2, Marks 12-5-24-1, Booth 10-5-13-0.

Somerset

N. F. M. Popplewell c Lawrence b Curran	44
N. A. Felton lbw b Curran	15
R. E. Hayward b Lloyds	12
R. L. Ollis b Graveney	19
S. C. Booth b Curran	10
I. V. A. Richards c Stovold b Walsh	27
*I. T. Botham not out	76
V. J. Marks c Graveney b Walsh	1
M. R. Davis c Athey b Graveney	14
J. Garner b Graveney	1
†T. Gard absent injured	
B 8, l-b 2, w 6, n-b 8	24

Total (57.1 overs)	243

1-63 2-72 3-107 4-107 5-147 6-159 7-184 8-229 9-243

Bowling: Lawrence 10-1-79-0, Walsh 19-3-65-2, Curran 15-5-52-3, Lloyds 5-2-12-1, Graveney 8.1-3-25-3.

FIRST CORNHILL TEST MATCH – ENGLAND v AUSTRALIA

At Headingley, June 13, 14, 15, 17, 18. England won by five wickets.

Umpires: B. J. Meyer and K. E. Palmer.

Australia

G. M. Wood lbw b Allott	14	(2) c Lamb b Botham	3
A. M. J. Hilditch c Downton b Gooch	119	(1) c Robinson b Emburey	80
K. C. Wessels c Botham b Emburey	36	b Emburey	64
*A. R. Border c Botham b Cowans	32	c Downton b Botham	8
D. C. Boon b Gooch	14	b Cowans	22
G. M. Ritchie b Botham	46	b Emburey	1
†W. B. Phillips c Gower b Emburey	30	c Lamb b Botham	91
C. J. McDermott b Botham	18	(10) c Downton b Emburey	6
S. P. O'Donnell lbw b Botham	0	(8) c Downton b Botham	24
G. F. Lawson c Downton b Allott	0	(9) c Downton b Emburey	15
J. R. Thomson not out	4	not out	2
L-b 13, w 4, n-b 1	18	B 4, l-b 3, w 1	8

Total	331		324

1-23 2-155 3-201 4-229 5-229 6-284   1-5, 2-144, 3-151, 4-159, 5-160, 6-192,
7-326 8-326 9-327   7-272, 8-307, 9-318

Bowling: *First Innings*—Cowans 20-4-78-1, Allott 22-3-74-2, Botham 29.1-8-86-3, Gooch 21-4-57-2, Emburey 6-1-23-2. *Second Innings*—Cowans 13-2-50-1, Allott 17-4-57-0, Botham 33-7-107-4, Gooch 9-3-21-0, Emburey 43.4-14-82-5.

England

G. A. Gooch lbw b McDermott	5	lbw b O'Donnell	28
R. T. Robinson c Boon b Lawson	175	b Lawson	21
*D. I. Gower c Phillips b McDermott	17	c Border b O'Donnell	5
M. W. Gatting c Hilditch b McDermott	53	c Phillips b Lawson	12
A. J. Lamb b O'Donnell	38	not out	31
I. T. Botham b Thomson	60	b O'Donnell	12
P. Willey c Hilditch b Lawson	36		
†P. R. Downton c Border b McDermott	54	not out	3
J. E. Emburey b Lawson	21		
P. J. W. Allott c Boon b Thomson	12		
N. G. Cowans not out	22		
B 5, l-b 16, w 5, n-b 14	40	L-b 7, w 1, n-b 3	11

Total	533	(5 wkts)	123

1-14 2-50 3-186 4-264 5-344 6-417 7-422   1-44 2-59 3-71 4-83 5-110
8-462 9-484

Bowling: *First innings*—Lawson 26-4-117-3, McDermott 32-2-134-4, Thomson 34-3-166-2, O'Donnell 27-8-77-1, Border 3-0-16-0, Wessels 3-2-2-0. *Second innings*—Lawson 16-4-51-2, McDermott 4-0-20-0, O'Donnell 15.4-5-37-3.

SURREY v SOMERSET

At The Oval, June 22, 24, 25. Match abandoned.

Umpires: J. Birkenshaw and R. A. White.

Somerset

N. F. M. Popplewell c Richards b Gray	30	c Lynch b Richards	35
P. M. Roebuck c Butcher b Gray	34	c Needham b Richards	0
N. A. Felton c Lynch b Pauline	21		
I. V. A. Richards b Pauline	5		
R. E. Hayward c Richards b Pauline	2		
*I. T. Botham c Richards b Gray	32	(3) not out	72
V. J. Marks c Needham b Gray	2		
†T. Gard c Jesty b Thomas	15		
M. R. Davis b Gray	11		
J. Garner c Lynch b Thomas	7		
M. S. Turner not out	0		
B 5, l-b 10, w 1, n-b 13	29	B 4, l-b 3	7

Total (63.2 overs)	188	(2 wkts dec)	114

1-44 2-85 3-100 4-117 5-118 6-122 7-168   1-4 2-114
8-170 9-184

Bowling: *First innings*—Thomas 20-4-55-2, Gray 20.2-4-69-5, Pauline 16-3-42-3, Butcher 7-4-7-0. *Second innings*—Clinton 6-0-46-0, Richards 8-1-42-2, Stewart 2-0-19-0.

Surrey

A. R. Butcher not out	6	c Richards b Botham	37
G. S. Clinton not out	4	not out	16
A. J. Stewart		not out	0
		L-b 5	5

Total (4 overs – 0 wkt dec)	10	(1 wkt)	58

1-54

Did not bat: *T. E. Jesty, M. A. Lynch, D. B. Pauline, A. Needham, †C. J. Richards, D. J. Thomas, P. I. Pocock, A. H. Gray.

Bowling: *First innings*—Garner 2-1-6-0, Davis 2-1-4-0. *Second innings*—Garner 7-1-30-0, Davis 7-0-21-0, Botham 0.4-0-2-1

SECOND CORNHILL TEST MATCH – ENGLAND v AUSTRALIA
At Lord's, June 27, 28, 29, July 1, 2. Australia won by four wickets.

Umpires: H. D. Bird and D. G. L. Evans.

England
G. A. Gooch lbw b McDermott	30	c Phillips b McDermott		17
R. T. Robinson lbw b McDermott	6	b Holland		12
*D. I. Gower c Border b McDermott	86	(5) c Phillips b McDermott		22
M. W. Gatting lbw b Lawson	14	(6) not out		75
A. J. Lamb c Phillips b Lawson	47	(7) c Holland b Lawson		9
I. T. Botham c Ritchie b Lawson	5	(8) c Border b Holland		85
†P. R. Downton c Wessels b McDermott	21	(9) c Boon b Holland		0
J. E. Emburey b O'Donnell	33	(3) b Lawson		20
P. H. Edmonds c Border b McDermott	21	(10) c Boon b Holland		1
N. A. Foster c Wessels b McDermott	3	(11) c Border b Holland		0
P. J. W. Allott not out	1	(4) b Lawson		0
B 1, l-b 4, w 1, n-b 17	23	B 1, l-b 12, w 3, n-b 4		20
Total	290			261

1-26 2-51 3-99 4-179 5-184 6-211 7-241 8-273 9-283

1-32 2-34 3-38 4-57 5-77 6-98 7-229 8-229 9-261

Bowling: *First innings*—Lawson 25-2-91-3, McDermott 29.2-5-70-6, O'Donnell 22-3-82-1, Holland 23-6-42-0. *Second innings*—Lawson 23-0-86-3, McDermott 20-2-84-2, O'Donnell 5-0-10-0, Holland 42-12-68-5.

Australia
G. M. Wood c Emburey b Allott	8	(2) c Lamb b Botham		6
A. M. J. Hilditch c Foster	14	(1) c Lamb b Botham		0
K. C. Wessels lbw b Botham	11	run out		28
*A. R. Border c Gooch b Botham	196	(5) not out		41
D. C. Boon c Downton b Botham	4	(6) b Edmonds		1
G. M. Ritchie lbw b Botham	94	(4) b Allott		2
†W. B. Phillips c Edmonds b Botham	21	c Edmonds b Emburey		29
S. P. O'Donnell c Lamb b Edmonds	48	not out		9
G. F. Lawson not out	5			
C. J. McDermott run out	9			
R. G. Holland b Edmonds	0			
L-b 10, w 1, n-b 4	15	L-b 11		11
Total	425	(6 wkts)		127

1-11 2-24 3-80 4-101 5-317 6-347 7-398 8-414 9-425

1-0 2-9 3-22 4-63 5-65 6-116

Bowling: *First innings*—Foster 23-1-83-1, Allott 30-4-70-1, Botham 24-2-109-5, Edmonds 25.4-5-85-2, Gooch 3-1-11-0, Emburey 19-3-57-0. *Second innings*—Allott 7-4-8-1, Botham 15-0-49-2, Edmonds 16-5-35-1, Emburey 8-4-24-1.

SOMERSET v LEICESTERSHIRE
At Taunton, July 6, 8, 9. Match drawn.

Umpires: A. A. Jones and B. Leadbeater.

Somerset
N. F. M. Popplewell lbw b Clift	24	c Taylor b Cook		53
P. M. Roebuck c Butcher b Taylor	21	b Clift		49
N. A. Felton c Balderstone b Taylor	112	c Garnham b Clift		58
I. V. A. Richards c Garnham b Taylor	47			
R. E. Hayward lbw b Cook	28	(4) lbw b Willey		8
*I. T. Botham st Garnham b Cook	48	(5) not out		50
V. J. Marks b Taylor	20	(6) c Cook b Clift		8
†T. Gard c Garnham b Agnew	15			
C. H. Dredge c Balderstone b Taylor	0			
S. C. Booth not out	17			
M. S. Turner st Garnham b Cook	18	(7) not out		15
B 5, l-b 5, n-b 7	17	L-b 6, n-b 1		7
Total (99.5 overs)	367	(5 wkts dec)		248

1-33 2-61 3-134 4-193 5-261 6-311 7-318 8-318 9-339

1-74 2-152 3-175 4-175 5-209

Bowling: *First innings*—Agnew 19-3-85-1, Taylor 28-4-77-5, Clift 23-3-86-1, Willey 10-1-32-0, Cook 19.5-4-77-3. *Second innings*—Taylor 7-2-13-0, Agnew 13-3-49-0, Cook 23-7-73-1, Willey 23-6-60-1, Clift 10-1-47-3.

Leicestershire
I. P. Butcher lbw b Dredge	38	lbw b Booth		3
J. C. Balderstone c Popplewell b Marks	27	b Marks		36
*D. I. Gower c and b Marks	4	c Felton b Marks		3
P. Willey c Gard b Marks	43	c Gard b Booth		80
J. J. Whitaker c Popplewell b Marks	105	c Dredge b Botham		19
N. E. Briers c Richards b Booth	34	run out		17
M. A. Garnham lbw b Marks	1	(9) not out		8
P. B. Clift not out	40	c Booth b Marks		0
N. G. B. Cook lbw b Marks	8	(10) not out		8
J. P. Agnew c and b Marks	17			
L. B. Taylor not out	20	(7) b Marks		8
B 1, l-b 4, n-b 1	6	B 3, l-b 5, n-b 2		10
Total (110 overs -- 9 dec)	343	(8 wkts)		192

1-66 2-66 3-76 4-152 5-241 6-242 7-269 8-283 9-321

1-26 2-29 3-88 4-127 5-167 6-175 7-176 8-178

Bowling: *First innings*—Botham 3-1-2-0, Turner 10-2-37-0, Marks 49-11-143-7, Booth 27-9-89-1, Dredge 15-1-50-1, Richards 6-0-17-0. *Second innings*—Dredge 3-0-12-0, Turner 3-1-8-0, Booth 17-3-63-2, Marks 27-8-65-4, Botham 12-5-32-1, Roebuck 1-0-4-0.

THIRD CORNHILL TEST MATCH – ENGLAND v AUSTRALIA
At Trent Bridge, July 11, 12, 13, 15, 16. Match drawn.

Umpires: D. J. Constant and A. G. T. Whitehead.

England
G. A. Gooch c Wessels b Lawson	70	c Ritchie b McDermott		48
R. T. Robinson c Border b Lawson	38	not out		77
*D. I. Gower c Phillips b O'Donnell	166	c Phillips b McDermott		17
M. W. Gatting run out	74	not out		35
A. J. Lamb lbw b Lawson	17			
I. T. Botham c O'Donnell b McDermott	38			
†P. R. Downton c Ritchie b McDermott	0			
A. Sidebottom c O'Donnell b Lawson	2			
J. E. Emburey not out	16			
P. H. Edmonds b Holland	12			
P. J. W. Allott c Border b Lawson	7			
B 12, w 1, n-b 3	16	B 1, l-b 16, n-b 2		19
Total	456	(2 wkts)		196

1-55 2-171 3-358 4-365 5-416 6-416 7-419 8-419 9-443

1-79 2-107

Bowling: *First innings*—Lawson 39.4-10-103-5, McDermott 35-3-147-2, O'Donnell 29-4-104-1, Holland 26-3-90-1. *Second innings*—Lawson 13-4-32-0, McDermott 16-2-42-2, O'Donnell 10-2-26-0, Holland 26-9-69-0, Ritchie 1-0-10-0.

Australia
G. M. Wood c Robinson b Botham	172
A. M. J. Hilditch lbw b Allott	47
R. G. Holland lbw b Sidebottom	10
K. C. Wessels c Downton b Emburey	33
*A. R. Border c Botham b Edmonds	23
D. C. Boon c and b Emburey	15
G. M. Ritchie b Edmonds	146
†W. B. Phillips b Emburey	2
S. P. O'Donnell c Downton b Botham	46
G. F. Lawson c Gooch b Botham	18
C. J. McDermott not out	0
B 6, l-b 7, w 2, n-b 12	27
Total	539

1-87 2-128 3-205 4-234 5-263 6-424 7-437 8-491 9-539

Bowling: Botham 34.2-3-107-3, Sidebottom 18.4-3-65-1, Allott 18-4-55-1, Edmonds 66-18-155-2, Emburey 55-15-129-3, Gooch 8.2-2-13-0, Gatting 1-0-2-0.

WARWICKSHIRE v SOMERSET

At Edgbaston, July 24, 25, 26. Match drawn.

Umpires: J. H. Hampshire and H. J. Rhodes.

Somerset

N. F. M. Popplewell c Gifford b Hoffman	4	c Amiss b Gifford	70
P. M. Roebuck c Humpage b Ferreira	40	c Amiss b Gifford	81
N. A. Felton c Humpage b Hoffman	10	b Gifford	8
I. V. A. Richards c Humpage b Lethbridge	65	(5) c Humpage b Pierson	53
B. C. Rose c Humpage b Ferreira	16	(6) run out	14
*I. T. Botham c Humpage b Lethbridge	5	(7) not out	138
V. J. Marks c Gifford b Ferreira	6	(8) not out	8
†T. Gard c Amiss b Ferreira	7	(4) c Dyer b Gifford	16
M. R. Davis c Humpage b Hoffman	1		
S. C. Booth c Dyer b Gifford	28		
C. H. Dredge not out	10		
B 4, l-b 3, w 7, n-b 1	15	B 10, l-b 18, w 2	30
Total (69.5 overs) 207		(6 wkts dec) 418	

1-4 2-30 3-120 4-121 5-126 6-133 7-155 8-164 9-168

1-112 2-132 3-188 4-213 5-249 6-345

Bowling: *First innings*—Hoffman 16-2-53-3, Smith 9-2-19-0, Ferreira 24-10-61-4, Lethbridge 19-4-62-2, Gifford 1.5-0-5-1. *Second innings*—Hoffman 5-0-33-0, Smith 7-2-33-0, Lethbridge 4-0-17-0, Ferreira 9-4-15-0, Gifford 42-20-128-4, Pierson 34-8-164-1.

Warwickshire

R. I. H. B. Dyer c Booth b Marks	106	c Botham b Davis	4
G. J. Lord b Davis	9	not out	17
A. I. Kallicharran c Rose b Dredge	48	not out	51
D. L. Amiss c Booth b Marks	14		
C. Lethbridge c Richards b Booth	47		
†G. W. Humpage c and b Botham	33		
P. A. Smith lbw b Botham	62		
A. M. Ferreira b Botham	4		
A. R. K. Pierson not out	2		
*N. Gifford run out	0		
D. S. Hoffman b Botham	0		
B 5, l-b 4, w 4	13	B 2	2
Total (118 overs) 338		(1 wkt) 74	

1-14 2-86 3-113 4-181 5-230 6-332 7-336 8-338 9-338   1-4

Bowling: *First innings*—Botham 22-7-63-4, Davis 14-2-56-1, Dredge 11-4-21-1, Richards 8-2-26-0, Marks 40-13-91-2, Booth 23-3-72-1. *Second innings*—Davis 3-1-3-1, Marks 12.4-5-22-0, Booth 2-0-15-0, Botham 8-1-32-0.

SOMERSET v ESSEX

At Taunton, July 27, 29 (no play), 30. Essex won by seven wickets.

Umpires: K. J. Lyons and R. Palmer.

Somerset

N. F. M. Popplewell c East b I. L. Pont	27
P. M. Roebuck c East b I. L. Pont	17
N. A. Felton c East b I. L. Pont	49
I. V. A. Richards c East b I. L. Pont	5
J. G. Wyatt c East b Pringle	50
*I. T. Botham c East b I. L. Pont	152
V. J. Marks c East b Pringle	17
†T. Gard not out	27
M. R. Davis c East b Pringle	7
C. H. Dredge b I. L. Pont	1
J. Garner not out	4
L-b 4, w 1, n-b 2	7
Total (100 overs – 9 wkts dec) 363	

1-36 2-45 3-56 4-148 5-162 6-246 7-343 8-352 9-353

Second innings forfeited.
Bowling: Pringle 30-2-90-3, I. L. Pont 24-2-103-5, Topley 24-3-86-0, K. R. Pont 11-0-45-1, Acfield 11-1-35-0.

Essex

G. A. Gooch c Gard b Wyatt	19	not out	173
B. R. Hardie not out	25	b Dredge	20
P. J. Prichard not out	18	b Dredge	44
K. S. McEwan		lbw b Dredge	0
D. R. Pringle		not out	45
L-b 4, w 2	6	L-b 11, n-b 3	14
Total (13 overs – 1 wkt dec) 68		(3 wkts) 296	

Did not bat: *K. W. R. Fletcher, K. R. Pont, †D. E. East, I. L. Pont, D. L. Acfield, D. Topley.

1-25

1-84 2-165 3-165

Bowling: *First innings*—Garner 1-1-0-0, Wyatt 6-0-40-1, Hoebuck 6-0-24-0. *Second innings*—Botham 8-0-61-0, Davis 16-2-65-0, Dredge 22-0-82-3, Marks 18-2-48-0, Wyatt 8-0-18-0, Popplewell 2-0-11-0.

FOURTH CORNHILL TEST MATCH – ENGLAND v AUSTRALIA

At Old Trafford, August 1, 2, 3, 5, 6. Match drawn.

Umpires: H. D. Bird and D. R. Shepherd.

Australia

K. C. Wessels c Botham b Emburey	34	(3) c and b Emburey	50
A. M. J. Hilditch b Gower b Edmonds	49	(1) b Emburey	40
D. C. Boon c Lamb b Botham	61	(5) b Emburey	7
*A. R. Border st Downton b Edmonds	8	not out	146
G. M. Ritchie c and b Edmonds	4	(6) b Emburey	31
†W. B. Phillips c Downton b Botham	36	(7) not out	39
G. R. J. Matthews b Botham	4	(2) c and b Edmonds	17
S. P. O'Donnell b Edmonds	45		
G. F. Lawson c Downton b Botham	4		
C. J. McDermott lbw b Emburey	0		
R. G. Holland not out	5		
L-b 3, w 1, n-b 3	7	B 1, l-b 6, n-b 3	10
Total 257		(5 wkts) 340	

1-71 2-97 3-118 4-122 5-193 6-198 7-211 8-223 9-224

1-38 2-85 3-126 4-138 5-213

Bowling: *First innings*—Botham 23-4-79-4, Agnew 14-0-65-0, Allott 13-1-29-0, Emburey 24-7-41-2, Edmonds 15.1-4-40-4. *Second innings*—Botham 15-3-50-0, Agnew 9-2-34-0, Allott 6-2-4-0, Emburey 51-17-99-4, Edmonds 54-12-122-1. Gatting 4-0-14-0, Lamb 1-0-10-0.

England

G. A. Gooch lbw b McDermott	74
R. T. Robinson c Border b McDermott	10
*D. I. Gower c Hilditch b McDermott	47
M. W. Gatting c Phillips b McDermott	160
A. J. Lamb run out	67
I. T. Botham c O'Donnell b McDermott	20
†P. R. Downton b McDermott	23
J. E. Emburey not out	31
P. H. Edmonds b McDermott	1
P. J. W. Allott b McDermott	7
J. P. Agnew not out	2
B 7, l-b 16, n-b 17	40
Total (9 wkts dec) 482	

1-21 2-142 3-148 4-304 5-339 6-430 7-448 8-450 9-470

Bowling: Lawson 37-7-114-0, McDermott 36-3-141-8, Holland 38-7-101-0, O'Donnell 21-6-82-0, Matthews 9-2-21-0.

SOMERSET v NORTHAMPTONSHIRE

At Weston-super-Mare, August 10, 12, 13 (no play). Match abandoned.

Umpires: C. Cook and B. Leadbeater.

Somerset

J. G. Wyatt run out	16
P. M. Roebuck c Ripley b Griffiths	53
N. A. Felton c Ripley b Mallender	9
I. V. A. Richards lbw b Griffiths	58
R. J. Harden b Mallender	10
*I. T. Botham c Cook b Mallender	134
V. J. Marks st Ripley b Harper	0
J. C. M. Atkinson c Larkins b Mallender	79
†T. Gard c Lamb b Griffiths	11
C. H. Dredge not out	25
A. P. Jones b Mallender	1
B 3, l-b 8, n-b 2	13

Total (104.2 overs) 409

1-23 2-40 3-143 4-144 5-193 6-194 7-371 8-371 9-393

Bowling: Mallender 26.2-5-83-5, Griffiths 29-4-127-3, Harper 24-4-52-1, Larkins 17-1-82-0, Williams 1-0-7-0, Wild 7-0-47-0.

Northamptonshire

*G. Cook not out	39
W. Larkins lbw b Dredge	29
R. J. Boyd-Moss not out	19

Total (29 overs – 1 wkt) 87

Did not bat: A. J. Lamb, R. J. Bailey, R. G. Williams, D. J. Wild, R. A. Harper, †D. Ripley, N. A. Mallender, B. J. Griffiths.

1-57

Bowling: Botham 1-0-4-0, Atkinson 5-1-22-0, Dredge 14-1-41-1, Jones 4-0-12-0, Richards 5-1-8-0.

FIFTH CORNHILL TEST MATCH – ENGLAND v AUSTRALIA

At Edgbaston, August 15, 16, 17, 19, 20. England won by an innings and 118 runs.

Umpires: D. J. Constant and D. R. Shepherd.

Australia

G. M. Wood c Edmonds b Botham	19	(2) c Robinson b Ellison	10
A. M. J. Hilditch c Downton b Edmonds	39	(1) c Ellison b Botham	10
K. C. Wessels c Downton b Ellison	83	c Downton b Ellison	10
*A. R. Border c Edmonds b Ellison	45	(5) b Ellison	2
G. M. Ritchie c Botham b Ellison	8	(6) c Lamb b Emburey	20
†W. B. Phillips c Robinson b Ellison	15	(7) c Gower b Edmonds	59
S. P. O'Donnell c Downton b Taylor	1	(8) b Botham	11
G. F. Lawson run out	53	(9) c Gower b Edmonds	3
C. J. McDermott c Gower b Ellison	35	(10) c Edmonds b Botham	8
J. R. Thomson not out	28	(11) not out	4
R. G. Holland c Edmonds b Ellison	0	(4) lbw b Ellison	0
L-b 4, w 1, n-b 4	9	B 1, l-b 3, n-b 1	5

Total 335   142

1-44 2-92 3-189 4-191 5-207 6-208 7-218 8-276 9-335   1-10 2-32 3-32 4-35 5-36 6-113 7-117 8-120 9-137

Bowling: *First innings*—Botham 27-1-108-1, Taylor 26-5-78-1, Ellison 31.5-9-77-6, Edmonds 20-4-47-1, Emburey 9-2-21-0. *Second innings*—Botham 14.1-2-52-3, Taylor 13-4-27-0, Ellison 9-3-27-4, Edmonds 15-9-13-2, Emburey 13-5-19-1.

England

G. A. Gooch c Phillips b Thomson	19
R. T. Robinson b Lawson	148
*D. I. Gower c Border b Lawson	215
M. W. Gatting not out	100
A. J. Lamb c Wood b McDermott	46
I. T. Botham c Thomson b McDermott	18
†P. R. Downton not out	0
B 7, l-b 20, n-b 22	49

Total (5 wkts dec) 595

Did not bat: J. E. Emburey, R. M. Ellison, P. H. Edmonds, L. B. Taylor.

1-38 2-369 3-463 4-572 5-592

Bowling: Lawson 37-1-135-2, McDermott 31-2-155-2, Thomson 19-1-101-1, Holland 25-4-95-0, O'Donnell 16-3-69-0, Border 6-1-13-0.

LANCASHIRE v SOMERSET

At Old Trafford, August 24 (no play) 26, 27. Lancashire won by six wickets.

Umpires: J. W. Holder and P. B. Wight.

Somerset

P. M. Roebuck lbw b Patterson	88
J. G. Wyatt lbw b Allott	5
R. L. Ollis c Simmons b Watkinson	4
I. V. A. Richards c Fairbrother b Simmons	120
R. J. Harden not out	19
*I. T. Botham not out	76
B 2, l-b 6, w 1, n-b 8	17

Total (81 overs – 4 wkts dec) 329

Second innings forfeited.

Did not bat: J. C. M. Atkinson, V. J. Marks, †T. Gard, J. Garner, C. H. Dredge.

1-8 2-23 3-229 4-230

Bowling: Patterson 15-3-61-1, Allott 16-4-58-1, Watkinson 21-3-52-1, Simmons 18-3-95-1, Fairbrother 11-0-55-0.

Lancashire

D. W. Varey b Atkinson	22
M. R. Chadwick c Dredge b Marks	132
K. A. Hayes c Roebuck b Garner	117
N. H. Fairbrother not out	31
G. Fowler c Harden b Marks	15
*J. Abrahams not out	2
B 1, l-b 3, w 1, n-b 6	11

Total (4 wkts) 330

First innings forfeited.

Did not bat: M. Watkinson, †C. Maynard, J. Simmons, P. J. W. Allott, B. P. Patterson.

1-73 2-249 3-309 4-324

Bowling: Garner 15-4-24-1, Dredge 18-2-79-0, Botham 5-1-14-0, Marks 43-10-125-2, Atkinson 15.5-2-54-1, Richards 8-0-30-0.

SIXTH CORNHILL TEST MATCH – ENGLAND v AUSTRALIA

At The Oval, August 29, 30, 31, September 2. England won by an innings and 94 runs. Umpires: H. D. Bird and K. E. Palmer.

England

G. A. Gooch c and b McDermott	196		
R. T. Robinson b McDermott	3		
*D. I. Gower c Bennett b McDermott	157		
M. W. Gatting c Border b Bennett	4		
J. E. Emburey c Wellham b Lawson	9		
A. J. Lamb c McDermott b Lawson	1		
I. T. Botham c Phillips b Lawson	12		
†P. R. Downton b McDermott	16		
R. M. Ellison c Phillips b Gilbert	3		
P. H. Edmonds lbw b Lawson	12		
L. B. Taylor not out	1		
B 13, l-b 11, n-b 26	50		

Total 464

1-20 2-371 3-376 4-403 5-405 6-418 7-425 8-447 9-452

Bowling: Lawson 29.2-6-101-4, McDermott 31-2-108-4, Gilbert 21-2-96-1, Bennett 32-8-111-1, Border 2-0-8-0, Wessels 3-0-16-0.

Australia

G. M. Wood lbw b Botham	22	(2) b Botham	6
A. M. J. Hilditch c Gooch b Botham	17	(1) c Gower b Taylor	9
K. C. Wessels b Emburey	12	c Downton b Botham	7
*A. R. Border b Edmonds	38	c Botham b Ellison	58
D. M. Wellham c Downton b Ellison	13	lbw b Ellison	5
G. M. Ritchie not out	64	c Downton b Ellison	6
†W. B. Phillips b Edmonds	10	c Downton b Botham	10
M. J. Bennett c Robinson b Ellison	12	c and b Taylor	11
G. F. Lawson c Botham b Taylor	14	c Downton b Ellison	7
C. J. McDermott run out	25	c Botham b Ellison	2
D. R. Gilbert b Botham	1	not out	0
L-b 3, w 2	5	B 4, n-b 4	8

Total 241   129

1-35 2-52 3-56 4-101 5-109 6-144 7-171 8-192 9-235   1-13 2-16 3-37 4-51 5-71 6-96 7-114 8-127 9-129

Bowling: *First innings*—Botham 20-3-64-3, Taylor 13-1-39-1, Ellison 18-5-35-2, Emburey 19-7-48-1, Edmonds 14-2-52-2. *Second innings*—Botham 17-3-44-3, Taylor 11.3-1-34-2, Ellison 17-3-46-5, Edmonds 1-0-1-0.

Acknowledgements

The Publishers are indebted to the following individuals and organisations for allowing their photographs to be reproduced in the book:

All-Sport	11
Associated Sports Photography	5(top),97(bottom),101,117,147,207
The Beldam Collection	88
Ian Bennett	162
Patrick Eagar	54,74,75,118,120,133,166,179(top and bottom)
Fotosports	104, 107(bottom), 181
David Frith	157
Alain Lockyer	13,15,18,34,37,40,42,43,79,80,82,83, 84(left),188(top and bottom),200,202
Phil Loftus	26
Peter Messit	2
Graham Morris	4,5(bottom), 8,9,135(top and bottom), 167,199,201
David Munden	94(top and bottom),95(top and bottom)
Adrian Murrell, All-Sport	20(bottom left),21(right),39,57,64,65,66, 90,97(top),107(top), 109,124,130,134,153, 154,164,174(top and bottom),175,185, 193,205,206(top and bottom)
National Portrait Gallery	208
Bob Thomas Sports Photography	20(top left, top right and bottom right), 21(left), 31,46,50,62,77, 84(right),127,144, 146,148,150,160
Steve Williams	141